REVISED EDITION

WJEC

Level 3 Applied Certificate & Diploma

CRIMINOLOGY

Carole A Henderson

Published in 2021 by Illuminate Publishing Limited, an imprint of Hodder Education, an Hachette UK Company, Carmelite House, 50 Victoria Embankment, London EC4Y 0DZ

Orders: Please visit www.illuminatepublishing.com
or email sales@illuminatepublishing.com

British Library Cataloguing-in-Publication Data

A catalogue record for this book is available from the British Library
ISBN 978-1-912820-98-6

Printed by Cambrian Printers, UK

02.22

The publisher's policy is to use papers that are natural, renewable and recyclable products made from wood grown in sustainable forests. The logging and manufacturing processes are expected to conform to the environmental regulations of the country of origin.

Every effort has been made to contact copyright holders of material produced in this book. Great care has been taken by the author and publisher to ensure that either formal permission has been granted for the use of copyright material reproduced, or that copyright material has been used under the provision of fair dealing guidelines in the UK – specifically that it has been used sparingly, solely for the purpose of criticism and review, and has been properly acknowledged. If notified, the publisher will be pleased to rectify any errors or omissions at the earliest opportunity.

The teaching content of this resource is endorsed by WJEC to support the WJEC Level 3 Applied Certificate/Diploma qualifications (4543QC/4543QD).

This resource has been reviewed against WJEC's endorsement criteria. As this resource belongs to a third party, there may be occasions where a specification may be updated and that update will not be reflected in the third party resource. Users should always refer to WJEC's specification and Sample Assessment Materials to ensure that learners are studying the most up-to-date course.

It is recommended that teachers use a range of resources to fully prepare their learners for the exam and not rely solely on one textbook or digital resource.

WJEC, nor anyone employed by WJEC, has been paid for the endorsement of this resource, nor does WJEC receive any royalties from its sale.

WJEC examination questions are reproduced by permission from WJEC.

Editor: Dawn Booth
Design and layout: Kamae Design
Cover design: Kamae Design
Cover image: domnitsky / Shutterstock

Photo acknowledgements
p1 domnitsky/Shutterstock; p10 michaeljung; p12 victorfusionart; p17 Bogdan Viga; p18 US Department of Justice/Public domain; p19 Nomad_Soul; p20 Everett Historical; p21 Andrey_Popov; p22 (top) chrisdorney; p22 (bot) ZUMA Press, Inc./Alamy Stock Photo; p23 WENN Rights Ltd/Alamy Stock Photo; p24 Diego Cervo; p26 IQonceput; p28 (top) SpeedKings; p28 (bot) FaysalFarhan; p29 (l) Photographee.eu; p29 (r) Mehaniq; p30 Nomad_Soul; p31 Alex Staroseltsev; p32 (top) ambronzinio; p32 (bot) Gavin Rodgers/REX/Shutterstock; p33 Creative Commons Attribution-Share Alike 3.0 Unported; p34 Aleksandra Duda; p35 chrisdorney/Shutterstock.com; p37 (both) News UK/News Licensing; p38 (top) Kathy Hutchins; p38 (bot) Robsonphoto; p39 (top) rvisoft/Shutterstock.com; p39 (bot) Pictorial Press Ltd/Alamy Stock Photo; p41 (bot) lonndubh/Shutterstock.com; p42 M-SUR; p43 Alice Day; p44 Ken Tannenbaum/Shutterstock.com; p46 TierneyMJ; p50 James Boardman/Alamy; p51 (top) Nigel Bowles/Alamy Stock Photo; p51 (bot) Sashkin; p52 Lenscap Photography/Shutterstock.com; p53 Shutterstock; p54 Steve Maisey/Shutterstock; p58 (top) VLADGRIN; p58 (bot) mrwebhoney; p59 (top) Jack the Giant Slayer; p59 (bot) WaterAid; p60 Featureflash Photo Agency/Shutterstock.com; p61 (top) Nigel Bowles/Alamy Stock Photo; p61 (middle) JessicaGirvan; p61 (bot) chrisdorney/Shutterstock.com; p64 (top) sliplee; p64 (bot) LuckyVector; p65 (top) aaelrahman89; p65 (bot) quinky; p66 Mile Atanasov; p67 wutzkohphoto; p68 nasirkhan; p71 (top) Kraphix; p71 (bot) Alex_Bond; p72 (top) Krafted; p72 (bot) Children in Need; p73 Courtesy of Declan Ballan, Ronan McDowell, Courtney Powell, Emily Anderson, Arisa Hudson; p75 eenevski; p78 Shishkin Dmitry; p79 happiness time; p80 (top) D.J.McGee; p80 (bot) Inna Ogando; p81 airi; p84 Sinart Creative; p86 kirazihu2u; p87 (top) hafakot; p87 (bot) Photographee.eu; p88 (top) Dmytro Zinkevych; p88 (middle) Christopher Gardiner; p88 (bot) thebigland/Shutterstock.com; p91 Alila Medical Media; p92 Sapann Design; p93 Reproduced in 'Rassenkunde des jüdischen Volkes' by Hans F. K. Günther 1929, J.F. Lehmanns Verlag, München. Scanned by MoritzB/Public domain; p94 (top) 'Tipi di delinquenti italiani'/Creative Commons Attribution 2.0 Generic; p94 (bot) robuart; p95 (top) Creative Commons; p95 (bottom r) Photograph by Jack and Beverly Wilgus of daguerreotype originally from their collection, and now in the the Warren Anatomical Museum, Center for the History of Medicine, Francis A. Countway Library of Medicine, Harvard Medical School - Own work, CC BY-SA 3.0, https://commons.wikimedia.org/w/index.php?curid=37613243; p95 (bottom l) Van Horn J.D., Irimia A., Torgerson C.M., Chambers M.C., Kikinis R., et al. (2012) Mapping Connectivity Damage in the Case of Phineas Gage. PLoS ONE 7(5): e37454. doi:10.1371/journal.pone.0037454/ Creative Commons Attribution 2.5 Generic license; p96 (top) vitstudio; p96 (bot) Magic Mushroom; p97 (top) ALMAGAMI; p97 (bot) Albert Bandura/Creative Commons Attribution-Share Alike 4.0 International license; p98 © Semhur/Wikimedia Commons/CC-BY-SA-3.0, or Free Art License; p99 (top) Roberto Herrett/Alamy Stock Photo; p99 (bot) Pretty Vectors; p101 (top) Max Halberstadt (1882-1940)/Creative Commons; p101 (bot) drawhunter; p102 Sirswindon at English Wikipedia - Creative Commons; p104 ProStockStudio; p105 Everett Historical; p106 Paul Fearn/Alamy Stock Photo; p107 Thierry Caro/Creative Commons; p110 Shutterstock; p111 CBW/Alamy Stock Photo; p112 RichardBaker/Alamy Stock Photo; p113 Visual Generation; pp114–120 (all thumbs) Oberon; p116 Reproduced in 'Rassenkunde des jüdischen Volkes' by Hans F. K. Günther 1929, J.F. Lehmanns Verlag, München. Scanned by MoritzB/Public domain; p123 bilha gotan; p124 (top) browndogstudios; p124 (bot) Paper Street Design; p125 Collection Christophel/Alamy Stock Photo; p126 Aleksandra Gigowska; p127 (top) Public domain; p127 (bot) Okeksandr Lysenko; p129 Tribalium; p130 astudio; p131 (top) Blan-k; p131 (bot) alice-photo; p132 (top) Jamie Bulger's killer to face child porn chargeses/YouTube; p132 (bot) WENN Ltd/Alamy Stock Photo; p134 (top) Granger Historical Picture Archive/Alamy Stock Photo; p134 (bot) Zefrog/Alamy Stock Photo; p135 Everett Historical; p136 (top) Anton Havelaar; p136 (bot) Darla Hallmark; p137 Ms Jane Campbell/Shutterstock.com; p138 Even Look/Shutterstock.com; p139 Brian A Jackson; p140 (top) World History Archive/Alamy Stock Photo; p140 (both bottom) Telegraph & Argus; p142 (top) Picture North News; p142 (bot) Police DVD; p143 (top) Clare's Law; p143 (bot) Lillian's law; p144 Arfan Afzal; p148 Bonezboyz; p149 (top) WENN Ltd/Alamy Stock Photo; p149 (bot) Kevin L Chesson; p150 Courtesy CPS; p151 (top) Shutterstock; p151 (middle) science photo; p151 (bot) Andrew Cowie/Alamy Stock Photo; p153 Art tools; p154 Shutterstock; p155 (top) Fair use; p155 (bot) researcher 97; p156 PA; p157 Richard Linnett Photography; p158 Atstock Productions; p159 (top) solar22; p159 (bot) Chuck Burton/AP/Shutterstock; p160 (top) oiriontrail; p160 (bot) Kaimen; p162 (top) BasPhoto; p162 (bot) munalin; p163 (top) Alexandr III; p163 (bot) Robsonphoto; p164 (top) WENN Ltd/Alamy Stock Photo; p164 (bot) WENN Ltd/Alamy Stock Photo; p165 Alexander_P; p166 hafakot; p167 Victim Support; p168 Courtesy CPS; p169 (top) Prath; p169 (bot) dnd_project; p171 Adam Murphy/Alamy Stock Photo; p172 Stuart Monk/Shutterstock.com; p173 (top) Rainer Fuhrmann; p173 (bot) Rex Wholster; p175 (top) kenny1; p175 (bot) Veva_31; p178 deepstock; p180 Scott Maxwell LuMaxArt; p181 Arthimedes; p182 Yayayoya; p184 hafakot; p185 SpeedKingz; p186 Henry Olden; p188 Nemanja Cosovic; p189 Pavel Rumme; p190 solar 22; p192 ibreakstock; p193 (top) Tomasz Guzowski; p193 (bot) Geoff Pugh; p194 WENN Ltd/Alamy Stock Photo; p195 (top) Trinity Mirror/Mirrorpix/Alamy Stock Photo; p195 (bot) kenny1/Shutterstock.com; p196 News UK/News Licensing; p198 James Boardman Archive/Alamy Stock Photo; p199 PA; p202 BCFC; p203 Richie Chan; p204 Jemastock; p205 Zolnierek; p206 Phil Holmes; p210 Graphic mooi; p211 Grasko; p212 hobbit; p213 Aquir; p215 hobbit; p216 (top) PeterSnow; p216 (bot) jesadaphorn; p217 (top) kenny 1; p217 (bot) hafakot; p218 StockCube; p221 Boris15; p222 pockygallery; p225 (top) Darran Whittingham; p225 (bot) nito; p228 karanik yimpat; p229 Alex Smith/Alamy Stock Photo; p230 (top) Darryl Sleath; p230 (bot) TotemArt; p234 Drop of Light/Shutterstock.com; p235 F-Stop boy; p236 The Crown Prosecution Service/Open Government Licence version 1.0; p237 file404; p238 (top) Andrey_Popov; p238 (bot) lazylama/Shutterstock.com; p239 Scott Maxwell LuMaxArt; p240 Paul J Martin; p241 (top) Mix3r; p241 (bot) Aquir; p242 Courtesy Prison Reform Trust; p243 (top) Out of Trouble; p243 (bot) Courtesy Howard League for Penal Reform; p244 christizimaging.com; p245 Adapted from Prison Reform Trust, Lewis; p246 The Works of Jeremy Bentham vol IV, 172–3/Public domain; p247 (top) HMP Berwyn, Wrexham's New Prison/wrexhamdotcom/YouTube; p247 (bot) Grim23/ GNU Free Documentation License; p248 Michael J P; p249 pockygallery; p250 Ka_Li; p251 (top) Lolostock; p251 (bot) Illustration Forest; p254 (top) cloki; p254 (bot) Feng Yu; p255 (top) Mohamad Zaid/Alamy Stock Photo; p255 (bot) TuckerBlade; p256 NACRO; p257 Maythaporn Plyaprichart; p258 Andrew Matthews/PA; p260 (l) Nigel Bowles/REX/Shutterstock; p260 (r) David Cairns/REX/Shutterstock; p261 Howard Sayer/Alamy Stock Photo; p262 (top) Surrey Police; p262 (bot) Tanasut Chindasuthi; p263 Office of National Statistics; p264 (top) REX/Shutterstock; p264 (bot) IQoncept; p265 Prison Reform Trust; p266 Adapted from Wright, P. & Paumbo (2016) 'UK Prisons Crisis: Five Graphs Showing Why Officers are Striking as Chaos Erupts behind Bars', International Business Times, 15 November; p267 Crown copyright; p268 (top) Prison Reform Trust; p268 (bot) Prince's Trust; p269 ActionFraud

Dedication

To my mam and dad – they would have been so proud of me.

CONTENTS

HOW TO USE THIS BOOK

The contents of this textbook are designed to guide you through to success in studying for the WJEC Level 3 Applied Certificate or Diploma in Criminology.

The structure of the book mirrors that of the specification and is divided into units that contain the assessment criteria. For the Applied Certificate in Criminology you must study Unit 1 and Unit 2. For the Applied Diploma, the additional Units 3 and 4 must also be studied.

The qualification is the same for learners in both England and Wales. The information and topics in the book reflect both the internal units (or controlled assessment) and the external exam units.

LEVEL 3 APPLIED CERTIFICATE IN CRIMINOLOGY			
UNIT NUMBER	UNIT TITLE	ASSESSMENT	
1	Changing awareness of crime	Internal	Mandatory
2	Criminological theories	External	Mandatory

LEVEL 3 APPLIED DIPLOMA IN CRIMINOLOGY			
UNIT NUMBER	UNIT TITLE	ASSESSMENT	
1	Changing awareness of crime	Internal	Mandatory
2	Criminological theories	External	Mandatory
3	Crime scene to court room	Internal	Mandatory
4	Crime and punishment	External	Mandatory

Internal Units 1 and 3

Units 1 and 3 are assessed by controlled assessments. Your school or college will decide when they want to hold the examination and make all the arrangements. In the controlled assessment you will be given a brief that contains a scenario and tasks. You are not able to see the scenario and task prior to the controlled assessment. Once the controlled assessment has started your teacher and friends cannot talk to you about any aspect of the tasks.

For both Units 1 and 3, your teacher selects a brief that has been prepared by the exam board. At the very start of your controlled assessment you will have access to it. It will contain a story involving criminal activity and links to all the different ACs in the unit. After the scenario there are a number of tasks, which again will not be shown to you until the start of the assessment. However, all the tasks are centred around the information you learn for each AC. You should pay particular attention to the wording of the task to ensure you refer to the brief when required to do so and that you address exactly what the question is asking. For instance, if it sets a required number, such as two crimes.

External Units 2 and 4

The sections of the book concerning the external exam, Units 2 and 4, contain the areas that could feature on an exam paper. While every learning outcome on each unit paper will be assessed, not every assessment criterion must appear. The questions may be answered by information that doesn't appear in this book but the main theorists or main aspects of topics are explored and nothing further has to be covered. However, credit will always be given for relevant information.

One very important thing to remember about each external unit is that it is **synoptic**. This means you may be required to draw on learning from a previous unit. So, for example, Unit 2 may draw on learning from Unit 1, while Unit 4 may draw on learning from Units 1, 2 and 3.

The 'amplification' section of the unit content in Units 2 and 4 indicate where you can draw on learning from other units. This can be found in the specification.

Skills

Please remember it isn't enough just to learn the detail for each examination; you must also address the skills demanded from the assessment criteria. This could be analysis, assessment, evaluation, etc. The particular skill is clearly outlined in each assessment criterion. You should also note the list of command terms later in this book.

Features

Alongside the key information for each assessment criterion, there is a variety of features that will help you to think and prepare you for the examination and controlled assessment:

- **Assessment criterion** and **Learner should** are taken from the specifications and contain details of the content to be covered, amplification and marks where available.
- **Synoptic links** include details of how the previous units link to the current AC and how they could feature in the external exam.
- **Activities** to help test your knowledge and reinforce important points of learning.
- **Key terms** are definitions of important words or terms used in the topic. They have been compiled in a glossary at the end of the book to help you with your revision.
- **Take it further** has ideas and activities to develop and extend your knowledge.
- **Handy hints** contain hints and advice on how best to approach the controlled assessment or what to include or not include.
- **Literacy skills** give examples of work to improve or address issues with spelling, punctuation and grammar.
- **Case studies** have examples of real-life scenarios.
- **Think theory** encourages you to apply theories to a specific crime or criminal in order to understand both the behaviour and the theory.
- **Example questions** from past exam questions to show typical questions in the area concerned, with example extract answers and appropriate mark bands to enable you to understand what is expected.
- **Tips** are suggestions on how to approach the controlled assessment.

METHODS OF ASSESSMENT

One of the many good things about this qualification is the way it is assessed. You will have both a controlled assessment and an external exam in each year of the course.

QUALIFICATION	UNIT	UNIT TITLE	ASSESSMENT METHOD	PERCENTAGE OF QUALIFICATION
Applied Certificate Year 1	1	Changing awareness of crime	Controlled assessment	50% of certificate or 25% of diploma
	2	Criminological theories	External exam	50% of certificate or 25% of diploma
Applied Diploma Year 2	3	Crime scene to court room	Controlled assessment	25% of diploma
	4	Crime and punishment	External exam	25% of diploma

Controlled assessments (Units 1 and 3)

What are controlled assessments?

Controlled assessments are exams and not coursework. They are carried out under specified conditions. They must be attempted on an individual basis and not in a group. There is an assigned brief or scenario that you will be able to access in the exam. It is a story about people and crime(s) being committed. After the brief will be a series of tasks that relate to the ACs studied in class. You will not know the brief or tasks until you are in the exam. The controlled assessment will be carried out in timed conditions. There cannot be access to your work outside the set times. Invigilators will oversee your exam. You must not talk to anyone or pass information to another during the exam. You cannot access any prepared work either electronically or in paper form. Everything must be answered in the assessment.

However, you will have access to:

- an assessment grid
- class notes
- ICT software
- the internet for Unit 1 during the designated period.

You cannot access:

- the internet at anytime for Unit 1 or Unit 3 for the non-designated time
- any textbooks
- any prepared material – everything must be produced in the exam time.

How long are the controlled assessments and how are they organised?

Both the assessments last for 8 hours and can be divided up in any way that suits you and your teacher. Many centres take you off timetable and spread the assessment over two days. Some organise it in class time but obviously this may take several weeks. Please also note that both controlled assessments for Criminology are summative assessments and can only be attempted once all teaching for that particular unit has ended.

At the start of your assessment, it is important to remember that you must take all class notes in with you on the first day of the exam. Everything is left in the exam room until you finish the exam. You do not take anything away each night, nor do you take anything else into the exam room once the assessment has started.

What is the focus of the controlled assessment?

The assessment focuses on a brief that contains a scenario involving the commission of different crimes. You will only use one of the briefs for each unit. Unit 1 focuses on under-reported crime and subsequent consequences and requires you to raise awareness of an under-reported crime. Unit 3 considers the investigation and prosecution of a crime, from the crime scene to the court room and beyond.

How much do I focus on the brief?

You should pay close attention to the tasks. They will indicate where a reference to the brief is required. Or, alternatively, they may ask you about crimes that take place in the scenario. It is imperative that you follow these instructions.

Do I type or write the controlled assessment?

You are able to sit the assessment using a computer or alternatively write it by hand. Unit 1 permits the use of the internet for parts of the assessment. However, for the remainder of the exam and for all of Unit 3 this facility will be disabled. Similarly, you will not be permitted to access anything electronically such as files and documents, to ensure that all work is produced in the 8 hours of exam time.

When is the controlled assessment?

The date of the controlled assessment is set by your teacher. Many centres sit it before the teaching of the external exam. So, typically, it is taught September–December, then the assessment takes place. The external exam is then taught from January to the summer (May/June).

Handy hints !

Remember, you will only be able to see the brief and tasks that follow it once you are in the exam room. They will be focused around the ACs taught in class.

Handy hints !

Note that all tasks are compulsory; there are no optional questions.

Handy hints !

A controlled assessment can only be attempted by candidates once all teaching for that particular unit has ended.

Other important information about sitting the controlled assessment

Please note the assessment is an exam and all work must be produced in the allocated time. There is no coursework. You cannot re-sit the assessment unless a different brief is used.

Can I re-sit a controlled assessment?

From 2019 you are allowed a second attempt at the controlled assessment. However, a different brief must be used for a second attempt. You cannot improve previously submitted work.

Your centre will have access to the alternative brief. Your teacher is not allowed to give you any feedback in between attempts. Both attempts must be sent to the exam board if selected for moderation.

The IT department in your centre may become involved and set up an exam account for you, which is likely to be time controlled to restrict access during non-exam times.

What happens after the controlled assessment?

After the exam your teachers will mark the assessment for you. They will have a system to ensure that all assessments are marked consistently and in accordance with the assessment criteria and the mark bands. They can tell you the raw mark you have achieved and an approximate grade. However, the WJEC Exam Board will require a sample of marked work to be sent to them. This is a process known as moderation, where experienced moderators ensure that there is consistency in marking across the country. Please be aware that, at this stage, your mark could change and go up or down. Mark bands involving raw marks or the mark your teacher can give you may vary each year, depending on the standard of the work produced. The grade boundaries for the 2019 controlled assessments are below.

Unit 1

Grade	A	B	C	D	E
UMS grade boundary	080	070	060	050	040
Raw mark grade boundary	081	071	061	052	043

Unit 3

Grade	A	B	C	D	E
UMS grade boundary	080	070	060	050	040
Raw mark grade boundary	084	074	064	054	045

Raw marks and UMS

The raw marks are converted into a mark from the uniform mark scale (UMS), which is the mark you will receive when results are available in August of each year. The overall qualification grade is calculated by adding together the uniform marks achieved in the individual units. This gives you a total uniform mark which converts to an overall grade based on the grade boundary.

Grade	Max.	A	B	C	D	E
Certificate	200	160	140	120	100	80
Diploma	400	320	280	280	200	160

For qualifications awarded from 2020 onwards, you must pass each unit in order to achieve a grade. For the Level 3 Applied Diploma, a Grade A* will be awarded to students who have achieved a Grade A (320 uniform marks) in the overall qualification and at least 90% of the total uniform marks for the two additional diploma units (Units 3 and 4).

External exams (Units 2 and 4)

Format of the external exams

Both external exams last 1 hour 30 minutes and are on set dates in the summer, May or June each year. These are more conventional exams and are organised and take place in a traditional way. The exam paper is set by the principal examiner who will be an experienced teacher and will be very familiar with the specifications. All the questions are compulsory as there will be no optional questions. The exams are available on paper or by way of an e-assessment. Which method is used will be decided by your centre.

Each exam paper is out of 75 marks and is divided into three main questions. Each question is worth a total of 25 marks, so each should be allocated 30 minutes. Each question will be divided into a series of part questions, carrying different marks that will total 25. The marks for a question can vary from 1–9. This is how they could appear on an exam paper:

1 mark available for point-based questions. For example, 'identify one feature …'

2 marks available for point-based questions. For example, 'identify two features …'

3 marks available for point-based questions. For example, 'identify three features …'

4 marks available for point-based questions. For example, 'identify four features …'

4 marks available for short-answer response questions, including those with the 'briefly' suffix.

6 marks available for mid-length response questions.

9 marks available for extended response questions.

Stimulus material

Each of the three main questions will start with stimulus response source material and have applied contexts. This could be a scenario, a quote or factual information. This will provide a prompt for each of the part questions that follow. Every learning outcome will be assessed in each question paper; however, not every assessment criterion may appear.

Command terms in questions

The following table outlines the command terms and the descriptors that will be utilised in Criminology examination papers from 2020 onwards. The list is not exhaustive as some other terms may be deemed necessary for syntactical reasons. However, generally, questions will include one of the following:

Analyse	You need to break down the set issue to its constituent components, determining its significance in the wider context.
Assess	You need to judge how, and how effectively, the set issue or issues achieve their objectives.
Compare	You need to give an account of the similarities and differences between two or more issues, referring to both, or all, of them throughout.
Describe	You need to give an account that addresses the features of the set issue and consider appropriate supporting material.
Discuss	You need to provide a commentary that includes a range of arguments and/or factors.
Evaluate	You will make a substantiated judgment based on the strengths and limitations of the relevant evidence.
Examine	You will review the relevant issue and consider the interplay between several factors.
Explain	You will identify, interpret and outline the key features of the set issue.

Answering the questions

The question papers are in booklets in which you also write the answers in a given space, extra sheets of exam paper will also be available, if needed. The number of marks available is given in brackets at the end of each part question. It is important that your answer is in good English and presented in an orderly way. The assessment will take into account the quality of written communication used in your answers. This will include the use of specialist terminology.

Mark scheme

Every exam paper will also have a mark scheme prepared to assist the specialist team of examiners mark each paper. The mark scheme for each question will differ but each one will show how the mark bands available must be applied to the answer. Past papers will be available for you to revise, as will the accompanying mark schemes.

From 2020 there will be the introduction of common mark bands. These fixed-mark tariffs are as follows:

1 mark available for point-based questions. For example, 'identify one feature ...'

2 marks available for point-based questions. For example, 'identify two features ...'

3 marks available for point-based questions. For example, 'identify three features ...'

4 marks available for point-based questions. For example, 'identify four features ...'

4 marks available for short-answer response questions, including those with the 'briefly' suffix.

6 marks available for mid-length response questions.

9 marks available for extended response questions.

The set mark bands are:

FOR A 1 MARK QUESTION

0 marks: the response does not meet any of the criteria specified.

1 mark: award 1 mark for a correct point.

FOR A 2 MARK QUESTION

0 marks: the response does not meet any of the criteria specified.

Up to 2 marks: award 1 mark for a correct point.

FOR A 3 MARK QUESTION

0 marks: the response does not meet any of the criteria specified.

Up to 3 marks: award 1 mark for a correct point.

FOR A 4 MARK QUESTION

0 marks: the response does not meet any of the criteria specified.

Up to 4 marks: award 1 mark for a correct point.

FOR SHORT ANSWERS

0 marks: the response does not meet any of the criteria specified.

1–2 marks: there is a limited focus on the question, with vague or no accurate support and little or no use of specialist vocabulary.

3–4 marks: there is a reasonable focus on the question with some accurate support and some use of specialist vocabulary.

FOR MEDIUM ANSWERS

0 marks: the response does not meet any of the criteria specified.

1–2 marks: there is a limited focus on the question, with vague or no accurate support and little or no use of specialist vocabulary.

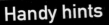

Handy hints !

Look out for Example questions and extract answers throughout this book, to help you refine your exam technique.

NOTE

The mark for each question will be specified on the exam paper.

Tip ✔

An indication of what may be included in an answer follows after each of the mark bands. However, any relevant material is credited.

3–4 marks: there is a reasonable focus on the question with some accurate support and some use of specialist vocabulary. The demands of the question may be only partially addressed.

5–6 marks: there is a clear and detailed focus on the question with mainly accurate support and an effective use of specialist vocabulary. The demands of the question are fully addressed.

FOR EXTENDED ANSWERS

Extended response mark scheme (NB as medium-length but with increased tariff)

0 marks: the response does not meet any of the criteria specified.

1–3 marks: there is a limited focus on the question, with vague or no accurate support and little or no use of specialist vocabulary.

4–6 marks: there is a reasonable focus on the question with some accurate support and some use of specialist vocabulary. The demands of the question may be only partially addressed.

7–9 marks: there is a clear and detailed focus on the question with mainly accurate support and an effective use of specialist vocabulary. The demands of the question are fully addressed.

Synoptic link

One very important thing about the external exams is that they are synoptic. Synoptic assessment is:

assessment which requires a candidate to identify and use effectively in an integrated way an appropriate selection of skills, techniques, concepts, theories, and knowledge from across the course content. **(Department for Education, cited in WJEC, 2015)**

This means that Unit 2 requires you to draw on learning from Unit 1 in order to successfully answer all questions. In addition, Unit 4 may require you to draw on learning from Units 1, 2 and 3 to complete the paper.

Let me explain how this might work. Unit 4 AC3.4 is all about evaluating the effectiveness of agencies in achieving social control, such agencies include the police. There could therefore be a question along the lines of 'Evaluate the effectiveness of the police.' To answer this question you could draw on information learned in Unit 1 AC1.6, where you 'evaluated methods of collecting statistics about crime', which included police recorded statistics. You will have discovered that the police do not record all crime that is reported to them and hence this affects the validity of police crime statistics. In addition, in Unit 3, AC1.1 'Evaluate the effectiveness of the roles of personnel involved in criminal investigations' will have contained advantages and limitations of the police. Hence, information from these ACs can contribute to the answer on the Unit 4 paper focused on AC3.4. It is therefore very important that when you are revising for Unit 2 or 4 that you remember to include Units 1 and 3 in your revision.

Grading external units

As in the controlled assessment units, the external exams are graded A, B, C, D and E. The UMS grade boundaries are also the same as the controlled assessments. In addition, the external exams are worth the same percentage of the overall qualification as the controlled assessment unit. Every year, after each exam paper is marked, the process will take place where raw marks are converted into UMS marks and for 2019 the grade boundaries were set as follows.

Unit 2

Grade	A	B	C	D	E	N
UMS grade boundary	080	070	060	050	040	030
Raw mark grade boundary	061	053	045	037	030	

Unit 4

Grade	A	B	C	D	E	N
UMS grade boundary	080	070	060	050	040	030
Raw mark grade boundary	061	053	045	032	029	

Re-sit opportunity

If you do not pass the Unit 2 exam or would like to try for a higher mark, you are allowed one re-sit opportunity. The higher grade will contribute towards the overall grade for the qualification. You should note that for qualifications awarded from 2020 onwards you must pass each unit in order to achieve a grade for the qualification. Otherwise, you will only achieve unit certification and not the full qualification. If you require further clarification you or your teacher can always contact the exam board.

Near pass

A 'near pass' rule has been introduced for all external units. This means that it is possible to pass the qualification despite not having achieved the normal minimum number of marks required for the external unit. It is possible to achieve a 'near pass' or an N grade if you meet the following two requirements:

1. Achieve the total UMS required at the relevant grade for the qualification. For example, 100 marks for the Certificate at grade D.

2. Obtained at least the minimum UMS for the relevant external units. For example, at least 30 UMS marks are needed for an N grade in Unit 2.

UNIT 1
CHANGING AWARENESS OF CRIME

This unit requires you to plan a campaign for change relating to crime.

You will learn about a variety of crimes that are under-reported and have a low level of public awareness. There are many reasons why people do not report crime and you will consider these and their impact.

You will learn how we record crime and whether it is an accurate system. There have been many campaigns that have changed the law and you will have the opportunity to explore them and the changes they have brought about.

The learning in this unit concludes with you planning a campaign to raise awareness of an under-reported crime. You will design materials linked to the campaign such as posters, leaflets and merchandise. You will also justify the whole campaign.

Assessment: 8-hour controlled assessment

LEARNING OUTCOME 1
UNDERSTAND HOW CRIME REPORTING AFFECTS THE PUBLIC PERCEPTION OF CRIMINALITY

AC1.1 ANALYSE DIFFERENT TYPES OF CRIME

ASSESSMENT CRITERION	MARK BAND 1	MARK BAND 2
AC1.1 You should be able to … Analyse different types of crime	Description of two types of crime evident in the assignment brief **(1–2)**	Analysis of two types of crime evident in the assignment brief **(3–4)**

CONTENT	AMPLIFICATION

Types of crime
 • white-collar, including:
   • organised
   • corporate
   • professional
 • moral
 • state, including:
   • human rights
 • technological, including:
   • e-crime
 • individual, including:
   • hate crime
   • honour crime
   • domestic abuse
	You should have knowledge of specific examples of different types of crime and be able to analyse them by:
	 • criminal offences
	 • types of victim
	 • types of offender
	 • level of public awareness
	
	 You should know that these acts may be deviant and/or criminal

Key terms

Criminal: Actions that will constitute an offence under English and Welsh law and are punishable by the state.

Deviance: Any behaviour that violates social or cultural norms or accepted standards. Much of society will generally disapprove of deviant behaviour.

Handy hints !

For this AC, be careful not to over-describe, as the skill required is analysis. In the controlled assessment, you need to select two crimes, but they must appear in the content of the brief. Therefore, ensure that you have analysed the full range of crimes during your studies, as you will then be able to manage the task.

White-collar crime

Criminal offences

White-collar crimes are generally non-violent crimes usually committed in commercial situations for financial gain. Examples could include:

- computer and internet fraud
- credit card fraud
- tax evasion.

Organised white-collar crime can concentrate on protection rackets but also involves illegal gambling and prostitution.

White-collar crime is usually committed by a business person who wears a shirt and tie.

Types of victim

People who are targeted by white-collar criminals are usually those who have funds to invest in a finance scheme, for example recently retired workers. Often, people are recruited by friends or acquaintances. This is particularly the case in Ponzi schemes, which are fraudulent investment scams promising high rates of return with little risk to investors. However, the returns are funded by money from new investors, as the offender keeps the initial investment for their own use.

Types of offender

White-collar criminals are usually people of respectability and high social status, who are trusted by the victims. They often work in commercial employment, hence the reference to wearing a white-collared shirt and tie. Offenders can also involve organised groups such as the Mafia (Italy, USA), Triads (China), Yakuza (Japan), as well as organised crime gangs in Eastern Europe and the UK.

Level of public awareness

Many white-collar crimes are difficult to prosecute because the perpetrators use sophisticated means to conceal their activities, through a series of complex transactions. The offender usually appears to be a respectable person and therefore suspicion is not aroused. Consequently, the level of public awareness is often low, especially as violence-related crimes are usually more widely publicised.

Deviant or criminal?

As part of the analysis, the exam specifications require comment on whether the offence is deviant or criminal or both. As regards white-collar crime, it is both criminal and deviant. It is criminal as such actions are against the law and deviant as the actions are against the norms of society.

CASE STUDY

BERNIE MADOFF

Bernie Madoff is an American businessman who, using a Ponzi scheme, defrauded investors of over $50 billion. Investors believed their money was being paid into various funds to make money. However, interest payments came not from the investments, which were never made, but from the payments made by new investors. Currently, he is serving 150 years in prison.

Bernie Madoff

Activity

Watch the film *Wall Street*.

This is the story about a young stockbroker who is willing to do anything to get to the top, including trading on illegal inside information.

Handy hints !

The brief given to you in the controlled assessment exam will be a story with a number of crimes being committed. However, not every under-reported crime will be present. The brief will change every academic year.

Moral crimes

Criminal offences

Moral crimes are crimes against the normal standard of morality within society. The following are all examples of what can be considered as moral crimes:

- prostitution
- vagrancy
- under-age drinking
- assisted suicide
- illegal gambling
- illegal drug use.

Types of victim

Moral crimes are often thought to be victimless. However, arguably the offender and the victim can often be the same person. For example, prostitution, vagrancy and under-age drinking can involve the offender and victim being the same person.

Types of offender

This can differ from crime to crime or even, as described above, be the same person. However, the offender is commonly in a difficult situation, for example financially or personally, such as a homeless vagrant or someone forced into, for example, prostitution for financial reasons.

Level of public awareness

This is often low as many of the offences are hidden from offenders' families. Alternatively, it is often a crime that the public ignore due to sympathy for the victims, rather than a desire to report them to the police. For example, vagrancy often brings sympathy for the victim for having to sleep rough.

Deviant or criminal?

Such acts are likely to be both criminal and deviant. Overall, society disagrees with the activities, which are all against the law.

State crimes

Criminal offences

State crimes are activities perpetrated by, or by order of, state agencies, such as governments that commit crimes in order to further their policies. For example:

- genocide
- war crimes
- torture
- imprisonment without trial.

Often such crimes are in breach of articles from the European Convention on Human Rights (ECHR), such as Article 2 a right to life or Article 3 freedom from torture and inhuman treatment.

Moral crime can mean that the offender and victim are the same person.

Activity

The crime of assisted suicide can be committed with a benign or kindly motive. Perhaps to ease someone's suffering or pain.

Research the following cases and consider:

1. Who the typical victim is.
2. Who the typical offender is.
3. What the level of public awareness of the crime is.
4. Under which law someone would be charged.
5. If it is deviant or criminal.

- Diane Pretty
- Debbie Purdy
- Daniel James

Key terms

Genocide: Any action with the intention to destroy, in whole or in part, a national, ethnic or religious group.

European Convention on Human Rights (ECHR): A treaty or agreement to protect human rights and fundamental freedoms in Europe.

Armenian orphans being deported from Turkey. Often referred to as the Armenian genocide, during World War I the Armenian people were ordered to be deported from Turkey. The Armenian people call it 'The Death March' as they had to flee across the Syrian desert leaving all their possessions behind. Many were killed by government soldiers or died of starvation and disease.

Types of victim

Victims of state crime are citizens of the country or potentially those of a different religion or political view than the government.

Types of offender

Offenders of state crime are usually high-ranking government officials under the orders of the country's regime. Examples of genocide include:

• Nazi Germany during the Holocaust
• Idi Amin's Uganda in the 1970s
• Bosnia in the early 1990s.

Level of public awareness

Given the speed of media and reporting in society, the level of public awareness is usually high, as the crimes are so extreme. For instance, most people have heard about the atrocities in Iraq carried out on the orders of Saddam Hussein.

Deviant or criminal?

Such acts are likely to be both criminal and deviant. They go against natural law and the moral compass of society.

Take it further ⟫

Research any one of the examples of genocide, noting the differences between the offenders and the victims.

Key term

Atrocity: A horrific and, usually, violent act.

Technological crimes

Criminal offences

Also known as cybercrime, technological crime is when the offence is committed using the internet or other technologies. The usual offences can include:

- internet-enabled fraud
- downloading illegal materials such as songs and images
- the use of social media to promote hate crimes.

Cybercrime has increased significantly over recent years.

Types of victim

The victim of a technological crime can be anyone who uses the internet, as there is a wide range of crime under this category that can affect many different people. It could be either individuals or large organisations. Often, vulnerable people are victims of phishing scams.

Types of offender

The type of offender can be anyone with access to and a basic knowledge of the internet. Many of the offenders are based overseas with the technical ability to gain access to bank accounts and credit cards. However, work carried out by the National Crime Agency suggests there is an increase in young people committing such crimes in order to impress their friends.

Key term

Phishing: A scam or an attempt to persuade someone to give out personal information, such as bank account numbers, passwords and credit card details.

Level of public awareness

Initially, the level of public awareness was low due to the new technological element. However, there has been a promotion of such crimes with increased publicity and an increase in the number of these offences. Often, victims do not know of the crime until they check bank accounts, etc.

Deviant or criminal?

Some of these crimes, such as internet fraud, are considered to be deviant and criminal as they break the law and go against the norms and values of society. However, crimes such as downloading songs are very common and may not be seen as a 'real crime' by many people. Illegal downloading of music etc, without the consent of the copyright owner, is not actually a criminal offence but part of civil law.

Activity

Have a class debate on the following:

'Technology does more to increase crime than solve it.'

Individual crimes – hate crime

Criminal offences

A hate crime is any crime that is perceived by the victim or any other person as being motivated by prejudice or hate based on a person's race, religious belief, sexual orientation, disability or if they are transgender. Any regular crime can be aggravated by having a hate element. For example, if you were assaulted, the offender would be charged with assault and the court would be told of the hate motivation behind the crime. The hate element would be an aggravating factor and the punishment is likely to be higher.

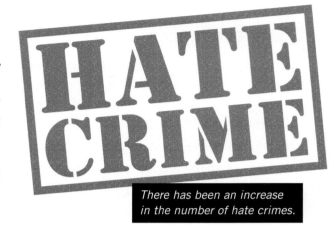

There has been an increase in the number of hate crimes.

Types of victim

Victims of hate crime could be anyone who falls under the five strands, stated above, or through association with someone under the strands. For example, Adam Pearson has experienced disability hate crime as a result of neurofibromatosis, which caused benign tumours to grow on nerve endings on his face. He has raised awareness of this crime in an attempt to educate people and seek acceptance in society.

Adam Pearson

Types of offender

The usual type of offender is anyone holding some form of prejudicial view against someone falling under the five strands and tends to be people with traditional views differing from those of the victim. An example of a racially driven hate crime is the Charleston Church Shooting in South Carolina, USA in 2015, where, during a prayer service, nine people were killed by Dylann Roof, a white supremacist, who targeted one of the oldest black churches in the USA.

Level of public awareness

The level of public awareness has grown recently due to a high media focus, particularly with hate crime for race, religious belief and sexual orientation. The Anti-terrorism Crime and Security Act 2001 added to previous legislation, ensuring religiously aggravated offences had an increased sentencing element. For example, assault is punishable with a maximum of six months in prison. However, this rises to two years if the assault is aggravated by a religious element. In addition, the Crown Prosecution Service ordered a crackdown on social media hate crimes in August 2017. This has added to raising the level of public awareness of these crimes.

Key term

Crown Prosecution Service: The principal prosecuting authority for England and Wales, which acts independently in criminal cases investigated by the police.

Deviant or criminal?

Hate crime is viewed as being both deviant and criminal as it goes against social norms to victimise someone regarding their identity.

Individual crimes – honour crime

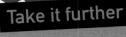

Take it further

Research the killing of American Matthew Shephard in 1998, an example of hate crime. Remember that the assessment criteria require relevant examples.

Criminal offences

Honour crimes are punishments on people for acts deemed to have brought shame on their families. Examples of honour crime include:

- acid attacks
- abductions
- mutilations
- beatings
- murder.

Types of victim

Typically, the victim of an honour crime is a young girl within the family, commonly a daughter from an Asian community.

CASE STUDY

SHAFILEA AHMED

One example of an honour crime is the case of Shafilea Ahmed, who was killed by her parents using a plastic bag to suffocate her after she refused to follow their strict Pakistani lifestyle.

Iftikhar and Farazana Ahmed were convicted of killing their daughter Shafilea, pictured here with their other daughter Mevish.

Types of offender

The offender of honour crime is usually a male member of the family, typically a father, brother or uncle of the one being targeted. These individuals usually come from Asian communities.

Level of public awareness

Generally, this type of crime has low levels of public awareness due to differences in culture. Within communities where honour crime occurs, it is viewed as the appropriate retaliation to 'shameful' behaviour. As a result, it is not reported to the authorities, so the wider community remains unaware of honour crime.

Deviant or criminal?

Any action that is aimed at punishing an individual for shameful behaviour is seen in wider society as both deviant and criminal. This is because, in the UK, it's socially frowned upon to harm individuals based on their life choices.

Take it further

Read the following article and consider if the level of public awareness is changing for honour crime:

'Ending the Silence on "Honour Killing"', at www.theguardian.com/society/2009/oct/25/honour-killings-victims-domestic-violence.

Individual crimes – domestic abuse

Criminal offences

Domestic abuse is any act targeted to be abuse against a partner/family member that happens within the home, often in secret. Domestic abuse can include physical violence such as:

- assault
- murder
- torture
- verbal abuse.

It can also cover emotional abuse to the victim, such as name calling or controlling behaviour.

Types of victim

Typically, women such as girlfriends or wives, or any females involved in intimate relationships, can be victims. However, men can be victims as well, albeit not as frequently as women. Victims are not restricted by age and circumstances. One example of domestic violence is the case of Clare Wood, a mother from Manchester, who became victim to the abuse of George Appleton after meeting him on an internet dating site. Unaware of his previous abusive history with women, she entered into a relationship with him. She was eventually raped, strangled and set alight in her own home.

Domestic abuse is an under-reported crime.

Types of offender

Typically, but not exclusively, offenders are men such as a boyfriend or husband in a relationship. Offenders typically keep their crimes hidden in the home and do not make them public knowledge. They also take steps to ensure their crimes are not reported and that their victims do not speak out.

Level of public awareness

The level of public awareness can be seen as low, despite publicity from notorious cases. The public often do not report such activity, preferring to turn a blind eye, and victims are frequently in fear of the consequences of reporting. Police are trained to take such crime seriously.

Deviant or criminal?

Domestic abuse is both deviant and criminal, being action that is regarded as against the law and also against the norms of society.

Activity

Research domestic abuse against males. Consider the following points:

(i) Is it different from abuse against females?

(ii) Try to record some statistics about male abuse.

(iii) Find a case to include in your notes.

Activity

Complete a table, like the one below, showing **similarities and differences** between honour killings and domestic abuse crimes.

Similarities	Differences

Handy hints !

In the controlled assessment, the brief will contain details of crimes. The specification contains a larger number of crimes than are in the brief.

Having an appreciation of all the crimes mentioned will allow you to know about the two crimes that you need to select from the brief.

AC1.2 EXPLAIN THE REASONS THAT CERTAIN CRIMES ARE UNREPORTED

ASSESSMENT CRITERION	MARK BAND 1	MARK BAND 2
AC1.2 You should be able to … Explain the reasons why certain crimes are unreported	Reasons for the two unreported crimes are limited in explanation **(1–2)**	Clear and detailed explanation of the reasons for the two unreported crimes **(3–4)**

CONTENT	AMPLIFICATION

Reasons
 	
 • personal, for example:
   • fear
   • shame
   • disinterest
   • not affected
 • social and cultural, for example:
   • lack of knowledge
   • complexity
   • lack of media interest
   • lack of current public concern
   • culture-bound crime (e.g. honour killing, witchcraft)
	You should have an understanding of the reasons why certain crimes are not reported to the police
	
	 Consider crimes such as:
	 • common assault
	 • domestic abuse
	 • vandalism
	 • rape
	 • perceived victimless crimes (e.g. white-collar crime, vagrancy, prostitution, assisted suicide)

Unreported crime

If you witness a crime would you always report it? Would it depend on the type of crime? If there are times when you may not want to report a crime, why is this?

For a crime to be recorded it must be against the law, someone must know the event took place; the crime must be reported and the police must record the event as a crime. If one of these factors does not occur, the act is referred to as being part of the dark figure of crime.

There are many reasons for unreported crime.

Personal reasons

Fear

Fear of potential consequences from the criminal, for themselves or their family, can be a reason for unreported crime. Examples of unreported crimes include:

- domestic abuse
- honour crimes
- hate crimes.

Shame

Shame or even embarrassment, especially if it involves a sexual act such as rape or indecent assault, can prevent someone from reporting a crime. This could be because the person might not want others to know they were vulnerable and unable to defend or protect themselves.

Disinterest

People do not always care about what has happened or feel upset about the crime that has been committed. For example, someone could walk past a homeless person who is drinking and high on drugs but not report it because they are disinterested.

Not affected

If an incident does not concern a person, they may feel it has nothing to do with them and that they should leave it to someone else to report. For example, criminal damage/vandalism may not concern people if it is not their property. Another example would be vagrancy. Homeless people can be ignored by members of society as it does not really affect them.

> **Key term**
>
> **Dark figure of crime:** The amount of unreported or unknown crime.

> **Handy hints !**
>
> To get into mark band 2 you will need to explain why both crimes defined in AC1.1 could go unreported. Answers may be brief for 4 marks but must include at least one personal and one social/cultural reason.

> **Activity**
>
> **Further research on male domestic abuse**
>
> Consider why males often fail to report this crime.
>
> Help can be found in the article 'Male Victims of Domestic Violence are Being Failed by the System', at
>
> www.independent.co.uk/voices/domestic-violence-male-victims-shelters-government-funding-stigma-a7626741.html.

> **Activity**
>
> Go to the *Guardian* article entitled 'Only 5% of "Honour" Crimes Reported to Police are Referred to CPS', at
>
> www.theguardian.com/society/2017/nov/07/only-5-of-honour-crimes-reported-to-police-are-referred-to-cps.
>
> Read the article and then produce a summary of the key points, including reasons for a lack of reporting to the police and some of the statistics involved.

Social and cultural reasons

Lack of knowledge

Lack of knowledge could be the reason why people do not report a crime. They may be unaware it is a crime or do not have knowledge of the procedures involved. For example, cyber-bullying via social networking and having to block people who might abuse you.

Key term

Cyber-bullying: A form of bullying using electronic devices, for example mobile phones, tablets or computers. It is becoming increasingly common, especially among teenagers.

People are not always aware of cyber-bullying.

Activity

In pairs, try to draw up a list of the ways in which a crime could be reported.

Complexity

The general public might not understand that a crime has been committed as it is too difficult to understand or follow. For example, white-collar crime is a complex crime where fraudulent transactions are hidden or carried out in private and are difficult to trace.

Lack of media interest

Some crimes are not widely promoted by the media as they believe there will be little public interest. For example, a murder will take precedence to being reported in preference to many moral crimes such as under-age drinking or prostitution.

Lack of current public concern

Lack of current public concern may occur if an offence is not considered an actual crime. Downloading illegal music, for example, is something that many people will do so they can listen to it free of charge. There is no real concern about it being an illegal act. Likewise, smoking of cannabis fails to attract the interest of many people and they may be reluctant to report it to the police on the basis that the offender should be allowed to smoke it if they so desire.

DOWNLOAD

Many people are not concerned about illegal downloading of music.

Culture-bound crime

Culture-bound crime can be acceptable in certain sections of society. For example, honour killings are accepted in some cultures or religions as they follow a certain tradition within family life. People who see different cultures as something mystifying may ignore this type of crime and not report it as they do not want to interfere.

Examples of why different crimes are not reported

Common assault

Common assault involves a very low level of physical contact with very little injury. It can be committed without any touching if a person apprehends violence. For example, shouting 'I am going to get you', but not doing anything else may result in an assault. In such a situation someone may feel it is not worth reporting it to the police or may feel that the police may not take them seriously.

Domestic abuse

Domestic abuse may not be reported, as the victim often cares about the offender due to their relationship. Alternatively, fear about future abuse may be the issue, or not having somewhere else to live for the victim and any children of the family may force someone to just put up with it. Male victims of abuse may be particularly embarrassed about reporting this to the police.

Vandalism

Officially known as criminal damage, vandalism may be considered someone else's problem and, unless the damage is against their property, many people would simply ignore it. If the damage is in the form of graffiti, people may feel it is not worth reporting to the police.

Take it further

The government promotes the reporting of vandalism. Go to www.gov.uk/report-vandalism and look at the electronic means of reporting.

Then consider if there was a financial reward for reporting a crime would that encourage you to do so?

Common assault can be committed without any physical contact.

Many people ignore vandalism.

Rape

Rape may not be reported due to embarrassment or shame. As a result of the intimate nature of this crime, many people may not want to re-live the experience by talking about it to the police. Men, in particular, may feel that they should have prevented such action from taking place and pride could prevent them reporting it.

Perceived victimless crimes

Perceived victimless crimes, for example white-collar crimes, may not be reported as people are unaware that they are happening. They are usually carried out in secret, hidden behind complex transactions that people cannot easily detect. Offenders are usually able to cover their tracks in unseen dealings.

Perceived victimless crimes include vagrancy, which is usually not reported as many people are unaware that sleeping rough is actually a crime. Legislation concerning this offence dates back to 1824 and sympathy for a person being homeless may prevent reporting.

Perceived victimless crimes include prostitution. Prostitution may not be reported as people understand that such activities occur and are willing for them to continue providing it does not affect them. It is also acknowledged that women earn a living from such activity and men receive a 'service'. As it is legalised in other countries, in certain situations many people may feel that, due to both parties' consent, it should not be illegal.

Many people are unaware that vagrancy is a crime.

Other perceived victimless crimes

Other perceived victimless crimes include assisted suicide. In assisted suicide the victim actually desires the action to take place. It is often a crime carried out due to compassion and love rather than a wish for financial gain or revenge. The government has produced guidelines to indicate when prosecutions are unlikely to take place, showing it is recognised that in certain circumstances no action will be taken.

Take it further

Research the Crown Prosecution Guidelines, which can be found online.

Literacy skills

Using the following words can you produce five separate sentences relating to unreported crime – each one using one of the following words:

- complexity
- disinterest
- controversial
- decriminalisation
- legalisation.

Then try to improve each sentence by adding an example to support your comment.

AC1.3 EXPLAIN THE CONSEQUENCES OF UNREPORTED CRIME

ASSESSMENT CRITERION	MARK BAND 1	MARK BAND 2
AC1.3 Explain the consequences of unreported crime	Limited explanation (may only list examples) of the consequences of unreported crime **(1–2)**	Clear and detailed explanation of the reasons why a range of crimes are unreported, using relevant examples **(3–4)**

CONTENT	AMPLIFICATION
Consequences • ripple effect • cultural • decriminalisation • police prioritisation • unrecorded crime • cultural change • legal change • procedural change	You should have an understanding of the positive and negative effects of unreported crime on the individual and on society

Handy hints !

To access mark band 2, all consequences must be covered, but it is expected that coverage will be brief. This may be little more than a definition of the consequence and an example.

Ripple effect

A ripple effect describes how the impact of crime can spread beyond the immediate victim throughout their family, friends and community. In other words, it ripples out much wider than the initial victims.

The ripple effect sees more than just the initial victim of the crime being affected.

Consider the offence of domestic abuse and the number of people this could affect. Abusers are often abused as children, or have witnessed the abuse of parents as children. If this goes unreported it can appear that it is acceptable, or children are socialised into this behaviour which goes unpunished and then repeat it as adults, causing a ripple effect. It can also affect other family members and neighbours who witness or hear incidents, or friends who may be distressed at the violence, or even work colleagues who will be affected if the victim is absent from work.

Children who are abused are much more likely to become adults who abuse.

Activity

Consider the impact of a house burglary. The consequences reach beyond just the people who live in the household. Who may they include?

Cultural

Sometimes there are cultural differences that make actions criminal in one country and not another. Cultural differences may mean that crimes are under-reported or not recognised. It can be difficult to understand cultures that are very different from our own. Often people will ignore or turn a blind eye to actions or customs that are alien to ours. They may feel it is not their place to interfere and therefore criminals and potential criminals may believe they can proceed without consequences.

Female genital mutilation is illegal in the UK but culturally there are some communities who believe it is an acceptable thing to do. Similarly, with honour killing, while alien to a Western society, there are many cultures that believe it is appropriate to take such drastic action.

CASE STUDY

KRISTY BAMU

The case of Kristy Bamu saw a 15-year-old boy being accused of involvement in witchcraft and then killed by members of his own family. The family were originally from the Democratic Republic of the Congo, where witchcraft or Kindoki is practised and exorcisms are carried out in some churches. Kristy was tortured over the course of several days before being drowned in a bath during an exorcism.

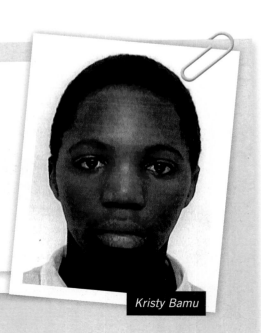

Kristy Bamu

Decriminalisation

Laws are frequently altered because they cannot be imposed or enforced. For example, the use of cannabis can be quite open in some places in the UK, because the police choose not to act. Eventually, the government has little choice but to decriminalise such offences because it has to accept that the criminal act cannot be controlled because people no longer take notice of the law.

When crimes go unreported, often it is due to lack of public concern and interest, or because it is seen as a victimless crime. This includes:

- drugs
- prostitution
- illegal downloads.

Such actions are common, widespread crimes that people do not see as 'real' offences so publically they become decriminalised. Although there are still laws against them, the punishments have been reduced, and less time and money are spent trying to find perpetrators of these crimes. In some cases these offences are even legalised. Eventually, the government has little choice over what can and cannot be controlled. They have no choice but to decriminalise some actions because they have to accept that people do not take notice of the law anymore.

Key terms

Decriminalise: Stop something from being illegal.

Perpetrators: People who commit criminal acts (offenders).

Legalise: Make an act legal within the law.

Police prioritisation

The police often prioritise certain crimes, ensuring that issues in a local area are addressed. This means that some crimes are not prioritised or are not investigated. For instance, in recent years there has been a rise in the number of sexual abuse cases, historic offences and reported domestic assault. The police have responded to the public's expectation for these crimes to be investigated. However, given the cost of both time and money on such investigations, the police do not have the capacity to deal with all crime. Hence, some offences can go unreported, as the public feel the police do not have the time to respond to their issue or where crimes are reported but due to police prioritisation they are not investigated. Alternatively, a swifter punishment may be dispensed such as a caution rather than a court case.

Key term

Historic offences: Crimes that were committed many years ago but are being prosecuted now, often due to a delay in reporting them to the police.

The police in County Durham have indicated that they will no longer actively pursue smokers and small-scale growers of cannabis in order to prioritise their resources against more serious crime. The aim is to reduce costs and keep users out of the criminal justice system so they could focus on organised crime and gang crime.

Hate crime, especially if it is carried out on social media, is currently a crime requiring police prioritisation. Two of the police priorities in South Wales are to reduce and prevent crime and anti-social behaviour and to work to make the local criminal justice system efficient and effective. These priorities can be found in the South Wales Police and Crime Plan for 2019–2023.

Social media hate crime

Hate crime has recently been a priority of the police. In 2016 a new unit was created in London's Metropolitan Police Force to investigate hate speech online. As part of a funded two-year project the unit will be responsible for the filtering and identification of hate crimes online, before informing regional police forces, which will take action against crimes committed online.

Rt Hon. Alun Michael, South Wales Police and Crime Commissioner

Unrecorded crime

Unrecorded crime involves crimes that are reported to the police but are not recorded by them as offences. This means an investigation into the alleged crime is unlikely to happen and the offender will not be punished or other crimes prevented. Clearly, the more serious these offences are, the more serious the consequences could be.

Activity

Watch 'Police Efforts Hampered by Unreported Crimes', at www.youtube.com/watch?v=78c6IXOKGpE and record the impact on the police in the USA for people failing to report crimes.

Activity

To support your comments on the above, research unrecorded crime and use statistics on different police-force areas in your controlled assessment. This will help develop and add detail to your work.

Cultural change

Within our own communities it may become the culture for crimes to be committed. Crime becomes a natural consequence of a culture shift, almost a way of life. For instance, illegal video streaming, from sports and movie channels, regularly takes place. Within a community many people may not see this as something that they should not do, so it is not reported and hence becomes acceptable.

When an area becomes run-down, for example properties have been vandalised or poverty turns people to petty crimes such as drug use or prostitution, the culture of the area can grow worse and more crimes are committed because no-one is reporting them so no-one is punished. This can lead to worse crimes such as drug dealing, rape and murder. If the area is cleaned up and smaller crimes are reported and properly dealt with, crime rates in the area will go down.

Take it further

Kelling and Wilson (1982) proposed the 'broken windows theory', which states that unchecked and unreported minor crime leads to further and more serious crime, for example an uncared for area of a town begins to act as a magnet for delinquent behaviour. Thus, they claimed that all crime should be tackled to avoid proliferation of further crime.

Activity

Create a poster explaining the broken windows theory.

The broken windows theory explains the consequences of failing to report crimes.

Legal change

Crimes may go unreported for a long time because they are perceived as human rights. For instance, homosexuality was illegal within the UK for many years. As the stigma towards homosexuality has reduced, legal changes have been made to the laws surrounding it. In October 2015 same-sex marriage was legalised. In this way, failing to report crime can have a positive consequence.

Similarly, there has been substantial legal change towards the smoking of cigarettes. At one stage smoking cigarettes was glamorised in the movies and even encouraged by the medical profession. However, as medical knowledge in this area developed, the risks of smoking prompted change. In 2007 smoking in enclosed public spaces become illegal and in 2015 it became illegal to smoke in a car with anyone under the age of 18 present. These were positive consequences from legal change.

Key term

Stigma: A mark of disgrace associated with something bad.

Procedural change

The actual procedural way of reporting crime has developed over the years to encourage reporting to take place. Traditionally, visiting the police station or, in an emergencey, telephoning 999 were the common methods of reporting a crime. Now other procedures have been introduced to report crime to the police. Some groups such as victim support can help people report offences. It is even possible to report a crime anonymously, for example through CrimeStoppers. There are specialised teams of police that deal with certain crimes such as hate crime, terrorism, fraud or anti-social behaviour that encourage crimes of that nature to be reported. There are also several apps that can be downloaded to a mobile phone to allow quick access to the police. In addition, some makes of mobile phones can connect to the police by shaking them or by quick pressing of the on/off button. These are positive consequences from procedural change.

Activity

Go to www.police.uk/pu/contact-the-police/what-and-how-to-report/how-to-report/ and discover how to report crimes committed in different situations such as:

- an emergency
- a non-emergency
- a terrorist act
- reporting anonymously
- fraud and cybercrime.

Report a crime anonymously through CrimeStoppers.

Literacy skills

Can you write sentences to appropriately include each of the following words?
- Culture
- Ripple effect
- Decriminalisation
- Hate crime
- Prioritisation

AC1.4 DESCRIBE MEDIA REPRESENTATION OF CRIME

ASSESSMENT CRITERION	MARK BAND 1	MARK BAND 2
AC1.4 You should be able to ... Describe media representation of crime	Limited description of the media representation of crime (1–3)	Detailed description of the media representation of crime, including relevant examples (4–6)

CONTENT	AMPLIFICATION
Media • newspaper • television • film • electronic gaming • social media (blogs, social networking) • music	You should have knowledge of specific examples of how different forms of media are used to portray fictional and factual representations of crime

Handy hints !

To reach mark band 2 you must include relevant examples of the media portrayal of crimes in the various types of media. You do not have to consider the impact of this portrayal.

Handy hints !

Make sure that you include all the content in your answer:

· newspapers
· television
· film
· electronic gaming
· social media
· music.

Newspapers

A vast amount of newspaper space is devoted to crime stories such as stabbings, shootings, murder and terrorist attacks. On a typical day, articles throughout a range of newspapers are related to reporting current crimes or concerned with the impact of crime. This relates to both local and national newspapers.

When a major incident occurs, the front pages of all newspapers and many sections inside contain the latest pictures and reports from the event. The August 2017 terrorist attacks in Barcelona were reported on the pages of all British newspapers, with dramatic headlines using words such as 'massacre', 'bloodbath', 'evil', 'terror', 'Barcelona Bastards' and 'slaughtered on the streets'. It is interesting that both tabloid and broadsheet newspapers reported this in a similar style. While terrorist attacks are atrocities and must never be condoned, it is interesting to note that often the media will sensationalise crime or over-exaggerate the event. Reporting often takes place in dramatic terms with a focus on the negative aspects, as if to scaremonger.

Key term

Tabloid: A type of popular newspaper with small pages, many pictures and short stories.

Broadsheet: A more serious newspaper that used to be printed on large sheets of paper but is now often printed on smaller sheets.

Scaremonger: Spread stories that cause the public fear.

Activity

Read the same crime-related story in two very different styles of newspaper and see in what ways the stories vary and in what ways they are similar.

Front pages from two British newspapers after the Barcelona terrorist attack in 2017.

Television

Television plays a major role in the portrayal of crime by the media. Television is used to portray both fictional and factual representations of crime. *Crimewatch* and *Police Camera Action!* are examples of factual programmes.

There have been many dramas based on high-profile crimes such as *Little Boy Blue*, based on the murder of Rhys Jones in 2007, and *The Moorside*, based on the kidnap of Shannon Matthews in 2008. There are also many fictional crime shows on television such as *The Bay*, *Line of Duty*, *Bulletproof* and *Strike*. According to Tim Newburn (2007) about 1/10th of prime-time television is concerned with crime and law enforcement from the 1950s. This has since increased, and is now roughly 1/4 of all output devoted to crime.

Activity

Review a television listing guide and discover the percentage of shows that relate to crime.

The Wolf of Wall Street, *one of many films about crime.*

Films

Films have a huge impact on the way people see crimes and the facts and fictions surrounding them. Films such as: *Suicide Squad*, *Die Hard*, *The Godfather* and *The Wolf of Wall Street* are all films that have a main focus on crime and corruption.

Electronic gaming

A form of media that is used to represent the fictional side of crime is gaming. The majority of crime games are aimed at over 18s. However, games can often trivialise crime, suggesting that violence is acceptable or that crime is appropriate. *Grand Theft Auto* is an example of a crime game, it encourages the players to steal cars, meet with prostitutes and kill people for game points.

Literacy skills ⚙⚙

How many words can you find that represent the way the media can over-exaggerate crime. For example, scaremonger, glorify, etc.

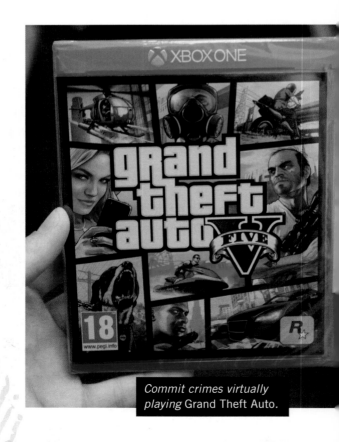

Commit crimes virtually playing Grand Theft Auto.

Social media (blogs, social networking)

The reporting of crime often appears on social media. Members of the public can raise awareness of crimes through postings. Police-force areas have Facebook and Twitter pages that allow increasing public awareness of particular crimes. They can also be used to enable the public to see what criminals are doing in their area or to make pleas for information from potential witnesses.

Social media sites offer the public a way of reporting crime.

Music

Many songs throughout the decades have been devoted to crime or criminals. Examples include 'I Fought the Law' by The Clash and 'Bonnie and Clyde' by Georgie Fame. Eminem has made several songs that allude to crime, sex and drugs, and Nirvana's 'Polly' is also based on crime. This happens worldwide, for example B.A.P, a Korean boy band, regularly use the concept of murder, theft and kidnapping in their music videos to portray gang culture.

The Clash had a hit with 'I Fought the Law'.

AC1.5 EXPLAIN THE IMPACT OF MEDIA REPRESENTATIONS ON THE PUBLIC PERCEPTION OF CRIME

ASSESSMENT CRITERION	MARK BAND 1	MARK BAND 2
AC1.5 You should be able to … Explain the impact of media representations on the public perception of crime	Limited explanation of the impact of media representations on the public perception of crime **(1–3)**	Clear and detailed explanation of the impact of a range of media representations on the public perception of crime **(4–6)**

CONTENT	AMPLIFICATION
Impact • moral panic • changing public concerns and attitudes • perceptions of crime trends • stereotyping of criminals • levels of response to crime and types of punishment • changing priorities and emphasis	You should be familiar with specific examples of media portrayal of criminality and the range of impacts given Understanding of these impacts should be based on theories

Handy hints !

In the controlled assessment make sure you not only explain the issues under each heading but also the **impact** of each one on the public perception of crime.

Moral panic

Research shows that the media exaggerate levels of serious crime and the risk of becoming a victim, which is known as moral panic. This has been found true for studies of newspapers (March, 1991, cited in Hale et al., 2013), television (Gunter et al., 2003, cited in Hale et al., 2013) and radio content (Cumberbatch et al., 1995, cited in Hale et al., 2013).

The sociologist Stanley Cohen, in his book *Folk Devils and Moral Panics* (1973), suggested that a moral panic occurs when a 'condition, episode, person or group of persons emerges to become defined as a threat to societal values and interests' (page 9).

One of the first moral panics occurred in the 1960s, with the media's portrayal of the clashes between Mods and Rockers. The media portrayed the event in a sensationalised way, with lawless gangs fighting.

Key term

Moral panic: Used to describe the consequence of the media presentation of something that has happened where the general public react in a panicky manner. The reporting is usually exaggerated and consequently the public reaction is inflated.

One headline read 'Wild Ones Invade Seaside – 97 Arrests'. In fact there were only 24 arrests.

Other examples of moral panic range from the risk of contracting HIV in the 1980s to the modern moral panic surrounding the reporting of terrorism and the subsequent result of Islamophobia.

The impact of a moral panic is to make the public think the issue is worse than it is in reality. This may bring about a more severe reaction to the issue and people involved, and an unreasonable desire for justice. For instance, the increase in punishments for crimes that occurred in the London riots of 2011.

Changing public concerns and attitudes

Over time, the public have been concerned about different types of crime. As seen in the previous section, at one stage the public were concerned about violence from the rivalry between Mods and Rockers. However, recently the threat of terrorism has caused a high level of concern to the public. This was fuelled by attacks such as those in London, Manchester and Barcelona in 2017. In addition, the media have reported a rise in knife-attack crimes and this causes alarm among the public.

The impact of changing concerns and attitudes reflects on the policing and government priorities. For instance, in response to terrorist acts the government may raise the threat level, for example from severe to critical following concerns after the Manchester attack in May 2017. Islamophobia also has an impact of the public's attitude towards terrorism. This is when Muslims are the victims of attacks just because of their religion. Alternatively, the concern about knife crime can result in a knife amnesty, involving the surrender of illegal knives without facing criminal action.

Take it further »

Watch the short clip on YouTube called 'Mods, Rockers and Moral Panics' to learn more about moral panics.

Key terms

Islamophobia: A dislike of or prejudice against Islam or Muslims.

Amnesty: To officially pardon or give official confirmation that no criminal action will be taken.

Memorial in St Ann's Square to the victims of the Manchester attack.

Perceptions of crime trends

Generally, the public's perception is that crime is on the increase. When the media report a high volume of crime stories, it impacts on the public, giving them a false belief about the amount of crime. This is because research suggests that crime is decreasing. According to the Crime Survey for England and Wales (ONS, 2020):

- *Total police recorded crime decreased by 4% in England and Wales to approximately 5.8 million offences in the 12 months ending June 2020;*

- *There were also falls in offences involving firearms (9% decrease) and knives or sharp instruments (1% decrease) across England and Wales;*

- *The number of victims of total TCSEW crime including fraud and computer misuse decreased by 19% in April to June 2020.*

It is important to note that some of this data may have been impacted by the Corona virus lockdown that began in March 2020.

However, crime statistics for England and Wales, year ending September 2019, suggest that levels are stable.

- *following a long-term reduction, levels of crime have remained broadly stable in recent years. While in the latest year there has been no change in overall levels of crime, this hides variation seen in individual crime types*

- *a 6% decrease in the overall number of homicides following a period of increases*

- *no percentage change in the number of police recorded offences involving firearms*

- *no percentage change in the number of police recorded offences involving firearms.* **(ONS, 2020)**

The impacts of the public perception of a rising crime rate are anxiety and stress about being a victim of crime and the subsequent repercussions. 'The Good Childhood Report' (Children's Society, 2020) found that the wellbeing and happiness of millions of children is being affected by concerns about crime in their local area. This report, based on a survey of 3,000 10- to 17-year-olds and their parents, found that two in five teenagers in the UK worry about anti-social behaviour and other crimes.

Take it further

Search for 'The Good Childhood Report' on the internet for more information about the survey.

Stereotyping of criminals

As a result of media reports, the public form stereotypes of criminals. Often they are seen as poor and uneducated members of society. In the USA many members of society see criminals as young black men. In the UK young people are seen by many, especially the older members of society, as 'hoodies' and thugs. They are labelled as juvenile delinquents who go around in gangs causing trouble.

The media's reporting of crime can produce stereotyping of criminals.

This stereotyping of criminals results in the public being mistrusting of people who fit the stereotypical image. The public may also become angry and fear crime, thus supporting harsher sentences.

Levels of response to crime and types of punishment

The media has an impact on the levels of response and punishment to certain crimes.

CASE STUDY

The London riots in 2011 are an example of how punishments can be affected by the media hype of reporting crime. According to the *Guardian* newspaper, the court gave prison sentences to the rioters that were on average 25% longer than normal. The *Guardian* newspaper's data also reported that

56 defendants of the 80 who have already been sentenced by magistrates were given immediate prison terms. This 70% rate of imprisonment compares with a 'normal' rate of just 2% in magistrates courts. **(Travis & Rogers, 2011)**

Other examples include a man sentenced to six months in prison for stealing a £3.50 case of water and two men sentenced to four years each for using Facebook to incite a riot that never took place. Such sentences would never have been given if they had not occurred during the riots. The media's representation of the events prompted the courts to get tough on the criminals.

The impact of this response to crime is to produce disproportionate sentences that fail to reflect the seriousness of the crime. The response is to show that crime of this nature will not be tolerated and to set a deterrent punishment to prevent similar conduct.

Take it further

Hold a class discussion about how to strike a balance between informing people about crimes and ensuring they are aware of them without over-reporting and scaring people. Use the example of reporting about Covid scams to support the discussion.

Literacy skills

Correct the spelling of the following words:
- responce
- steotype
- dilinquent
- purception
- Islamophobia
- morel panic.

Changing priorities and emphasis

Certain major criminal events are world changing, producing new priorities and policies. For example, the 9/11 attacks on the Twin Towers, New York, in 2001, have had a lasting impact, with new policies made that affect everyone:

- The Anti-terrorism Crime and Security Act 2001 allows the bank accounts of suspected terrorists to be frozen.
- The Counter Terrorism Act 2008 gives the police more powers to take finger prints and DNA samples.
- There is heightened security at airports, tube stations and train stations.
- The government has produced a counter-terrorism or prevent strategy to challenge extremism in all aspects of our lives.

The impact of changing priorities can be far-reaching, including travel and education, and the curbing of civil liberties.

Handy hints

Make sure you include all the identified content to reach the top mark band:

- moral panic
- changing public concerns and attitudes
- perceptions of crime trends
- stereotyping of criminals
- levels of response to crime and types of punishment
- changing priorities and emphasis.

Key term

Civil liberties: Basic rights and freedoms granted to citizens of a country by the law.

World Trade Center Memorial Plaza, remembering the 9/11 attack in New York.

AC1.6 EVALUATE METHODS OF COLLECTING STATISTICS ABOUT CRIME

ASSESSMENT CRITERION	MARK BAND 1	MARK BAND 2
AC1.6 You should be able to … Evaluate methods of collecting statistics about crime	Limited (may only list methods/ sources of information) evaluation of two methods of collecting information about crime **(1–3)**	Clear and detailed evaluation of two methods/sources of information used to collect information about crime, with clear evidence of reasoning Detailed and relevant reference to specific sources **(4–6)**

CONTENT	AMPLIFICATION
Evaluation criteria • reliability • validity • ethics of research • strengths and limitations • purpose of research **Information about crime** • Home Office statistics • Crime Survey for England and Wales	You should evaluate the methods used to collect and present the two sources of information about crime given in the content. The evaluation should use the criteria specified in the content

Measuring and tracking trends in crime

There were traditionally two main methods of measuring and tracking trends in crime:

1. Recorded crime statistics collected by the police (Home Office).

2. Information collected in the Crime Survey for England and Wales (CSEW) (formally called the British Crime Survey).

Handy hints

Make sure that in the controlled assessment, wh you write about this AC, yc comment on both methods measuring crime througho the evaluation.

Police recorded crime

The Home Office provides police recorded crime (PRC) in tables that contain recorded crime figures broken down by offence type, geography and time period. This information can be accessed by the public. It should be noted that these figures can be affected by changes in recording policy and practice.

Activity

Go to the Police UK website (www.police.uk/), type in your postcode and look at the crimes in your local area. Consider which crimes the police should be focusing their resources on. For instance:

- Are there any common crimes?
- Should resources be used to combat them?
- Are there serious offences that require resources?
- Should patrols be diverted to certain areas? Are certain streets being targeted for burglaries?

The answers may be different in various parts of the country.

Crime Survey for England and Wales (CSEW)

This is a victim survey that asks a sample of the population in England and Wales about their experiences of crime. It includes crimes against households and adults, also including data on crime experienced by children as well as crimes against society and businesses. An important feature of this survey is that it includes crimes that are not reported to the police. This makes the survey potentially a more accurate recording measure than surveys that just ask about crimes reported to the police. As well as information about the nature of the crime, it includes location and timing, characteristics of the offender and relationship between offender and victim.

Activity

Go to the Office for National Statistics (ONS) website for the CSEW ending with the latest date and record some of the statistics. Such data can be used in your controlled assessment to show the types of crimes that are taking place. Such statistics can also be compared to police recorded crime. Consider the two sets of measures of crime recording and ask if they produce the same or different results.

Key term

Victim surveys: Occur where the intention is to interview a representative sample of a particular population and to ask a series of questions about their experience of victimisation. These surveys started in the USA; the first such survey in the UK was in 1972. It later became the British Crime Survey and from 2012 has been called the Crime Survey for England and Wales.

The CSEW is a victim survey.

SURVEY

Reliability of methods of collecting statistics about crime

Reliability is the consistency of results when the experiment is replicated under the same conditions. Any statistic has its limitations and no source can tell us with complete accuracy what is happening with crime. However, as the CSEW also considers crime not reported to the police, it may be more reliable. The methods of recording crimes by the police have changed over the years and are acknowledged to have affected data and hence the reliability; comparing yearly statistics will have its limitations.

Validity of methods of collecting statistics about crime

Validity is described as the degree to which a research study measures what it intends to measure. If the results of a study are not deemed to be valid then they are meaningless. If a crime survey is meant to record the amount of crime that has taken place it may not be truly valid. For example, the victim may be unaware of the offence or the crime may be victimless. In addition, not all crime is reported and reporting a crime to the police does not always mean it is recorded by them.

Ethics of methods for collecting statistics about crime

Ethics of methods for collecting statistics about crime concerns moral rules and codes of conduct to the collection, analysis, reporting and publication of information from the research. In particular, it means active acceptance of the right to privacy, confidentiality and informed consent. The CSEW is entirely confidential and the details are only used for research purposes. They are not passed on to any other organisation.

Strengths and limitations of methods for collecting statistics about crime

STRENGTHS	LIMITATIONS
• CSEW captures unreported crime • CSEW relies on first-hand victim knowledge and may be more accurate than police-interpreted information • CSEW identifies those most at risk, so informs crime prevention schemes • CSEW looks at people's experience of anti-social behaviour and how it affects their quality of life • Police can use the information provided to detect crimes • CSEW looks at a large sample of participants	• Police do not record all crime reported to them • Police recorded crime does not contain details on unreported crime • Variation in recording practices reduces effectiveness of yearly comparisons • CSEW fails to capture victimless crimes such as drug sales and hidden crimes such as domestic abuse • CSEW relies on the accuracy of the victim's memory • CSEW does not ask every member of the public • Victims may be reluctant to speak about crime and being a victim out of fear, embarrassment, etc. • Lack of parity between the two recording methods resulted in the police reporting a 10% rise in crime and the CSEW reporting a reduction in crime of 7% in 2017

Purpose of the research of methods for collecting statistics about crime

- Provides trends in offending, especially where the two methods show similar results.
- Allows the evaluation and development of crime reduction policies.
- Informs resource management by government and police.
- Provides information on a geographical basis.
- Enables the protection of potential victims.
- Allows the public to voice their views.
- Shows the police workload.
- Shows the emergence of 'new' crimes, for example the use of social media to promote hate crime.

Potential ideas, reliability and validity

Reliability

The reliability of statistics is the consistency of the results when the experiment is replicated under the same conditions. Every statistic has its limitations and no source can be completely accurate. However, the Crime Survey for England and Wales is now based on multiple sources, which indicates that police data alone must have its limitations and may even be unreliable.

Validity

If surveys do not measure what is wanted, then they cannot be used to answer questions about crime and are meaningless and inaccurate. There are several reasons why a crime survey may not record the amount of crime taking place:

- the victim may be unaware of the offence
- there may be no victim
- people decide not to report a crime
- social attitudes towards different offences change
- reporting an offence does not automatically mean it will be recorded by the police.

Handy hints !

When addressing this AC in the controlled assessment, to reach the top mark band make sure you add a lot of detail. Evaluate the methods and don't just describe them, and ensure that you explain how or why the methods affect the statistics. Also use headings such as 'reliability', 'validity', 'strengths and limitations' and 'purpose of research'. These will enhance the look of your answer, make it easier to read and mark and, importantly, ensure that all the relevant points are covered.

LEARNING OUTCOME 2

UNDERSTAND HOW CAMPAIGNS ARE USED TO ELICIT CHANGE

AC2.1 COMPARE CAMPAIGNS FOR CHANGE

ASSESSMENT CRITERION	MARK BAND 1	MARK BAND 2	MARK BAND 3
AC2.1 You should be able to … Compare campaigns for change	Limited awareness of campaigns for change Evidence is mainly descriptive **(1–3)**	Some comparison of a range of campaigns for change There are some links to planned campaigns to support decision making **(4–7)**	Clear and detailed comparison of a range of relevant campaigns for change Explicit links to planned campaign with reference to specific and appropriate sources to support conclusions **(8–10)**

CONTENT	AMPLIFICATION
Campaigns for change, for example: • change in policy • change in law • change in priorities of agencies • change in funding • change in awareness • change in attitude	You should be aware that campaigns for change may have different purposes You should compare examples of campaigns for change and examine their effectiveness in achieving their objectives Campaigns could include, for example, classification of drugs, euthanasia, abortion, smoking, etc.

Key term

Campaigns for change: Relate to a set of planned activities that people carry out over a period of time in order to achieve something such as social or legal change.

Purposes of campaigns for change

There are many campaigns for change, with a range of subjects and aims or purposes that are desired by people. Many relate to a change in law or policy. As required by this AC, a range of campaigns must be compared, which means that similarities and differences need to be considered. Select campaigns that interest you or are easy to understand. To ensure a range of relevant campaigns is selected, it is suggested that a minimum of four or five should be studied. However, this depends on the detail provided. The more campaigns you include the more opportunity you will have to include comparisons.

Some campaign suggestions are listed below, but remember that these are suggestions only, as any appropriate campaign can be selected for comparison in the controlled assessment and at this stage does not have to relate to a crime as a comparison of campaigns; however, their methods and other features are required:

- Sarah's law (child sex offence disclosure scheme)
- Clare's law (disclosure about domestic abuse)
- Helen's law (murderer kept in jail if fails to disclose location of body)
- campaign to abolish the rule against double jeopardy for murder
- Bobby Turnbull's campaign regarding gun licensing
- anti-smoking campaigns
- abortion campaigns
- Brexit
- Lillian's law (drug-driving laws)
- campaign to introduce a Minister for Suicide Prevention.

Let's look at some of the campaigns to gain ideas on how they can be compared.

Sarah's law campaign

In 2000, while she and her family were visiting her grandparents, Sarah Payne, then aged eight, was abducted and murdered by a man called Roy Whiting. Whiting had a previous conviction for abduction and sexually assaulting a young girl. Her mother, Sara Payne, insisted that if she knew someone with such a previous conviction was in the area she would never have consented to her daughter being left to play in the local fields without an adult being present. In other words, she felt that she was unable to make an appropriate decision about the care of her daughter because relevant information was not available. Therefore, Sara started a campaign, based on the American Megan's law, seeking a requirement for the police to make information about local sex offenders available to the parent or carer of a child at risk.

Campaign methods and relevant issues for comparison with other campaigns:

- The campaign was for a change in the law to provide a legal right for parents or carers to formally ask the police if someone with access to a child has a record for child sexual offences.
- Use of the media: the *News of the World*, a Sunday newspaper at that time, backed the campaign and launched a petition backing Sarah's law. Seven-hundred-thousand members of the public showed their support by signing it.

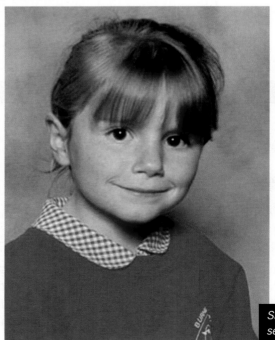

Sarah Payne was abducted and sexually abused.

Key term

Petition: A formal written request, typically one signed by many people, appealing to authority in respect of a particular cause.

This was a controversial campaign, which was opposed by some childcare agencies. The 'name and shame' tactics of the *News of the World,* when it printed 100 pictures of alleged sex offenders, fuelled the opposition. This saw vigilante attacks where, for example, in Portsmouth, 300 people attacked the home of a local taxi driver who had been named by the paper. Also, innocent people were attacked as they looked like people in the published photographs and the home of a paediatrician was attacked due to confusion over the word paedophile.

This campaign arose from a tragic incident involving the death of eight-year-old Sarah Payne. Her parents, Sara and Michael, were the main supporters of the campaign for change, which they helped drive forwards. In particular, Sara spoke at numerous events such as the Police Federation Conference and numerous fund raising events that publicised the campaign. She was awarded the MBE in 2008.

Key terms

Vigilante: A person who tries an unofficial way to prevent crime occurring or to catch and punish a criminal, usually as they believe the police are unable to do so.

Paedophile: A person with a sexual attraction to children.

Sara and Michael Payne were key campaigners.

The campaign could be deemed a success, as the Child Sex Offender Disclosure Scheme (CSODS) was piloted in 2008 and rolled out across England and Wales in 2011. According to the BBC News (2013) website, in 2013 nearly 5,000 applications seeking disclosure of the sex offenders living in the area had been made and more than 700 paedophiles had been identified since the introduction of the Scheme in 2011.

Take it further

Read the Parliamentary Research Briefing Paper 'Sarah's Law: The Child Sex Offender Disclosure Scheme', which can be found online at https://commonslibrary.parliament.uk/research-briefings/sn01692/. This will provide you with further details of this scheme.

Brexit campaign

The United Kingdom joined the European Economic Community (former name for the European Union) on 1 January 1973. This was after two previous applications for membership had been rejected. Brexit is an abbreviation for 'British exit', which refers to the referendum, on 23 June 2016, whereby British citizens voted to exit the European Union.

Brexit

Brexit and the media

Brexit campaign methods and relevant issues for comparison with other campaigns include:

- **The Brexit campaign**: was for a constitutional change in the membership of Britain in the European Union, unlike Sarah's law which sought to change freedom of information.

- **Use of a referendum**: to allow democracy to take place. This rare technique was used to allow the public to speak and make a decision that would have a major impact on the country and the European Union.

- **Key characters:** Boris Johnson and Michael Gove, two politicians who were at the forefront of Brexit. Whereas, Sarah's law campaign was fronted by her parents, particularly her mother Sara Payne.

- **Successful vote outcome:** on 23 June 2016 the UK voted by a majority of 52% to 48% to leave the EU.

- **Use of celebrities:** the actors Elizabeth Hurley, Michael Caine and Joan Collins and President Donald Trump were all very vocal in supporting Brexit.

- **Use of the media:** this included prime time televised debates and newspapers such as the *Sun*, the *Daily Telegraph* and the *Sunday Times* that readily provided headlines supporting Brexit. However, it was the former Sunday newspaper, the *News of the World*, that spearheaded Sarah's law campaign.

> ### Key term
>
> **Referendum:** A general vote by the electorate on a single political question that has been referred to them for a direct decision.

Assisted dying campaign

Assisting a person to die or helping them commit suicide is a criminal offence under section 2 of the Suicide Act 1961. This would involve an act capable of assisting the suicide or attempted suicide of another person, for example administering a lethal dose of medication. It is punishable with up to 14 years in prison. However, there has been a series of attempts to change the law by applications to both the courts and to Parliament.

The assisted dying campaign methods and relevant issues for comparison with other campaigns include:

- The campaign sought a change in the criminal law with the abolition of the criminal offence under section 2 of the Suicide Act 1961. This is unlike Brexit, which sought a change to constitutional law.
- **Key characters:** Diane Pretty, Tony Nicklinson and Debbie Purdy, who all made applications to the High Court, seeking the right to die at the time and method of their choosing. All were suffering from a terminal illness. However, all were unsuccessful.
- This was a highly controversial issue where there were two sides and no middle ground. In this way it is similar to the Brexit campaign.
- Partial success was achieved when, as a result of Debbie Purdy's case, the Director of Public Prosecutions produced guidance and a list of factors explaining when a prosecution for assisted suicide would not be likely. The law, however, remained unchanged. In contrast, the campaign for Sarah's law was fully successful.
- **Uses of celebrities:** Sir Patrick Stewart (actor, including *Star Trek*), Zoë Wannamaker (actress) and Sir Michael Holroyd (author) are all patrons of the Dignity in Dying group. As was the late Sir Terry Pratchett (author), who campaigned for assisted suicide after being diagnosed with Alzheimer's disease.
- The campaigning resulted in a bill (proposed law) being put before parliament to try to legalise assisted dying. Lord Falconer's 'Assisted Dying Bill' was rejected in September 2015 by Parliament, so the law remains unchanged.

Debbie Purdy and her husband Omar

Change to the double jeopardy law campaign

The law concerning double jeopardy states that an offender cannot be tried twice for the same offence. This is to protect individuals from endless prosecutions or multiple attempts at securing a conviction for the same incident.

The double jeopardy campaign methods and relevant issues for comparison with other campaigns include:

- The campaign sought a change to the criminal law with an abolition of the double jeopardy rule for serious offences such as murder and manslaughter. This change in criminal law compares to the criminal law change requested in the assisted dying campaign.
- The campaign was lead by a mother whose daughter had been killed in tragic circumstances: similar to the Sarah Payne campaign. Ann Ming's daughter, Julie Hogg, was murdered by her partner, Billy Dunlop. Dunlop was charged with the murder and appeared in two trials where the jury failed to reach a decision. However, he later confessed to the killing but thought he was protected by the double jeopardy law. When the law was changed he became the first person to be charged under the new rules. He was convicted of murder and is still serving his life sentence.

> ### Key terms
>
> **Constitutional law:** The fundamental principles according to which a state is governed.
>
> **Dignity in Dying:** A campaign group who believe that assisted dying for terminally ill, mentally competent adults should be legal in the UK.
>
> **Bill:** A proposed piece of legislation that attempts to proceed through the stages of parliamentary law making.

Ann Ming and her husband Charlie

- Ann Ming's campaign was supported by the media and in particular the *Northern Echo* newspaper, which ran stories in support and kept the issue in the public eye.
- Ann Ming's campaign was successful and the Criminal Justice Act 2003 brought in the changes to this area of law. This is similar to the Sarah's law campaign but differs from the assisted dying campaign, which did not change the law.

Ideas for comparisons:

- People behind campaign, for example family or groups.
- Focus of campaign, for example change in criminal law or constitutional law.
- National/country-wide.
- Arose out of a tragic incident.
- Support given, for example personalities or politicians.
- Use of media coverage.
- Was it successful? Did it make any changes? If so state them.

Extract answer

An answer for AC2.1 in the controlled assessment could be:

There are several campaigns that could be considered as being successful. Sarah's law, a campaign that resulted from the killing of Sarah Payne, produced a disclosure scheme to allow parents to find out if any paedophiles live in the area. Also, the campaign, supported by Ann Ming, to abolish the rule of double jeopardy for murder, was also successful when it got the law changed. However, the campaign for Scottish independence was unsuccessful and Scotland is still part of the UK.

Many campaigns have come about after a tragic event. These include Sarah's law, Lillian's law and Claire's law, all of which involved the killing of a young girl. In addition, the campaigns were all led by family members. However, the Brexit campaign resulted from the wish of the people to leave the EU. It was led by politicians.

Many campaigns wanted a change in the criminal law. These included Sarah's law, Lillian's law and Claire's law. They were also all national campaigns.

Many campaigns use the media to help promote their cause. For example, Sarah's law was helped by the former newspaper the News of the World. It also used a petition, as did the Campaign for Scottish Independence and Lillian's law.

Handy hints !

✓ Do not write too much about the story behind the campaign. It is the issues concerning how the campaign came about, how it was run and how it can be compared with other campaigns that are important.

✓ Try to name the change in law or policy that the campaign brought about.

✓ 'Compare' can mean look at differences as well as similarities.

✓ Introduce statistics, where available, to support your conclusions.

Assessment

Mark band 2 (4–7 marks)

This answer would reach mark band 2 as it contains a range of campaigns and a number of comparisons. A further positive is that there is some mention of differences as well as similarities. Changes are mentioned but lack specific detail, for instance the name of the act that changed the double jeopardy law or the name of the scheme introduced as a result of the Sarah's law campaign. There is also an overall lack of detail, which could be added, such as the use of statistics on the result of the Scottish independence campaign, details of who lead the various campaigns and information about the changes sought could be added. Finally, to achieve the top mark band it is necessary to have explicit links to your planned campaign, see the handy hints below.

Handy hints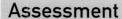

It is important to note the criterion in mark band 3, namely *'explicit links to planned campaign with reference to specific and appropriate sources to support conclusions'*. To gain the higher marks there must be a reference to your campaign. Although the campaign is formed in LO3, make sure you link your campaign to some of the campaigns compared. Consider such issues as:

- What type of change does your campaign seek? Is it a change in law or policy? If not, make the point that your campaign has a different aim from the researched campaigns and is to raise awareness of a crime.
- Consider campaign methods. Are they similar to your campaign, for example a petition, social media page or merchandise? Or are they different and you have written a song or arranged a concert. Has a local or national newspaper agreed to support the campaign?
- Make reference to the researched campaign's sources or sources from your campaign to help with drawing of comparisons.
- It is very important that the unreported crime at the centre of your campaign is a crime that is also identified in the brief.

Take it further

Research some of these recent campaigns:

- P.C. Harper's family campaign (Andrew's law)
- Helen McCourt's family campaign (Helen's law)
- the Assisted Dying Coalition formed in 2019 to support a change in the law
- Covid 19 campaign – stay home, protect the NHS and save lives
- Marcus Rashford's campaign for free school meals.

AC2.2 EVALUATE THE EFFECTIVENESS OF MEDIA USED IN CAMPAIGNS FOR CHANGE

ASSESSMENT CRITERION	MARK BAND 1	MARK BAND 2	MARK BAND 3
AC2.2 You should be able to … Evaluate the effectiveness of media used in campaigns for change	Limited evaluation of the effectiveness of media used in campaigns for change Evidence is mainly descriptive and limited in range **(1–5)**	Some evaluation of the effectiveness of a range of media used in relevant campaigns for change Response is largely descriptive but includes some appropriate judgements **(6–10)**	Clear and detailed evaluation of the effectiveness of a range of media used in relevant campaigns for change Clear evidence of well-reasoned judgements to support conclusions **(11–15)**

Handy hints !

Note that the links do not have to be with the campaigns used in AC2.1.

Handy hints !

To reach this mark band the evaluation must contain both positives and negatives, and provide examples on their effectiveness. This could be the number of likes or shares with regard to social media.

Handy hints !

Note that you need to include a range of media. You could be asked to refer to a set number in the controlled assessment so, to ensure you achieve high marks, make sure you consider five or six campaigns in class. In addition, it is important that they each have their own evaluation rather than general comments about the effectiveness of media.

CONTENT	AMPLIFICATION
Media • blogs • viral messaging • social networking • advertising • radio • television • film • documentary • word of mouth • events • print Please make sure you select your media from this list.	You should have knowledge of the media and specific materials used in campaigns, and be able to evaluate their effectiveness in promoting a campaign for change

Handy hints !

You must link these types of media methods back to a range of real-life campaigns to give them context and address whether or not they have been used effectively. To do this, provide a range of different campaigns and at least four media types in detail.

Under each type of media make sure you include the following information:

· definition of method
· effectiveness of method
· limitations of method
· examples of use of media and an explanation as to whether each is used effectively. This could include statistics showing awareness, for example the number of shares or likes on social media or amount of money raised by a campaign.

The use of blogging can be a very effective media method in a campaign.

Blogs

A blog is a regularly updated website or web page, typically run by an individual or small group, which is written in an informal or conversational style.

An advantage of using a blog in a campaign is that anyone can set blogs up and they are free of charge. As well as this, they allow people to express their views and opinions on specific topics. There are up-to-date information and statistics on blogs that will keep the content fresh and interesting. Usually, there will be links to social media pages, which allow readers to find out more and donate to the campaign. Furthermore, they do not just contain writing; they also have video links, pictures and links to other similar websites that may also be of interest to the reader.

However, blogs are extremely hard to keep up to date and they can become quite time-consuming for the author. As well as this, it is becoming an out-of-date method because many people prefer to use social media as it can be more appealing to a younger audience. A blog has to be found in order to find information, so generally there will be a limited audience of people who are really interested in the cause or the campaign.

The environmental campaign group Greenpeace uses a blog that has videos, images and articles included on it, and the majority of posts have been shared via social media platforms, helping to widen their audience. Some of the things have been shared nearly 1,000 times, which shows that the blog can be effective in raising awareness to the public.

Handy hints !

Make sure you give well-reasoned judgements to support conclusions. Statistics or data help with such justifications.

Social networking

Social networks are websites such as Facebook and Twitter, which are dedicated to allowing people to communicate with one another.

When used for campaign purposes, social networking allows videos, information and other forms of communication to spread quickly and reach a wide audience. Approximately 2.3 billion people use social media, so a campaign on one of these platforms will raise a great deal of awareness in a short space of time and in a very cost-effective way.

Around 500 million Tweets are sent every day.

However, hackers can get onto the network pages and alter information. There is also the possibility of internet trolls, who send upsetting messages that can deter people from using the sites.

The ice bucket challenge was used to raise money and awareness of ALS (amyotrophic lateral sclerosis) disease. The campaign posted on Facebook and other social networking sites, requesting people to pour a bucket of ice-cold water over their head and nominate others to do the same. In turn, people would donate money to see this happen. By the end of the campaign it had proved to be a very effective media method as $115 million was raised.

TV advertising

Television advertisements are a span of television programming that are produced and paid for by an organisation. They convey a message, or market a product or service.

Advertisements are usually a very effective use of moving imagery and sometimes include music that fits with the product or campaign. Additionally, they can make issues more memorable for the audience by the use of celebrity endorsement to seize their attention. Also, they will reach a wide audience due to the number of viewers, especially during prime-time slots.

However, adverts can be extremely expensive to make, costing thousands of pounds. The cost of the advert increases if scheduled for a prime-time slot. Moreover, many people skip adverts if a programme is watched on catch-up or simply ignore them if they are not interested in the content. Sometimes, the adverts can be quite graphic with scenes of death occurring in a horrific way, and may upset younger and more vulnerable viewers who may be concerned or associated with the topic. This may have a negative effect on the campaign.

The ice-bucket challenge was a very effective example of a campaign using social networking.

CASE STUDY

WATERAID

The WaterAid campaign in 2014–2015 used TV advertising very effectively. It allowed two million people to receive safe water and 3.1 million people in India were provided with sanitation in their villages. This campaign was supported by actors from the television period drama, *Downton Abbey*. The stars from the show posed with water bottles for a photograph, to raise funds for the charity, as previously a promotional picture for *Downton Abbey* had mistakenly been taken with a plastic bottle in the background. Given that *Downton Abbey* is a period drama, a modern-day bottle of water in a scene was clearly a mistake. The picture was used to raise awareness of this issue and people were also invited to make a donation to WaterAid.

Event

An advantage of public events is that they may be shown on a news programme, which increases publicity, allowing more people to become aware of the campaign. Often the event involves a well-known celebrity attending, helping to raise awareness of the campaign. People are able to contribute to the campaign without having to attend the actual event. For example, they can donate by telephone or over the internet.

Disadvantages of public events include things not going according to plan, for example people may not attend or watch the event in the numbers anticipated. They may also need funding before the event can take place. One of the biggest charity events was the Live Aid concert, organised by Sir Bob Geldof in 1985, to support famine relief in Africa.

Key terms

Event: An occasion that takes place, especially one of importance, to promote a campaign's cause.

Funding: Money provided for a particular purpose.

CASE STUDY

CHILDREN IN NEED

The yearly 'Children in Need' fundraising evening is very effective. By providing an evening of TV entertainment, coupled with raising an awareness of the issues, a large sum of money has been raised. In 2020 this amounted to £37 million.

Pudsey Bear is easily recognised by many people as being associated with the 'Children in Need' campaign.

Public appearances

Public appearances are often used to support a campaign; they involve the promoters attending an event to talk in public to raise awareness of the aims of the campaign.

This method provides a personal approach and a realistic touch to the campaign. This in turn generates public interest and support. The information provided will be informative and true to life.

The weaknesses include a reluctance of some people to appear and speak in public. If they cannot generate interest and a following, the campaign is unlikely to be successful. In addition, people attending may not be supportive and may even be disruptive.

CASE STUDY

SARAH'S LAW

A campaign that used public appearances was Sarah's law campaign. Sarah's parents, Sara and Michael Payne, made many public appearances to try and find their missing daughter. In addition, once the campaign for Sarah's law was launched her mother attended many events such as the Police Federation Conference to share awareness of the campaign and the need for a child sex offender disclosure scheme. This proved effective, as the scheme was introduced throughout England and Wales in 2011.

Sara Payne used public appearances to promote her campaign.

Print leaflets

Leaflets are printed materials that contain information about a campaign. The benefits of using leaflets in a campaign include:

- contact numbers or links to social media to allow readers to contact them or donate
- a great deal of information, including pictures and imagery, so readers can get a full insight of the campaign
- they do not rely on technology such as the internet, which may not be accessible to all.

However, a limitation with leaflets is that they may contain too much information, so the reader might be reluctant to spend a long time reading one and therefore be put off donating funds. In addition, they may be expensive to print and can be easily ignored and thrown away.

STAY HOME

PROTECT THE NHS

SAVE LIVES

This Covid 19 image was used in TV advertisements and government briefings.

CASE STUDY

CANCER RESEARCH

A charity such as Cancer Research uses leaflets for its campaigns to spread awareness, which are sometimes handed out in doctors' surgeries. This is an effective method as the charity raised £634 million in 2017–2018.

CANCER RESEARCH UK

Extract answer

An answer for AC2.2 in the controlled assessment could be:

TV advertising is a popular method to promote a campaign. A TV advert is a clip on the TV that promotes a campaign in some way or form. TV adverts can help get the message across, they can be very precise. A lot of adverts are straight to the point, this is likely due to the cost of TV time. Billions of people watch TV every day, meaning that the audience is almost limitless, this allows the advert to reach a large range of people and promote the campaign even further. A disadvantage to TV advertising is that it is incredibly expensive to have an advert on prime-time TV, it costs around £300,000, for a two-minute commercial during the day, Another disadvantage is that some adverts might not be appropriate for younger viewers and it may unsettle them: this is bad for the campaign as many families will turn over instead of watching it. Also, another disadvantage is being able to record shows and skip the adverts. The majority of people own a remote device that allows them to skip adverts and breaks, meaning that the advert may rarely get seen. Some THINK! campaign adverts are sometimes deemed unwatchable by a young audiences due to the level of violence. The THINK! campaign relates to road safety and can contain quite graphic images of death occurring in road traffic accidents.

Social networking is a common method used to promote a campaign. Social media is used to broadcast many campaigns around the world. Millions of people use social media every day, meaning that your message will reach up into millions of people. Putting a post on Facebook or Twitter is free, meaning that it costs no money to put up a campaign post, but someone will likely need to update it regularly. While many people use social media, many people do not, many above the age of 40 do not use social media, meaning that a large portion of people don't ever see the message. Many people brush past the adverts and messages to look at what their friends were doing, etc. Again meaning many people don't see or read them. A campaign that used social media was the 'Yes Scotland' campaign.

Assessment

Mark band 2 (6–10 marks)

There is a clear attempt at evaluating the effectiveness of two types of media used in campaigns for change. The evaluation is at its best when examples contain detail such as costing for the television advertisement. However, at times, the response is largely descriptive and judgments need to be developed. This is especially the case in the examples of campaigns, as they lack detail about their effectiveness. Also, at times the quality of the communication could be improved. However, the biggest issue is that it only considers two types of media methods.

Activity

Improve the above answer above by rewriting it, developing the evaluation and improving the terminology used, then add in at least two more media methods.

LEARNING OUTCOME 3
PLAN CAMPAIGNS FOR CHANGE RELATING TO CRIME

AC3.1 PLAN A CAMPAIGN FOR CHANGE RELATING TO CRIME

ASSESSMENT CRITERION	MARK BAND 1	MARK BAND 2	MARK BAND 3
AC3.1 You should be able to … Plan a campaign for change relating to crime	Plan for a campaign relevant to selected assignment brief is limited in detail Appropriate actions, sequences and time are briefly outlined **(1–3)**	Plan for campaign relevant to selected assignment brief has evidence of some appropriate actions in a relevant time sequence in some detail **(4–7)**	Detailed and appropriate plan for campaign, relevant to selected assignment brief, includes clearly described actions in a relevant time sequence **(8–10)**

CONTENT	AMPLIFICATION
Plan • aims and objectives • justification of choice of campaign • target audience • methods to be used • materials to be used • finances • timescales • resources needed	You should identify an appropriate campaign for change and produce a comprehensive plan of action

Where to start

In this AC you are to plan a campaign to practise your skills. These skills will then be used in the controlled assessment to plan a campaign that links to the Brief. Your teacher will guide you on which crime to select. They may even insist on using the crime that you work on during lessons. You will then follow the heading for this AC and learn the best way of planning a campaign. You may find out information that helps and guides your plans and choices. You will then produce a plan but this will be different from what is produced in the controlled assessment.

In the controlled assessment you will be given an assignment brief with a story or scenario involving different crimes. Your campaign and its plan must be one of those crimes indicated in the brief, hence you will not know the nature of the plan until the day of the assessment. However, you can practise before and look at useful websites for aspects such as finances, etc.

Your plan should contain:

- aims and objectives
- justification of choice of campaign
- target audience
- methods to be used
- materials to be used
- finances
- timescales
- resources needed.

A detailed plan is required for your campaign.

Aims

Aims are long-term or overall goals. Examples of aims could include:

- encourage victims to report domestic abuse
- raise awareness of the signs of violence in the family or a relationship
- educate and inform the public about hate crime
- raise awareness and encourage people to seek support about male domestic abuse.

You should briefly explain why you have selected the aims for your campaign. However, full justification is made in AC3.3 (see page 74).

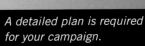

Objectives

Objectives are short-term plans that enable you to reach the aims you have decided on. Make them SMART:

S – Specific (be detailed about what you want to do)

M – Measurable (provide a percentage or a target that you can give evidence for when you meet it)

A – Achievable (you are not going to cure cancer! Create objectives that you will be able to do)

R – Realistic (you only have a few hours, you will not be able to be too ambitious)

T – Time (know how long it will take you. In your objective give a timeframe).

Examples of objectives could include:

- Create 150 leaflets to distribute to community centres in the town.
- Raise £1,500 to use towards producing merchandise/holding an event.
- Create a social media account on Twitter/Facebook and achieve at least 500 re-tweets or likes and shares.

Activity

Consider the Women's Aid campaign 'Change that Lasts', at www.womensaid.org.uk/our-approach-change-that-lasts/.

Answer the following questions:

- What is the focus of the campaign?
- What are the aims of this campaign?
- What could the objectives of the campaign be?

Justification of choice of campaign

Here you need to explain why you have selected the crime in the campaign. It can include both personal and more objective reasoning. Make sure you comment on matters such as:

- Your own connection to this crime, if relevant.
- Details of a lack of awareness.
- Statistics on reported and actual crime.
- Why it is generally under-reported.
- Real-life examples of the crime taking place.
- Are offences of this type increasing? If so, give statistics in support.

REASONS

Remember that full justification of all campaign aspects is required in AC3.3.

Target audience

A target audience is a particular group at which the campaign is aimed.

Activity

Consider the following campaigns and identify the target audience of each one. You can find them by searching the internet:

- Women's Aid: Nowhere to Turn
- Essex Police: Hate Crime
- Centers for Disease Control and Prevention: Tips From Former Smokers
- ManKind Initiative.

You should consider the following questions:

- Who is your target audience?
- Why has this group of people been selected as your target audience? Perhaps think about the crime you have chosen to focus on. Does it relate to a particular gender, age group, etc.?
- How do your campaign methods and materials relate to this group?

Methods and materials

The next part of this campaign plan requires you to think about methods and materials that you wish to plan for and produce.

Activity

Before you start selecting methods, you should research some campaigns and the methods that they have used. Look at the following to give you some ideas for research:

- 'White and Gold Dress: Salvation Army Launches Powerful Campaign against Domestic Violence Using "that Dress"', *Daily Mirror*: www.mirror.co.uk/news/uk-news/white-gold-dress-salvation-army-5284119.
- 'Drug Drive TV ad "Eyes"': www.youtube.com/watch?v=dytCWrf92zc.
- 'THINK! Drink Drive: in the Doghouse #butalive': www.youtube.com/watch?v=-VCAwsWli5g.
- York LGBT Forum: www.yorklgbtforum.org.uk/hate-crime/.
- Help for Heroes: www.helpforheroes.org.uk/.
- Campaign for Dignity in Dying: www.dignityindying.org.uk/.

Using the information you have found from the above websites, choose the methods you are going to use in your campaign, for example:

METHOD [IDENTIFY THE METHOD]	WHY YOU HAVE CHOSEN IT [JUSTIFY YOUR CHOICE, THINK ABOUT TARGET AUDIENCE, AUDIENCE IN GENERAL, COST, ETC.]	HOW YOU WILL USE IT [HOW WILL THIS METHOD BE USED IN YOUR CAMPAIGN?]	MATERIALS TO BE USED [WHAT MATERIALS WILL BE NEEDED TO ENABLE THE METHODS TO BE IMPLEMENTED?]
Poster	To gain people's attention and make younger people understand this crime	Place poster in places young people will notice it, for example schools, colleges, toilets	Computer, printer and paper

Keep in mind that you are going to have to create some of them, so try to be practical and not be too ambitious.

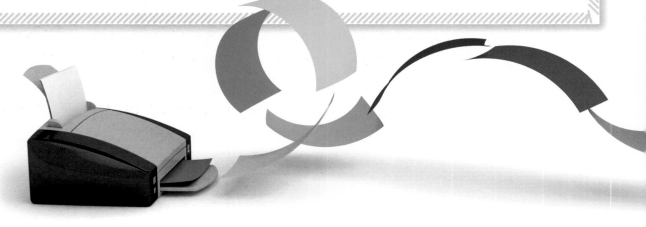

Finance

Once you have decided on your methods you then need to research the pricing of them. This will help you to justify the methods in AC3.3. For example, social media may be cost-effective, therefore your finance can go towards other methods.

Think about:

✓ Where will you get your materials from?

✓ Cost of materials?

✓ How many will you produce?

✓ Overall cost?

✓ Price sold for?

✓ Potential profit made?

✓ Allocation of profits?

✓ How to raise initial funding required?

Here is an example of a finance plan:

A finance plan is essential to the campaign.

I need to purchase:

- 500 posters for £9 from cheapestprintonline.com. I am going to hand these out for free.
- 40 hoodies for £8.00 each from Mypersonalisedclothing.com. I am going to sell these for £11.95 each.
- 36 badges for £8 from mine4sure.com. I am going to sell these for £1.50 each.
- 40 t-shirts for £1.88 each from Mypersonalisedclothing.com. I am going to sell these for £6 each.
- 100 wristbands for 13p each from adband.com. I am going to sell these for £1.50 each.

Social media is free to set up.

The total price I will have spent is £425.20. To help fund this I am going to approach local businesses to ask for a donation. If further capital is needed I will hold a coffee morning and tombola fundraiser.

Potentially I can make a profit of £226.80. Any profits will go to purchase more materials to further promote the campaign.

Timescales

When planning a campaign you need to consider the following:

- research time
- design of materials for use with the campaign
- creation of the materials
- implementation of the campaign, for example delivery and training.

Stage 1 – Research

Think about what research you need to carry out:

- research into the crimes being committed
- research what effects the crimes are having
- research statistics on the crime (victims, etc.)
- research existing support available for victims
- research real-life cases
- time required – approx. one month.

Stage 2 – Design

Think about how you will design your materials:

- Which materials will you be designing?
- How will you design/mock-up your materials?
- Use of websites. There are also various templates of social media sites available, on the internet, for you to add in details of your campaign (simitator?).
- Use of programs on the computer (Publisher?).
- Will you include links to other campaigns for support?
- Will you use images/information to put on your design materials from the research stage?
- Time required – approx. one month.

Key term

Simitator: A website that allows you to produce a fake Facebook or Twitter account.

Stage 3 – Creation of materials

Think about how you will create your materials:

- Will you approach a local business to request a donation for your campaign to set it up? (You could mention this in the finance plan.)
- What materials will be produced?
- Which company will produce your materials? Link to research from finance plan.
- Will the profit from merchandise allow you to continue buying more leaflets, etc.?
- How long will you leave for creation and delivery?
- Time required – approx. two months.

Stage 4 – Implementation

Think about how you will set your campaign up:

- How long will it take to launch your campaign?
- How will you launch the campaign?
- How will you distribute leaflets/posters (where, target audience, when)?
- How long will it take to set up the social media account?
- How will you promote and sell the merchandise?
- Will you launch all campaign materials at the same time or will you spread them out? Why?
- Time required – approx. three weeks.

Complete an overall timeline for your campaign. You can use the details above to help you. Ensure that you develop the timeline for your campaign and the materials you are using.

Resources needed

- Do you require any resources when planning your campaign in general?
- Think about your timescale (opposite). For example: include research, materials, time, training, finance, etc.

Activity

In small groups discuss campaigns that easily come to mind. Consider why they are so memorable.

- Is it their name? Is it a catchy sound, for example with alliteration such as 'Justice for Julie'?
- Is it because they're cute such as Pudsey bear.
- Is it because they're supported by a famous person?
- Are they frequently seen on the media?
- Do they involve something that affects a large part of society in some way?

Literacy skills

Improve the sentences below by adding in more provocative language.

For example:
'Helps to support others' could become 'Act now to prevent serious harm and millions of deaths every year.'

Improve the following:
- 'Help sick children.'
- 'Those animals need our support.'
- 'They deserve more.'
- 'Can you please donate some money?'

AC3.2 DESIGN MATERIALS FOR USE IN CAMPAIGNING FOR CHANGE

ASSESSMENT CRITERION	MARK BAND 1	MARK BAND 2	MARK BAND 3	MARK BAND 4
AC3.2 You should be able to … Design materials for use in campaigning for change	Materials are basic/simple in design Limited clarity of purpose for the materials **(1–5)**	Some evidence of materials that are designed with relevant content and which stimulate some interest Some evidence of persuasive language and clarity of purpose **(6–10)**	Attractive materials are designed with relevant content which stimulates interest Evidence of persuasive language and clarity of purpose Some evidence of technical skills **(11–15)**	Well-designed attractive materials are presented Content is appropriate for changing behaviour Materials are visually and verbally stimulating and technically accurate **(16–20)**

CONTENT	AMPLIFICATION
Design • structure of information • use of images or other accentuating features to capture attention • use of persuasive language • promotion of action • consideration of target audience • alignment with campaign	You should consider the design of materials such as: • leaflets • advertisements • posters • blogs • social network pages

Handy hints !

You cannot take previously designed materials into the controlled assessment with you. However, you do have access to the internet.

Handy hints !

You need to design materials for the campaign that you plan in the controlled assessment. It is suggested that you design a minimum of three materials to enable access to mark band 4. For example:

· a poster with an attention-grabbing image
· a social media site with posts and comments
· a piece of merchandise such as a t-shirt showing both front and back images.
Try to keep consistency using the campaign logo, name, colouring, etc.

Structure of information

Consider what is best to make sure you capture your audiences' attention without confusing them or giving them too much information. This is particularly important with regard to posters and leaflets. You also need to make sure your information follows the typical conventions of whatever you plan to make, so look at the layout/structure of similar items for ideas. For example, regarding a poster, how much information does the typical one carry? What information does it contain? How large or small is the imagery?

Consider the design of your poster/leaflet carefully.

Use of images or other accentuating features to capture attention

This could be your own image/feature, or something you find while researching that seems to capture the essence of your campaign. It could, for example, be an image of a person, but does not have to be. Consider how the image or feature links to your campaign and how it will grab attention.

Take it further

Research campaigns in support of anti-smoking. Why and how were they hard-hitting and designed to shock? Consider the images used and terminology involved, as well as the use of children to promote their message.

Use of persuasive language

The point is to promote an awareness of the campaign and bring about a change, so you need to encourage your audience to act or help bring about a change. Persuasive language is essential, for example, 'You should', 'You'd be better off …', 'Look after your …', 'You don't deserve to be …'. Try to play on people's emotions where appropriate and use direct language, i.e. 'you', 'your'.

Use persuasive language to encourage an audience to act.

Promotion of action

Try to include verbs to direct people to act. For example:

- stop
- get help now
- do something about it
- join in.

Consideration of target audience

Your target audience is fundamental, so you must consider who are you aiming the materials at and how your methods, approach and design will target them. Use an image that they can relate to and wording that they will use and understand. If it becomes confusing the audience will not react.

Alignment with campaign

Your materials should have consistency with each other and they must also link to the other parts of your planned work. This is appropriate even if you plan but do not design or carry out other aspects of the campaign. Consider using the same images, campaign logo and colouring across your designs for instant recognition of your campaign by the public. For example, the image of Pudsey Bear with his spotted eye patch instantly tells people it is the 'Children in Need' campaign.

This is instantly recognisable as the image for 'Children in Need'.

Activity

Look at the following examples of materials. Decide what you like about them, what works well, what you would change or how you would improve them.

Radio advert

Woman on a phone to her friend, you hear the woman speaking:

Hello? He did it again ... he ...*sniffs and breaths heavily* ... he threw the remote at me this time, it hit me in the eye ... that's both eyes bruised now. *Pauses* What am I going to do?! *Cries when speaking* I can't get away! *The door sounds* That's him now ...*The phone cuts off.*

In a different female voice you hear.

Do you know anyone who suffers at the hands of domestic abuse? Help them, act now! Report it at 0808 2000 247, that's 0808 2000 247. **(Student)**

The radio advert on the previous page will create one of those occasions when listeners may not want to change the radio station. It is dark and meaningful and therefore will gain their attention, perhaps while they are in a car. It gives the number for Women's Aid to help promote the campaign's aims and provides assistance to promote action to bring about change.

The following are all materials designed by Criminology students and are typical of the images that should be produced during the controlled assessments. You should pay attention to the use of images, colouring, language used, etc.

By Declan Ballan

By Ronan McDowell

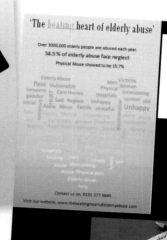

By Courtney Powell

Emily Anderson

Secondly I have created my merchandise; I have three different types of merchandise I am going to produce.

This is my pen.

This is my USB.

Finally this is my poster which will also be printed on an acrylic keyring.

By Emily Anderson

By Arisa Hudson

Handy hints !

You are allowed to access the internet to research images to help you carry out this task; however, you must ensure that your final design is all your own work.

AC3.3 JUSTIFY A CAMPAIGN FOR CHANGE

ASSESSMENT CRITERION	MARK BAND 1	MARK BAND 2	MARK BAND 3
You should be able to … Justify a campaign for change	Limited justification of a campaign for change Evidence is largely descriptive with few judgements **(1–5)**	Some justification is well-reasoned Response is largely descriptive but includes some appropriate judgements Persuasive language is used **(6–10)**	Clear and detailed justification which is well-reasoned Conclusions are supported by relevant judgements, including the use of persuasive language **(11–15)**

CONTENT	AMPLIFICATION
Justify • presentation of a case for action • use of evidence in support of a case • use of persuasive language	You should justify the approach and the need for a campaign for change

Handy hints !

Do not just describe your campaign; make sure you justify all your actions.

Handy hints !

Make sure your justification relates to your entire campaign, not just the specific materials you have created.

Presenting a case for action

Presenting a case for action involves explaining why your campaign is necessary and what impact it hopes to achieve. Outline your campaign focus, give reasons and present your supporting evidence. Make sure you link into your specific aims and target audience. Supporting statistics and real-life case examples should be included. Use sentence starters such as:

- I chose to focus on … because …
- This is an important area to address because …
- Without a campaign like this, it is likely that …
- However, with a campaign highlighting this issue, it could result in …

Use of evidence in support of a case

Use your statistics and other research from AC3.1 to help give evidence in support of a case. Go over the concept for your campaign and justify your choices for aspects such as name, logo, audience, etc. This includes justification of your materials, explaining the choice and design. The imagery used, colouring and details must be justified. You can refer to other campaigns and particularly the aspects of them that have proved successful. You could refer to things such as:

- I decided upon … for the campaign name. I chose this because … What's more, it meets my aim of … as well as targeting my audience because …
- I chose to use a range of methods including … I chose these because my audience … I also felt that these would be effective in promoting my aim because … If I had chosen … or … it might not have been so successful.
- The target audience would be most likely to respond to this because … It also offers a good link to the topic because …
- I chose to use images of … This is highly effective because …
- The colouring is effective as it …
- I used other features such as … and … These are good for meeting my aims because …

Use of persuasive language

Discuss the materials you designed in AC3.2 and how effective they are in relating choices to the persuasive language you have used. Useful sentences could include:

- I used the term …. because it conveys …
- I focused on … because … This is convincing to the audience because …
- I designed the layout to include … This is because …
- The language is persuasive as it …

Remember to justify all aspects of your campaign.

UNIT SUMMARY

By working through this unit you will:

- have gained skills to differentiate between myth and reality when it comes to crime and to recognise that common representations may be misleading and inaccurate
- have gained the skills to understand the importance of changing public perceptions of crime
- be able to use and assess a variety of methods used by agencies to raise awareness of crime so that it can be tackled effectively
- have gained the skills to plan a campaign for change in relation to crime; for example, to raise awareness, change attitudes or change reporting behaviour.

UNIT 2
CRIMINOLOGICAL THEORIES

In this unit you will apply your understanding of the public perceptions of crime and campaigns for change, studied in Unit 1, with criminological theories to examine how both are used to set policy.

You will consider why people commit crime and whether these theories are credible. Then the theories will be applied to real-life situations and this will allow you to discover answers to questions such as 'what makes someone a serial killer?'

You will discover when an act is criminal and when it is deviant, and the similarities and differences between them.

Assessment: 1 hour 30 minutes external exam

Synoptic: Unit 1

AC1.1 COMPARE CRIMINAL BEHAVIOUR AND DEVIANCE

ASSESSMENT CRITERION	CONTENT	AMPLIFICATION
AC1.1 You should be able to … Compare criminal behaviour and deviance	**Criminal behaviour** • social definition • legal definition • formal sanctions against criminals • variety of criminal acts **Deviance** • norms, moral codes and values • informal and formal sanctions against deviance • forms of deviance	You should have an understanding of: • how criminality and deviance is defined • acts that are criminal • acts that are deviant • acts that are both criminal and deviant • the implications of committing a criminal and/or deviant act

Synoptic links

You should also understand the impact of reporting on public perceptions of crime and deviance. Familiarise yourself with the following areas from Unit 1, LO1, AC1.5:

• moral panic
• changing public concerns and attitudes
• perceptions of crime trends
• stereotyping of criminals
• levels of response to crime and types of punishment
• changing priorities and emphasis.

Criminal behaviour

Social definition

Sometimes crime is a label from 'social interaction' or a wrong against the community. If a society has said that an act is a crime, then it becomes one. Crimes have consequences that are detrimental in some way to the community at large or one or more people within it. Certainly, in our society some crimes are universally disapproved of, for example sex offences, especially those involving children. However, some acts are crimes in some countries but not in others. For instance, most people in the UK would think it is it wrong to have sex with a 14-year-old. However, forced marriages exist in some countries, such as Bangladesh, where children must become child brides. Hence, a social definition of the word criminal is difficult to find as it can vary.

Legal definition

In our society it is the legal system that defines a crime. For example, behaviour that breaks the law and for which you are punished by the legal system. Examples would include the offences:

- theft
- fraud
- murder.

In law a crime must have two elements: an actus reus, which means the guilty act, and a mens rea, meaning guilty mind. If A takes a gun and deliberately shoots B through the heart and B then dies, the actus reus is the act of shooting and the mens rea is the intention to kill, as evidenced by shooting through the heart. There are, however, offences of strict liability that do not require a mens rea, for example many food and hygiene regulations. Even if both elements were present, a defence such as self-defence could mean a person was not found guilty. Hence, a legal definition of the word crime is difficult to find, as it can vary.

Formal sanctions against criminals

Non-court sanctions:

- **Cautions** are administered by the police for minor crimes such as writing graffiti on a bus shelter. You have to admit an offence and agree to be cautioned; otherwise you could be arrested for the offence. A caution is not a criminal conviction.

- **Conditional cautions** are given by the police but you have to agree to certain rules and restrictions, such as receiving treatment for drug abuse or repairing damage to a property.

- **Penalty notices** for disorder are given for offences such as shoplifting, possessing cannabis, or being drunk and disorderly in public. You can only get a penalty notice if you are aged 18 or over.

Writing graffiti is a minor crime.

Court sanctions:

- **Custodial sentences** are where you are immediately sent to prison. There are mandatory and discretionary life sentences and fixed term and indeterminate prison sentences.

- **Community sentences** can be a combination order including unpaid work, probation, curfew and orders such as having drug testing and treatment.

- **Fines** are financial penalties; the amount depends on the seriousness of the offence and the financial circumstances of the offender.

- **Discharge** can be either conditional, when if the defendant reoffends during a set time period the court can give an alternative sentence, or absolute, when no penalty is imposed as the defendant is technically guilty but morally blameless.

An example of a court sanction is imprisonment.

Variety of criminal acts

Below is a table of criminal acts and common examples.

TYPES OF CRIMINAL ACT	EXAMPLES
Fatal offences against the person	Murder, manslaughter
Non-fatal offences against the person	Assault, battery, actual and grievous bodily harm
Offences against property	Theft, robbery, burglary
Sexual offences	Rape, indecent assault
Public order offences	Riot, affray, violent disorder
Drug offences	Possession of a controlled drug or possession with intent to supply

Deviance

Deviance is behaviour that goes against the dominant social norms of a specific group or society, which causes some kind of critical reaction or disapproval.

Norms, moral codes and values

Norms, moral codes and values are basically unwritten rules of acceptable behaviour, which are often used interchangeably in society. However, they do have specific meanings:

- **Norms** are social expectations that guide behaviour and explain why people act in the way that they do. Norms keep in check deviant behaviour. While it is expected behaviour, it could vary from one culture to another. For instance, in the UK we often wear dark sombre colours for a funeral but in China the colour of mourning is white.

- **Moral codes** are morals or good ways of behaving. Breaking a moral code would generally be considered serious in society, an example would be murder.
- **Values** are rules shared by most people in a given culture. It is what people feel should happen. They are more general guidelines than norms. So, for example, most people feel we should respect the elderly.

Activity

Consider how norms, moral codes and values have changed over the years. You could research examples such as cigarette smoking, homosexuality and women's rights.

Respecting the elderly is considered a value in society.

Informal and formal sanctions against deviance

Informal sanctions can include:

- frowning upon behaviour
- name calling, etc.
- ignoring behaviour
- labelling behaviour
- parents grounding a child.

Also, there are more formal sanctions such as fines; even imprisonment may be appropriate for some deviant acts.

If students fail to hand their homework in on time, the teacher may keep them back after school by way of detention, and the rest of the class may laugh at such a punishment. Here, failing to hand in the homework is the deviant act and the sanction is the detention. In addition, the classmates' laughing could also be an indirect sanction.

The classroom environment provides many examples of both formal and informal sanctions.

Forms of deviance

It should be noted that deviant behaviour is not always something negative, nor is it always frowned upon by society. This can be seen by the various basic forms of rule-breaking behaviour in terms of three basic ideas:

- **Admired behaviour:** deviant but considered good or admirable, for example saving a life while putting own at risk, as most people would not do so.
- **Odd behaviour:** deviant by being odd or different from what is considered the norm, for example living with an excessive number of cats.
- **Bad behaviour:** deviant because it is bad, for example assaulting a pensioner.

There is an overlap between some of these types, for example behaviour that is both odd and bad such as exposing yourself in public. Therefore, it is important to note that:

- Some acts may be deviant but not criminal, for example shouting in a library.
- Some acts are classed as criminal but may not be deviant, for example keeping excess change given by mistake.
- Some acts are considered both criminal and deviant, for example murder.

Activity

Draw a Venn diagram (two overlapping circles as shown in the figure below right). Label one circle as 'Deviant' and the other as 'Criminal', then place the following acts in the relevant circle. Some of the acts may be considered both deviant and criminal, and these are entered where the two circles overlap:

- speeding
- burglary
- naked sunbathing
- robbery
- smoking
- theft
- stealing from a friend
- hoarding newspapers
- excessive washing of hands.

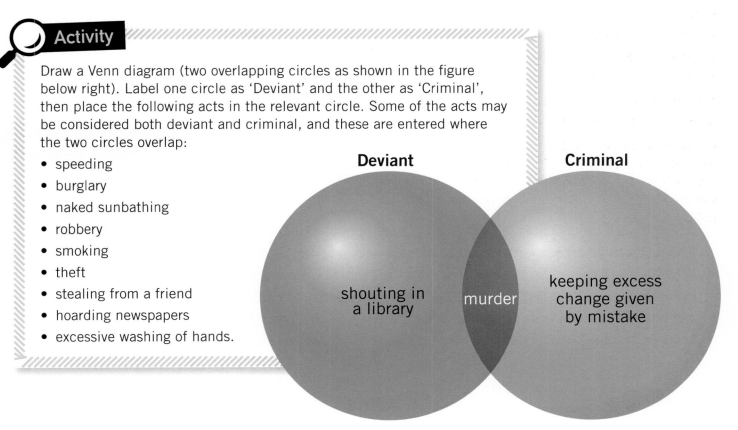

Deviant

Criminal

shouting in a library

murder

keeping excess change given by mistake

Example questions

The following are exam questions from this AC:

Unit 2 Exam 2017
Compare criminality and deviance with reference to relevant examples. **[5 marks]**
NOTE that from 2020 the changes in the mark bands would mean that this question would be out of either 4 or 6 marks.

Unit 2 Exam 2019
Describe the difference between formal and informal policy making. **[2 marks]**

Unit 2 Exam 2018
Describe what is meant by the term 'deviance'. **[3 marks]**

Using examples from the scenario, explain behaviour that could be described as criminal, deviant, or both. **[5 marks]**
NOTE that from 2020 the changes in the mark bands would mean that this question would be out of either 4 or 6 marks.

Tip ✓

Always read the question carefully. Each part of the scenario is there for a reason. Look for the deviant or criminal acts and mention them in your answer as an example of each type.

Unit 2 Exam 2017

Compare criminality and deviance with reference to relevant examples. **[5 marks]**

A deviant act is one that goes against society's shared norms and values. However, it isn't necessarily against the law. An example of a deviant act is committing adultery, as cheating on a partner is significantly frowned upon in many societies, yet is not illegal. It can be said that not all criminal offences are examples of deviance, such as possession of cannabis, which is arguably becoming more acceptable in society, with some American states legalising it.

Literacy skills ⚙

Can you improve this answer by adding in terminology that conveys comparisons being made?

Assessment

NOTE that from 2020 the changes in the mark bands would mean that this question would be out of 6 marks and would lie in the mark band 3–4. There is a reasonable focus on the question with some accurate support and some use of specialist vocabulary.

This answer contains a definition of the word deviance but not criminality. However, it does give an example of both a deviant and criminal act and attempts to compare the two terms. Terminology could be improved by using words such as 'whereas', 'alternatively' and 'however' to enhance the comparison aspect.

Exam question and answer

Explain, with examples, the connection between the terms crime and deviance. **[6 marks]**

The following answer would achieve the top mark band 5–6. There is a clear and detailed focus on the question, with mainly accurate support and an effective use of specialist vocabulary. The demands of the question are fully addressed.

Crime is a behaviour that breaks the formal laws of a society and can lead to formal sanctions or punishment. For example, a life sentence for the offence of murder. Deviance is any violation of society's norms or going against expected behaviour; for example, shouting in the library. Most crimes are seen as deviant, for example most people do not steal or go around hitting other people. However, it does not follow that all or even most deviant acts are crimes. For instance, shouting in the library or excessive storage of newspapers is not illegal but would be considered deviant. Some deviant acts can become the norm and be accepted, for example speeding. Some behaviour once accepted may be seen as deviant over time, for example smoking of cigarettes, which in certain circumstances, such as at a place of work, can also now be seen as illegal. However, not all smoking of cigarettes is illegal. Prostitution is a deviant act, which at one stage was unacceptable behaviour (although technically not illegal). However, there have been calls for it to be decriminalised. There have also been calls to decriminalise possession of cannabis, which is still today a deviant and illegal act.

Activity

In pairs, try to write a short scenario involving both deviant and criminal actions. Then swap your work with another pair and see if you can identify the acts that are criminal, acts that are deviant and acts that are both criminal and deviant.

AC1.2 EXPLAIN THE SOCIAL CONSTRUCTION OF CRIMINALITY

ASSESSMENT CRITERION	CONTENT
AC1.2 You should be able to … Explain the social construction of criminality	**Social construction** • how laws change from culture to culture • how laws change over time • how laws are applied differently according to circumstances in which actions occur • why laws are different according to place, time and culture

Synoptic link

You should understand how media and campaigns for change contribute to social constructions of criminality and unreported crime. These can be found in Unit 1, LO1, AC1.5

Handy hints !

You need to know how and why laws are different in terms of culture, place and time. What was once a crime may have changed over time or the same act may be a crime in one area or culture but not in another.

How laws change from culture to culture

You should approach the discussion of any criminal act by considering:
• What the definition is of the act.
• What is the situation with regards to legality in the UK?
• Cultures where it is legal.
• Cultures where it is illegal.
• Why the law varies in different cultures.

Key term

Civil partnership: Legally recognised agreement for both same-sex couples and heterosexual couples.

Adultery is not a crime in the UK.

	Adultery	Honour crimes	Homosexuality
WHAT THE DEFINITION IS OF THE ACT	Sexual relations between a married person and another, with the exception of their spouse	Crimes where the accused has brought shame on their family Can include killings for conduct such as refusing to enter an arranged marriage or being in a relationship that displeases the family	Involving or characterised by sexual attraction between people of the same sex
WHAT THE SITUATION IS WITH REGARDS TO LEGALITY IN THE UK	Not considered a criminal offence but may have legal consequences in divorce proceedings	Such actions are crimes and if a killing is involved it is murder	Once it was illegal but was partially decriminalised in 1967 with the age of consent, i.e. to participate legally in sexual relations, was set at 21 years The age of consent was lowered to 18 and then 16 Initially, civil partnerships were allowed and now same-sex marriages can also take place
CULTURES WHERE IT IS LEGAL	UK and all other European countries	Most honour crimes take place within South Asian and Middle Eastern families	UK, Europe, USA and Canada
CULTURES WHERE IT IS ILLEGAL	Many countries governed by Islamic law such as Saudi Arabia and Pakistan Almost half of the states in the USA consider it a crime but in most it is only a misdemeanour (minor offence)	UK, Europe, USA, Pakistan, etc. The issue is usually one of evidence	India, Saudi Arabia, Iran, Yemen and Nigeria
WHY THE LAW VARIES IN DIFFERENT CULTURES	One reason is religion: the Bible states that adultery is a sin Could also relate to the status of women, who are owned by their husbands and could be treated as property Some politicians may not wish to be seen as opposing moral laws, so are reluctant to revoke them	Such crimes are thought to have originated from tribal customs, where an allegation against a woman can besmirch (damage) a family's reputation None of the world's major religions condone (forgive) honour-related crimes but perpetrators have sometimes tried to justify their actions on religious grounds	Religion is a major reason as, for example the Bible says that homosexuality is a sin In some cultures it is more of a taboo and something against the norm, resulting in intolerance or bigotry (prejudice)

Over time, and to reflect a changing society, opinion and moral views change, hence changes in the law are made to reflect these.

OVER TIME

How laws change over time

Capital punishment

Capital punishment is the practice of executing someone as punishment for a specific crime after due process, going through the correct legal proceedings, or a legal trial. In the 18th century there were over 200 offences for which the death penalty could be given. Such crimes included picking pockets and shooting rabbits. Laws were made by the rich to protect themselves and their property. The laws were often focused on the poor who were viewed as lazy and agents of their own misfortune. Such a view faded as all people were given rights and freedoms, and the opportunity to progress in society. Hence, some of the reasons for capital punishment faded too. Eventually, it remained purely for the very serious crimes of murder and treason.

Key terms

Execute: To kill someone as a legal punishment.

Statute: An Act of Parliament or legislation

CASE STUDY

MISCARRIAGES OF JUSTICE

In the 1950s, cases such as Derek Bentley and Timothy Evans were regarded as a miscarriage of justice, leading to a change in public opinion about the death penalty and also to a change in the law. As DNA evidence developed, it became apparent that many people were being wrongly convicted, but after a person was dead it was impossible to put this right. Hence, the law was out-dated and in need of reform. Capital punishment, for murder, was temporarily abolished in the UK in 1965 and fully abolished in 1969. However, it remained on the statute books for treason, and this too was abolished in 1998 with the Crime and Disorder Act.

Take it further

Research what happened in these two cases to discover the miscarriage of justice that took place.

Key term

Miscarriage of justice: The conviction and punishment of a person for crime that they had not committed.

Therefore, as shown above, this law changed over time due to the changing status of various social groups in society and their increased rights under the law. Also, cases that showed miscarriages of justice were happening and these could not be put right if the person was deceased.

Law against double jeopardy

The law regarding double jeopardy has changed over time. As a result of, among other reasons, Ann Ming's campaign, the law that prevented a person being tried again for the same offence was abolished for serious offences. A provision in the Criminal Justice Act 2003 came into force, which stated that where there is 'new and compelling evidence' pointing to the guilt of a former defendant, the Court of Appeal may quash an acquittal and order a retrial.

This change was necessary as the law at the time was inadequate to bring justice. Also, technologies and medical knowledge became more advanced and allowed for certainty of evidence, including, for example, the successful prosecution of Gary Dobson and David Norris for the murder of Stephen Lawrence.

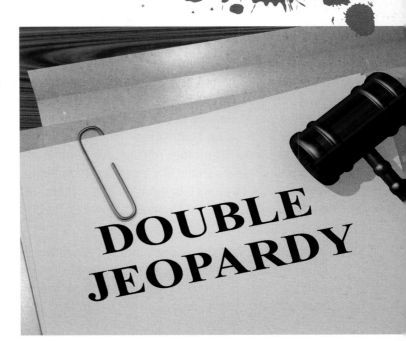

Laws concerning prostitution

Prostitution, or the selling of sexual services, is the world's oldest profession. Prostitution itself is legal but many of the connected activities are illegal. This includes soliciting in a public place, kerb crawling or owning a brothel. Once prostitution had a stigma attached to it and the women involved were thought to be immoral due to the idea of having sex for money. Many women became prostitutes because it provided a source of income at a time when they had few other options for jobs. However, society's view slowly changed. There are now calls for it to be decriminalised with appropriate regulation. The concern is for the safety of the woman and how to protect vulnerable people who become involved in prostitution, sometimes against their will.

Society changed its view of prostitution due to a decline in people believing in religion and an increased moral tolerance. In addition, the status of women changed and, with increased equality, more occupations and training opportunities became available.

Key terms

Acquittal: Verdict of a court when someone is found not guilty of a crime they have been charged with doing.

Soliciting: To offer sex for money, usually in a public place.

Kerb crawling: Driving slowly along a road, close to a pavement or walkway, in order to ask a prostitute for sex.

Brothel: A place where men go to pay to have sex with a prostitute.

Prostitution is known as the world's oldest profession.

Vagrancy

Vagrancy relates to having no visible means of support and travelling from place to place. Often termed sleeping rough and begging, it is illegal under the Vagrancy Act 1824. Originally, the law was passed in order to clear the streets of beggars, rogues and vagabonds, and prevent further crime from being committed. The Act fell into disuse as society accepted there were legitimate reasons for homelessness. However, over the last couple of years there has been an increase in the number of prosecutions, due to people begging in the streets, representing themselves as homeless when this was not the case. However, such circumstances allowed them to make money.

Views surrounding vagrancy have changed since the 19th century and no longer is it looked upon with disapproval. Now there is sympathy and concern for the vagrants. There is an acceptance that there are many genuine reasons for homelessness and that it is not connected to laziness or idleness.

Vagrancy is still a criminal offence in England and Wales.

Take it further

Research recent cases involving the Vagrancy Act 1824 and consider why they have been brought before the court.

How laws change in different places

The same actions are not necessarily criminal offences in all places throughout the world or even policed in the same way within England and Wales.

Possession of cannabis

Possession of cannabis is an offence and is illegal in England and Wales, but there have been calls to decriminalise it and allow its use, particularly for medical reasons. However, in some countries such as Columbia and Uruguay it is legal. Within England and Wales the law is enforced differently, according to the regional police priorities and resources. For instance, Durham Constabulary does not prioritise people who grow cannabis plants for personal use; whereas, the police in Cumbria do prosecute.

Views on the use of cannabis are different according to place: some countries view it as a recreational drug, while others consider that the medicinal properties should take precedence over its legality.

Possession of cannabis can be policed differently within various areas of the UK.

Jaywalking

Jaywalking is when pedestrians cross a road without regard to traffic regulations, for instance they step out anywhere other than a specified crossing, or without a green light. Jaywalking is an offence in most urban areas in the USA, Canada, Singapore and Poland. However, in the UK there is no such offence as it is considered a personal responsibility to cross the road safely.

Jaywalking is not a crime in England and Wales.

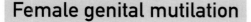

Female genital mutilation

Female genital mutilation or FGM is the deliberate mutilation of female genitalia for non-medical reasons. It is usually carried out on girls under the age of 15, prior to them entering into sexual activity, and is illegal in the UK. It is carried out in many parts of Africa, the Middle East and Asia, and is connected to cultural, religious and social reasons. It is believed it will benefit the girl and preserve her virginity ready for marriage.

The law surrounding FGM is different in different places due to the views and understanding of it. In the UK, the painful nature of the operation and health implications and problems relating to sex and mental illness after having it done are understood.

How laws are applied differently according to circumstances in which actions occur

The rule of law states that everyone is subject to the law and that it should be applied equally to all. There are, therefore, few instances of when laws are applied differently. One example is concerned with age:

- The age of criminal responsibility in the UK is ten. This means any child under ten years of age cannot be arrested, charged or prosecuted for a criminal offence, no matter how much blame can be attributed to them.
- In Canada no person can be convicted of an offence committed under the age of 12 years.
- In Bangladesh the age is nine years.
- In China generally it is under 16 years.

There are occasions when, despite murder taking place with the appropriate actus reus (guilty act) and the mens rea (guilty mind), the law allows an alternative charge of manslaughter to be made. This only happens in specified circumstances, including when the offender is said to have suffered from diminished responsibility or acted under a loss of control. The stated circumstances act as a partial defence and, rather than face a mandatory life sentence, the law allows the charge of manslaughter, where all the sentencing options are open to the judge.

These partial defences are only available to the charge of murder. However, there are other defences which show that a person is not guilty of an offence. The defences of consent, self-defence and automatism, if successful, mean that a person is not guilty of a crime.

Key terms

Manslaughter: An unlawful killing, without malice or aforethought and in circumstances when it is not murder.

Diminished responsibility: A partial defence for murder resulting in a conviction for manslaughter instead of murder.

Mandatory: Required by law.

Consent: A defence in law that proves permission was provided by the appropriate person for the crime to occur.

Self-defence: A defence in law allowing the use of reasonable force to avoid a conviction.

Automatism: A defence in law where the defendant is not in control of their actions.

Why laws are different according to place, time and culture

There are numerous reasons why laws are different. For example, changes may reflect changing social and moral views; views on prostitutes have changed significantly over the last 100 years.

Also, opinions change over time and campaigns can change opinions.

Can you remember any campaigns from Unit 1 that have changed opinions or the law? For example, Sarah's law, Lillian's law, law on double jeopardy, etc.

The status of women in different societies can reflect on how laws vary. For example, in some countries men can have more than one wife; or jaywalking is a crime in some countries but not others, where it may be considered a personal responsibility to cross the road safely.

Religion can have a significant impact on different laws. The religious guidance in some books of faith can dictate which actions are criminal. If a country becomes less religious, then laws can change too.

Knowledge, especially regarding health and safety, can make laws change. For example, the changing laws concerning the smoking of cigarettes over the last 50–60 years.

Take it further

Consider a law that you believe should be reformed (changed) or abolished (removed). Then consider why you believe this to be the case. For example:

· Is it outdated as society has changed its view since it was originally created?
· Does it discriminate against some groups in society?
· Does it prevent freedom of choice?
· Does it relate to a medical issue about which we are now more knowledgeable?
· Are there any campaign groups to support a change to the law?
· Does this law vary around the world or in different cultures?

Understanding the reasons for wanting to change the law will help you understand why laws are different according to place, time and culture.

LEARNING OUTCOME 2
KNOW THEORIES OF CRIMINALITY

AC2.1 DESCRIBE BIOLOGICAL THEORIES OF CRIMINALITY

ASSESSMENT CRITERION	CONTENT	AMPLIFICATION
AC2.1 You should be able to … Describe biological theories of criminality	**Biological theories** • genetic theories • physiological theories	You should have knowledge of a range of genetic theories, such as: • Jacob's XYY study • twin and adoption studies • Lombroso • Sheldon

Biological theories focus on the idea that physical characteristics make some people more likely to commit crime than others. Such criminal tendencies can be genetic and therefore inherited. Hence, it could be said that the person is born bad.

Genetic theories

Genetic theories as an explanation for criminal behaviour emerged with modern criminology in the 1700s. In recent times there has been an increase in research on the genetics of behaviour, including anti-social behaviour.

XYY theory

This theory of criminality suggests that some crime might be attributable to a chromosomal abnormality. Chromosomes are structures in cell nuclei and humans usually have 46 chromosomes, 44 of which determine the shape and constitution of our body, and two determine sex.

Sex is determined by the pattern of a person's sex chromosomes: XX in a woman, XY in a man. It is a Y chromosome that makes a person male. There are a variety of chromosome abnormalities, some of which involve the presence of extra chromosomes, one such condition, known as 'XYY', involves the presence of an extra Y chromosome.

> **Tip** ✓
>
> This book includes the theories that are given as examples in the specification. However, other theories may also be relevant and could be used to answer an external exam question.

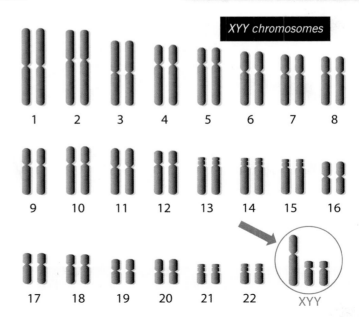

XYY chromosomes

XYY men, sometimes called super males, have been of interest to criminologists because of the suggestion that they are more aggressive and more inclined to be violent than males with a single Y chromosome.

Jacob et al. (1965) suggested that men with the XYY syndrome were more aggressive than normal 'XY' men. There are also some studies that suggest XYY men are over-represented in the prison population. There are 15 sufferers per 1,000 in prisons and one per 1,000 in the general population.

The serial killer John Wayne Gacy is said to have XYY syndrome. He sexually assaulted, tortured and killed at least 33 men in the USA.

Twin studies

Twin studies support the contention that a heritable trait may increase risk for criminal behaviour. Identical twins are monozygotic (MZ) as they are from one fertilised egg. Such twins share 100% of their DNA, whereas dizygotic (DZ) twins are from two separate eggs and share 50% of their DNA. When both of the twins share a characteristic there is said to be a concordance rate. In order to assess the role of genetic and environmental influences, or the nature versus nurture debate, various twin studies have taken place and there is some evidence to suggest that genetics or nature may play a role in criminality to the extent that concordance in MZ twins is greater than that in DZ twins.

One of the earliest twin studies was reported by the German physician Johannes Lange (1929). He found that MZ twins showed a much higher degree of concordance than DZ twins for criminal behaviour. Ten of the 13 MZ twins had both served time in prison, whereas only two of the 17 DZ twins had such concordance.

Christiansen (1977) studied 3,586 twin pairs from the Danish islands and found concordance rates of 35% (MZ) and 13% (DZ) for male twins and 21% (MZ) and 8% (DZ) for female twins.

Key terms

Monozygotic: Identical twins.

Dizygotic: Non-identical (fraternal) twins.

Concordance: In agreement or harmony.

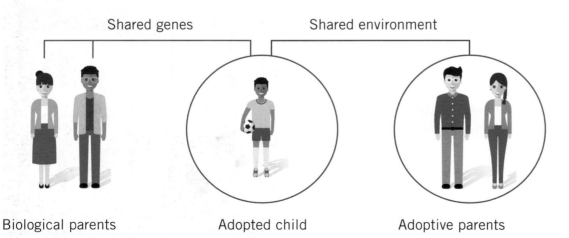

Shared genes   Shared environment

Biological parents   Adopted child   Adoptive parents

Twin studies look at the impact of genetics on criminality.

Adoption studies

The underlying principle of adoption studies in explaining criminal behaviour is the comparison of criminals with both their biological and adoptive parents. Such studies look at the impact of nurture on children who are raised by their non-biological parents. If, in criminal behaviour, the child is more similar to their biological parents than to their adoptive parents, with whom they share the same environment, a genetic basis of criminality may be suggested. On the other hand, if the child is more similar to their adoptive parents than their biological parents, an environmental argument for criminality is preferred.

Hutchings and Mednick (1975) studied 14,000 adopted children and found that a high proportion of boys with criminal convictions had biological parents with criminal convictions too, suggesting a link between aggression and genetics. Mednick et al. (1994) found no relationship between the number of criminal convictions of adoptive parents and their adopted children but did find a significant correlation between the number of criminal convictions of the biological parents and their offspring.

Handy hints !

As it is possible to consider both twin and adoption studies you can easily get confused and think that adoption studies involve twins who have been adopted. Twin and adoption studies are separate research techniques, as adoption studies do not usually involve twins. Twins are usually placed for adoption together rather than separated.

Physiological theories

These theories focus on a person's physical form as an indicator of criminality. The most widely known are those of Lombroso and Sheldon.

Cesare Lombroso – 'Father of Modern Criminology'

Lombroso was an Italian psychiatrist and military doctor who developed theories about criminals. Known as the 'Father of Modern Criminology', he pioneered the use of scientific methods in criminology. He argued that the criminal is a separate species, a species that is between modern and primitive humans. He also argued that a 'born criminal' could be determined by the physical shape of the head and face. He claimed that criminality was heritable and those who committed crimes had atavistic or primitive features. Such features were 'throwbacks' from an earlier stage of human development that manifested as a tendency to commit crimes.

Key term

Atavistic: Relating to something ancient or ancestral.

Cesare Lombroso (1835–1909)

Examples of atavistic features include:

- large or forward projection of the jaw
- high cheekbones
- flattened or upturned nose
- low, sloping forehead
- long arms relative to lower limbs
- large ears.

Lombroso examined the facial and cranial features of 383 dead criminals and 3,839 living ones, and concluded that 40% of criminal acts could be accounted for by atavistic characteristics. According to Lombroso, you can tell what kind of crime someone will commit by the way they look, for example murderers had bloodshot eyes and curly hair, and sex offenders had thick lips and protruding ears.

Besides physical traits, Lombroso suggested there were other aspects of the born criminal including insensitivity to pain, use of criminal slang, tattoos and unemployment. His theory was published in the book *L'uomo Delinquente* or *Criminal Man* (2006).

It is noteworthy that a study from a university in China has produced research that suggests facial features really can give a criminal away. ID photos of 1,856 Chinese men, half of whom had a previous conviction, were entered into an artificial intelligence programme. They found it wrongly flagged innocent men as criminal 6% of the time but correctly identified 83% of the real criminals.

Photographs from Lombroso's collection showing atavistic features.

William Sheldon

William Sheldon (1949) advanced a theory that shares with Lombroso's principle the idea that criminal behaviour is linked to a person's physical form. As a result of a meticulous examination of photographs showing the front, side and back views of 4,000 scantily clothed men, Sheldon put forward that there were three fundamental body types or somatotypes:

1. **Endomorphic** (fat and soft) tend to be sociable and relaxed.

2. **Ectomorphic** (thin and fragile) are introverted and restrained.

3. **Mesomorphic** (muscular and hard) are more aggressive and adventurous.

Sheldon, using a correlation study, found that many criminals prone to committing violent and aggressive acts were mesomorphic, and the least likely to be were ectomorphic. He used a sample of photographs of college students

> **Key term**
>
> **Somatotype:** Body shape.

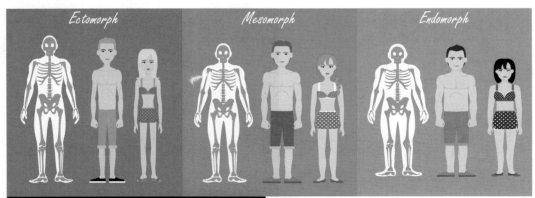

The three types of body shapes or somatotypes

and delinquents rated on a scale of 1 (low)–7 (high) their resemblance to mesomorphy. The results showed that the delinquents had a higher average mesomorphy rating than the college students (4.6–3.8).

Sheldon was inspired to produce his research while growing up watching his father breed poultry and dogs competitively; observing the correlation of genetics combined with his wish to breed a better species. His findings linking body shape to delinquents were produced in his book *Atlas of Men* (1954).

Brain abnormality

Several research studies have suggested that damage to the pre-frontal cortex of the brain may cause individuals to have an altered behaviour pattern, making them more immature and having an increased loss of self-control as well as having an inability to modify behaviour. Raine et al. (1994) used PET scans to study the living brains of impulsive killers. Damage was found in the pre-frontal cortex in the brains of the criminals: the part of the brain that controls impulsive behaviour.

Key term

PET scan: Positron emission tomography (PET) scans are used to produce detailed three-dimensional images of the inside of the body.

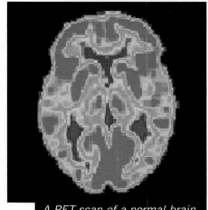

A PET scan of a normal brain.

CASE STUDY

PHINEAS GAGE

Gage was a railroad worker who survived an accident in which a large iron rod went through his head, destroying much of the left frontal lobe of the brain. Gage's personality and behaviour were greatly affected, with friends reporting that he was no longer Gage. He became extravagant and anti-social, used bad language, had bad manners and became a liar. The part of the brain that he had lost was associated to the mental and emotional functions that had changed. His doctor believed that the balance between his intellectual faculties and animalistic behaviour was destroyed in the accident.

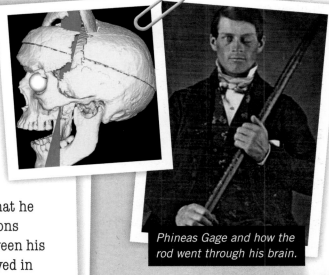

Phineas Gage and how the rod went through his brain.

Take it further

Read the research carried out by the Disabilities Trust – a foundation briefing paper: 'The Prevalence of Traumatic Brain Injury among Adult Male Offenders in the UK'.

A more modern Canadian study (McIsaac et al., 2016) found that people who have suffered serious head injuries are twice as likely to end up in prison (0.5% compared to 0.2%). Female prisoners were even more likely to have survived traumatic brain injuries. For women with these injuries, the risk of winding up in a Canadian federal prison was 2.76 times higher than it was for uninjured women.

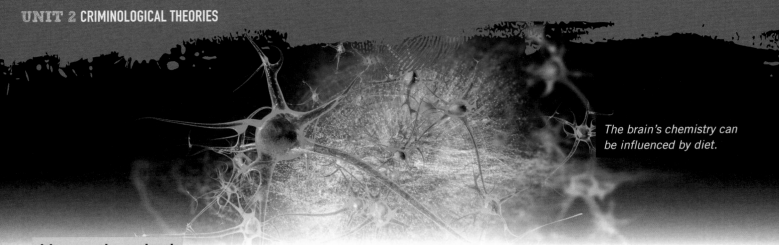

The brain's chemistry can be influenced by diet.

Neurochemical

The brain's chemistry can be influenced by diet, for example food additives, pollution or hypoglycaemia (low blood sugar levels associated with forms of diabetes).

Some studies show that low levels of serotonin are linked with higher aggression. Serotonin regulates signals between neurons and is said to control a person's mood. Scerbo and Raine (1993) conducted a meta-analysis on 29 studies into anti-social adults and children, finding low levels of serotonin in all of them. Control of serotonin levels by diet is possible, as some foods, including dark chocolate, cheese, nuts, salmon, turkey and chicken, can help raise serotonin levels.

People who take large amounts of steroids can become extremely violent (known as 'roid rage'). Steroids, often taken to increase muscle growth, also increase testosterone levels. Horace Williams, an American body builder, beat a man to death after taking 2,000 times the recommended dosage of steroids.

Roid rage

Example questions

Exam questions in this area are as follow:

Unit 2 Exam 2017
With reference to the text above, describe the main features of one physiological theory of criminality. **[6 marks]**

Explain one genetic theory of criminality. **[5 marks]**
NOTE that from 2020 the changes in the mark bands would mean that this question would be out of either 4 or 6 marks.

Unit 2 Exam 2018
Describe one physiological theory of criminality. **[5 marks]**
NOTE that from 2020 the changes in the mark bands would mean that this question would be out of either 4 or 6 marks.

Unit 2 Exam 2019
Describe one biological theory of criminality. **[5 marks]**
NOTE that from 2020 the changes in the mark bands would mean that this question would be out of either 4 or 6 marks.

Think theory

In the exam read all the questions before attempting to answer any. You may be asked to describe a theory in one question and later apply or evaluate the selected theory to the scenario in another question. In other words, the theory carries forward to another question.

AC2.2 DESCRIBE INDIVIDUALISTIC THEORIES OF CRIMINALITY

ASSESSMENT CRITERION	CONTENT	AMPLIFICATION
AC2.2 You should be able to … Describe individualistic theories of criminality	**Individualistic theories** • learning theories • psychodynamic • psychological theories	You should have knowledge of a range of theories, for example: • Bandura • Eysenck • Freud

Learning theories

Learning theories are based on the assumption that offending is a set of behaviours that are learned in the same way as other behaviours.

Many of the studies that we will look at emphasise the family and peer group as potential sources of criminal behaviour.

Think about what you have learned from your teachers. What happens if you fail to hand in your homework? Are you punished perhaps with detention? So, have you learned not to repeat such behaviour? Have you ever received a treat for positive behaviour? This is the same principle for learning theories.

Learning theories can account for criminality.

Albert Bandura – social learning theory (SLT)

Bandura believes that people learn by watching the behaviour of others. If children watch adults gaining pleasure from an activity, or being punished for an activity, they will either repeat or reject those behaviours. So, aggression can be learned from watching others behave in an aggressive manner. To prove his ideas, Bandura conducted a series of experiments involving a bobo doll.

Albert Bandura (1925–)

CASE STUDY

BANDURA AND THE BOBO DOLL EXPERIMENT (1963)

Bandura carried out a series of tests involving a bobo doll (see McLeod, 2014). The experiment involved exposing children to two different adult models: an aggressive model and a non-aggressive one. In the aggressive model adults were seen to kick and pummel the doll and also hit it with a mallet and throw it in the air. After witnessing the adults' behaviour, the children would then be placed in a room without the model and were observed to see if they would imitate the behaviours they had witnessed earlier. The experiment showed that children exposed to the aggressive adults tended to copy such behaviour. They even came up with new ways to hurt the doll, for example using a toy gun to shoot it or throwing darts at it. Children who watched the non-aggressive version demonstrated far less aggression towards the bobo.

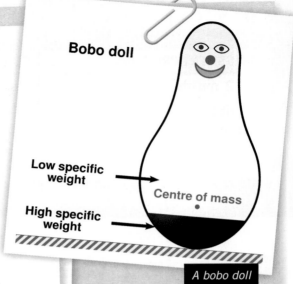

A bobo doll

Violence and aggression are produced by:

- an arousal event (provocation)
- learned aggressive skills
- expected success and rewards
- pro-violence values.

People pay attention to models and copy their behaviour. If imitating a model's behaviour is rewarding, we are more likely to continue performing the behaviour.

How do the findings for the bobo doll experiment account for criminality?

Criminal behaviour, like any other, can be learned from observation. Some people learn criminal behaviour from those around them, for example family. We term this observational learning. This is where viewers learn behaviours from watching others and may imitate them; many behaviours are learned from the media.

Observational learning is thought to take place primarily in three contexts:

1. In the family.
2. In the prevalent sub-culture, for example peers.
3. Through cultural symbols such as television and books.

Consider the impact of the media.

CASE STUDY

Are we influenced by the television, films or video games? Do we copy what we see on the media? These questions were debated as a result of the murder of James Bulger by two ten-year-old boys: Robert Thomson and Jon Venables. They are said to have watched the film *Child's Play 3* before the murder. The judge in this case said:

It is not for me to pass judgment on their upbringing, but I suspect exposure to violent video films may in part be an explanation. **(Mr Justice Morland, Trial Judge)**

The trial judge made comments about the influence of video films on the killers of James Bulger.

Supporting Bandura is the theory advanced by Sutherland (Sutherland et al., 1992) who considers differential associations or different learning experiences. This theory suggests that people learn their values and techniques for criminal behaviour from associations with different people or differential associations. If more favourable attitudes about crime are learned rather than negatives, then people see criminal behaviour as acceptable. They learn methods of how to commit crimes from those around them, whether the crime is theft or fraud, etc. The learning experiences or differential associations will vary in frequency and importance for each individual. The process of learning criminal behaviour is no different from the learning of any other behaviour. This theory also accounts for the high reoffending rate of released prisoners in our country. While in prison criminals learn from those around them and become more versed in certain criminal techniques and offences. Thus, this is the reason why prisons are known as 'universities of crime'.

Key terms

Observational learning: When an observer's behaviour changes after viewing the behaviour of a model.

Differential associations: Interactions with others.

Research shows that criminality is concentrated in a small number of families. Research by Osborn and West (1979) considered sons of criminal fathers and those of non-criminal fathers. They found that where the father had a criminal conviction, 40% of the sons also acquired one by the age of 18. However, only 13% of sons where the father was not criminal had a criminal conviction. While not conclusive, it is consistent with a genetic view on offending.

Exam question Unit 2 2019

Describe one individualistic theory of criminality.   **[5 marks]**
NOTE that from 2020 the changes in the mark bands would mean that this question would be out of either 4 or 6 marks.

Albert Bandura's social learning theory proposes the idea that people will learn from those around them. People often do this by observing their peers and family, and using their conduct as a model that is then imitated. Children are often most influenced by the adults around them and will repeat behaviours or reject certain behaviours based on the consequences they see for those adults. For example, if an adult enjoys a particular activity, a child may mimic this to experience the same pleasure; whereas, if an adult is punished for a particular activity, a child is less like to copy it. This is known as observational learning and can take place within the family, in prevalent sub-cultures and via the media (film, television, books, video games, etc.). Modelled aggression was illustrated in Bandura's bobo doll experiment, which suggested that violence and aggression are produced by an arousal event. Children exposed to the aggressive modelling picked up hostile language and increased their attraction to guns. People can also learn from those around them how to commit crimes and effective methods to carry out criminal behaviours, such as committing a robbery or fraud.

Handy hints !

In an exam, a 4 mark question will start with the word 'briefly', for example 'Briefly describe one individualistic theory of criminality.' A 6 mark question, which would require more information, would read as 'Describe one individualistic theory of criminality.'

Assessment

This would reach the top mark band 5–6 marks.

This answer is detailed and uses appropriate terminology. It refers to research such as the bobo doll experiment and includes the support of Sutherland's work. An improvement area could be to develop the bobo experiment, citing the variations used and subsequent results. However, for a 6 mark question this is not essential.

Psychodynamic theories

Sigmund Freud

Sigmund Freud believed the best way to understand behaviour is to examine early childhood experiences and that criminality was linked to guilt. He suggested that much of our mind was in an unconscious region, similar to an iceberg where only the tip can be seen. It is our unconscious mind that controls behaviour, including criminality.

Freud developed a structure of the mind or psyche containing our personality divided into three parts:

- the **id**, which controls our selfish and animalistic urges
- the **ego**, which seeks rational and sensible control
- the **superego** being our moral conscience.

The id wants instant gratification and represents our basic needs. It is the most primitive part of our personality and is found in the deep unconscious part of the brain. The id would tell you to ignore your homework and go to the party instead.

The superego is what people think of as our conscience. Concerned with social rules and morals it tells us what is right and wrong. It would tell you to stay home and complete all your homework, as that is more important than going to a party.

The ego is less primitive than the id and tries to be practical and realistic. Acting as a mediator between the id and the superego it would suggest you spend some time completing your homework and then go to the party. It is in the partly conscious and partly unconscious mind.

Sigmund Freud (1856–1939)

Freud's theory of personality

Superego　　**Ego**　　**Id**

A healthy personality needs a balance between all three parts. When these parts have an unresolved conflict the result is a disturbed personality. If the id dominates, the mind may be uncontrollable and this is when criminality takes place. However, if the superego is dominant someone would be very moralistic, expecting perfection and being rather judgemental if this was not achieved. A dominant ego can result in someone being incapable of accepting change and desiring a very fixed and rigid lifestyle.

Children need to progress from the pleasure principle, being id dominated and therefore needing instant gratification, to the reality principle, where the ego is dominant. Criminals are those children who do not make this transition. According to Freud, the child needs a stable home environment in order to successfully make this transition. Research has supported the fact that most criminals come from unstable homes. John Bowlby's (1944) study looked at maternal deprivation by studying 44 juvenile delinquents and comparing them with non-criminal disturbed juveniles. Of the delinquents, 39% had experienced complete separation from their mothers for six months or more during the first five years of their lives compared with 5% of the control group.

Psychological theories

Hans Eysenck

Eysenck believed that certain personality types are more likely to commit crime because they crave excitement, but are slow to learn that crime has bad consequences. He based his results on analysis of responses to a personality questionnaire. He carried out the questionnaire with 700 soldiers who were being treated for neurotic disorders at the hospital he was working in. He believed that the answers suggested there were a number of different personality traits revealed by the soldiers' answers.

Hans Eysenck (1916–1997)

He then identified, initially, two 'dimensions' of personality, namely extraversion/introversion (E, I) and neuroticism/stability (N, S). These had different personality traits or characteristics.

- **Extraversion/introversion:** concerns the amount of stimulation a person needs. An extrovert is sociable but can become bored very quickly, if there is a lack of stimulation. Whereas introverts are reliable and in control of their emotions.
- **Neuroticism/stability:** concerns the level of emotional stability of a person. Neurotics are very anxious and often irrational. Whereas a stable personality is calm and emotionally in control.

Eysenck later added a third dimension he called psychoticism (P), a cold, uncaring and aggressive personality, and this further indicates a tendency towards criminality.

Key terms

Juvenile delinquent: Someone under the age of 18 years who has broken the law.

Control group: A group in an experiment or study that does not receive treatment by the researchers and is then used as a benchmark to measure how the other subjects tested did.

Take it further

Research the Oedipus and Electra complexes to discover some of Freud's theories about the impact of our upbringing.

Key terms

Extraversion: Being mainly concerned with and gaining pleasure from things outside of the self.

Introversion: Directing your interests inwards or to things within the self.

Neuroticism: To have feelings of anxiety, worry, anger or fear.

Stability: Unlikely to move or change.

Psychoticism: A personality pattern that is typified by aggression and hostility towards other people.

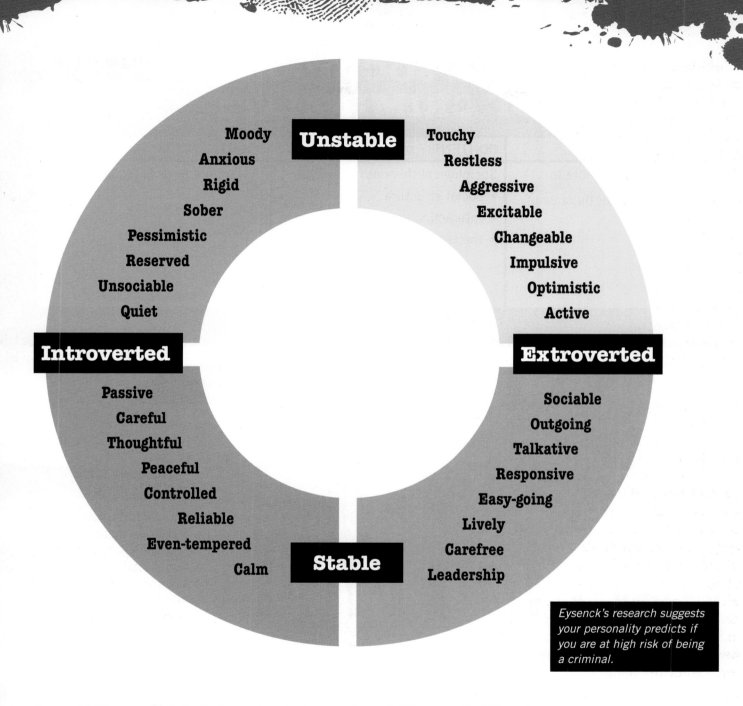

Moody
Anxious
Rigid
Sober
Pessimistic
Reserved
Unsociable
Quiet

Unstable

Touchy
Restless
Aggressive
Excitable
Changeable
Impulsive
Optimistic
Active

Introverted

Extroverted

Passive
Careful
Thoughtful
Peaceful
Controlled
Reliable
Even-tempered
Calm

Stable

Sociable
Outgoing
Talkative
Responsive
Easy-going
Lively
Carefree
Leadership

Eysenck's research suggests your personality predicts if you are at high risk of being a criminal.

Eysenck's theory predicts that people who have extrovert (E), neurotic (N) and psychotic (P) personalities are more likely to offend because it is difficult for them to learn to control their immature impulses. Hence, criminals are more likely to be impulsive, thrill-seeking, and unable to accept and understand the rules of society.

Activity

Take the personality test to discover your type of personality.
See http://similarminds.com/eysenck.html.

AC2.3 DESCRIBE SOCIOLOGICAL THEORIES OF CRIMINALITY

ASSESSMENT CRITERION	CONTENT	AMPLIFICATION
AC2.3 You should be able to ... Describe sociological theories of criminality	**Sociological theories** • social structure • interactionism • realism	You should be able to summarise the key points of a range of theories, for example: • Marxism • labelling • functionalism • left and right realism

Society can cause criminality.

Sociological theories of criminology believe that society influences a person to become a criminal.

Social structure

Sociological theory assumes that a disadvantaged social class is the primary cause of crime and that criminal behaviour begins in youth. Crime is largely a result of unfavourable conditions in a community, for example unemployment, single-parent families, etc.

Marxists essentially see crime as something being inevitable in a capitalist society and is used by the ruling class, or bourgeoisie, as a means of social control. If someone does not conform then they will be punished. Institutions such as the police, the criminal justice system, prisons, schools, the family and religion are there to

Key terms

Marxism: The political and economic theories of Karl Marx, which state that capitalism is unequal and undemocratic, being based on the exploitation of the working class by the capitalist class/ bourgeoisie.

Capitalism: The social system in which the means for producing and distributing goods (the country's trade and industry) are controlled by a small minority of people for profit (the capitalist class). The majority of people must sell their ability to work in return for a wage or salary (the working class/proletariat).

encourage you to conform. They argue that white-collar crimes, which tend to be committed by the more powerful in society, are ignored, while crimes committed by the less powerful, such as street crime, are focused on and seen as more serious.

Marxists would also argue that different social classes are policed differently, with the working class, or proletariat, heavily policed in the expectation that they will be more criminal and therefore raising the chances of their crimes being detected.

In addition, Marxists hold the view that, when it comes to crime, governments fabricate statistics to suit their purposes and get public support for any action taken that might be construed as trespassing on freedoms. Marxists believe that on average 42% of the statistics presented by the government are false and misleading.

Karl Marx (1818–1883)

Exam question

Unit 2 2018/9

Describe one sociological theory of criminality. **[6 marks]**

or

Unit 2 2020

Briefly describe one sociological theory of criminality. **[4 marks]**

NOTE that in this type of exam question the 4 mark would ask for a brief description and the 6 mark would want a mid-length answer.

Describe one sociological theory of criminality. **[6 marks]**

Synoptic link

Think back to Unit 1 AC1.6 'Evaluate methods of collecting statistics' and the criticisms about the accuracy of crime statistics.

This theory is **1** that society makes **2** a person become a criminal. It assumes that the disadvantaged social class is a primary cause of crime and that criminal behaviour begins in youth. It says that crime is largely a result of unfavourable conditions in a community. The views of Marx essentially see crime as something used by the ruling class **3** that is used as a means of social control.

The **4** police are there to encourage you to conform and that the working class **5** are heavily policed. **6** They also believe that governments lie about **7** statistics to suit their purposes. **8** Marxists believe that loads of the statistics **9** presented by the government are not right. **10**

1 asserts

2 influences

3 bourgeoisie

4 Institutions such as

5 proletariat

6 Develop to consider a lack of policing on white-collar crimes.

8 Develop to include gaining support for their intervention and possible trespass on freedoms.

7 fabricate

9 qualify, e.g. 42%

10 false and misleading

Assessment

Mark band 3–4

While the theory in this answer is correctly stated, the detail is limited. Also, more specialist terminology could be used. See the comments around the answer for alternative suggestions and ways of improving it.

Crime and a functionalist approach

This theory begins with society as a whole and the suggestion from Émile Durkheim that crime is inevitable as not every member of society can be equally committed to the collective sentiments or values and beliefs. Socialisation and social control help to achieve solidarity in society.

Crime is considered to be functional and only becomes dysfunctional when the rate of it is high or low. If in society collective sentiments are too strong, there will be little change. This can be seen in the changes in the law of homosexuality. If there was no opposition to this law there would have been no change and practising homosexuality would still be illegal. If collective sentiments are too weak there will be too much crime and the status quo breaks down with chaos possibly resulting.

Crime also strengthens social cohesion or the willingness of members of society to cooperate with one another. It maintains boundaries with society, reacting and uniting, and reinforcing their commitment to the value consensus. An example of this can be seen following the abduction of Shannon Matthews in 2008, when members of the Moorside Estate united in expressing their views of the crime, organising searches, marches and other public displays of boundary maintenance.

Émile Durkheim (1858–1917), also known as the 'Father of Sociology', believed that crime itself serves a function.

Merton's strain theory

Robert K. Merton argues that society encourages us to subscribe to the goals of material success, but society is unable to provide the legitimate means for us all to achieve such successes, as not everyone can gain qualifications and not everyone can access jobs. Working-class people are more likely than others to be denied these material benefits. Their opportunities are blocked and, consequently, they experience feelings of strain and anomie, when they strive for goals of material success, but do not have the opportunities to reach the goals through legitimate means. If people cannot achieve their goals they can:

- conform and accept the situation
- innovate by adopting non-conventional or criminal ways to gain material success
- become ritualistic, where sight of goals is lost
- become retreatists and drop out of conventional society
- become rebels, who set alternative, opposing goals and values rather than those promoted by society.

Key terms

Anomie: Loss of shared principles or norms.

Ritualistic: Performing in the same way.

Retreatist: Rejection of society's prescribed goals and the conventional means of attaining them.

Interactionism

Interactionism refers to how people in society interact with one another. Interactionists such as Howard Becker use the labelling theory to explain criminality. They argue that official statistics on crime are socially constructed and they believe that crime is also a social construction. Becker put forward the argument that crime is a subjective concept; agents of social control, such as the police and judges, label certain acts and behaviour as deviant or criminal. Behaviour will then be punished accordingly.

The sociologist Edwin Lemert referred to two specific types of deviance: primary deviance, which is an act of deviance that has not been socially labelled as deviant; and secondary deviance, which is an act that has been labelled as deviant.

Once a particular act/behaviour has been labelled as deviant, the deviant person starts to view themselves as a deviant. This becomes their 'master status' and can lead to a self-fulfilling prophecy, which means that they start to internalise the label and begin acting and behaving in a way that mirrors the label. In short, the person then becomes the label, in this case a deviant or criminal.

The media can contribute towards this, as they may 'demonise' people who have been socially labelled as deviant, creating moral panic in society, and in turn making those labelled as deviants appear as folk devils, marginalising and alienating them further. This process is referred to as deviancy amplification, as it amplifies the situation, making it more difficult for the deviant person to change public opinion towards them. This is the impact of labelling and can often lead to stereotyping.

Howard Becker (1928–)

Key terms

Folk devils: A person of bad influence on society (see Cohen (1973), page 40).

Deviancy amplification: A process often performed by the media, in which the extent and seriousness of deviant behaviour is exaggerated, creating a greater awareness and interest in deviance.

Stereotyping: A widely held but fixed, over-enlaraged image or idea of a type of person.

Activity

Discuss as a class: Is it likely that being labelled a trouble-maker is enough to make someone turn into a criminal?

Realism

Synoptic link

Refer back to Unit 1 and how the media portray crime.

Right realism

Right realism considers crime from the perspective of political conservatism, with the standpoint of getting tough on crime.

Charles Murray is a leading right realist who states that everyone is tempted to commit crime but it is the amount of social bonds that often prevent us from doing so. Murray talks about the development of the 'underclass' such as single parents, where young boys grow up without appropriate role models and crime is a way of proving they are men.

Left **Right**

Right and left realism follow the political structure of the UK.

Right realists question the view that economic factors, such as poverty or unemployment, are the reason behind rising crime rates. Instead, it was believed that individuals are more likely to commit crime when the social constraints on their behaviour are weakened. So crime is linked to inadequate social control.

Left realism

Left realism suggests that crime lies in the inequalities created by a capitalist society. Left realists believe that both practical measures to reduce crime and a long-term change towards a more equal, caring society are needed. Capitalism encourages levels of consumption but is unable to deliver to all. So some people are motivated by consumerism and materialism and turn to crime to make up the shortfall. But what is needed is gradual social change along with practical solutions to the problem of crime.

Handy hints !

The theory you select will be guided by the scenario at the start of the question. This will include prompts or clues pointing towards at least one sociological theory. The choice of theory will be down to you. However, before you decide the theory read all the other part questions that follow. This is because you may have to analyse the selected theory in relation to the circumstances in the scenario. In addition, you may also have to evaluate it. Hence, the chosen theory could span more than one part of the question.

Activity

Create a revision aid on left and right realism. For example, a poster or chart showing the comparisons between each theory. Try to include the following points:

- a summary of the key aspects of the theory
- theorists linked to the theory
- key terminology for each theory
- positives of each theory
- weaknesses of each theory
- crimes that could be associated with each theory
- the main focus of crime prevention in each theory.

LEARNING OUTCOME 3
UNDERSTAND CAUSES OF CRIMINALITY

AC3.1 ANALYSE SITUATIONS OF CRIMINALITY

ASSESSMENT CRITERION	CONTENT	AMPLIFICATION
AC3.1 You should be able to … Analyse situations of criminality	Situations relating to: • different types of crime • individual criminal behaviour	You should have knowledge of a range of crimes, for example crimes against the person/property, white collar, corporate crime, etc. You should be able to analyse a range of crimes and criminal behaviour and understand possible causes through the application of the theories learned for LO2

Handy hints !

Here you have to consider why crimes have been committed, looking at both types of crimes and individual behaviour. You can apply the theories considered in ACs2.1, 2.2 and 2.3.

Activity

Copy and complete the table.

CRIME	POSSIBLE REASONS FOR CRIMINALITY	RELEVANT THEORY
Crimes against property (theft, robbery, burglary)		
White-collar crimes		
Crimes against the person (assault, battery, ABH and GBH)		
Honour crimes		
Murder		
Public Order Act offences, such as affray, riot and violent disorder		

ABH = actual bodily harm   GBH = grievous bodily harm

CASE STUDY

ROBERT NAPPER

Robert Napper was convicted of the brutal murder of Rachel Nickell, and the double murder of Samantha Bisset and her four-year-old daughter Jazmine. He was also thought to be the 'Green Chain Rapist', who carried out a series of at least 70 attacks across South London over a four-year period ending in 1993.

Background

During the early years of his life, Napper witnessed his father's violence against his mother. He and his siblings were placed in foster homes and Napper, who suffered from a psychiatric and behavioural disorder, became a paranoid schizophrenic who also suffered from Asperger's syndrome. At the age of 12 he was raped by a family friend, and in school he did not have any friends and was teased by other children. He was found to have had only average intelligence. Napper would bully his brothers and went on to confess to his mother to raping a woman.

Robert Napper

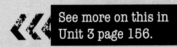
See more on this in Unit 3 page 156.

Key term

Paranoid schizophrenic: Someone with an illness of psychosis of varying intensity, which makes them lose touch with reality.

Relevant theories of criminality – Robert Napper

Bowlby's theory of attachment

Given the case study information about Napper's life, there are a number of theories that could be relevant to his criminality. For example, we can consider Bowlby's (1944) theory of attachment, which supports the proposition that a child needs a stable home environment to develop appropriately. However, it may be argued that the separation experienced in childhood has led to affectionate psychopathy where individuals feel no remorse for their victims or guilt for the crime they have committed.

Social learning theory

In addition, the social learning theory as put forward by Bandura would suggest that Napper has learned from those around him. In particular, he witnessed his father's violence towards his mother. In later life he inflicted brutal violence on women in both rapes and murders. In addition, aged 12, Napper was raped in the woods near his home. This was echoed by his crimes in later life.

CASE STUDY

FRED WEST

Fred West, from Gloucestershire, was thought to have committed at least 12 murders of young females, many with his wife Rose, between 1967 and 1987. The murders involved both Fred and Rose's sexual gratification and included rape, bondage and torture. There was also dismemberment of bodies, with some being buried under the patio area of their home. This included Heather West, their daughter, whose body was found with the head severed from the body and bones chopped up to reduce the space in which the skeleton could be buried. Eventually, the pair were arrested and charged with the murders. However, Fred hung himself in prison before trial. Rose was convicted of ten counts of murder by a jury in November 1995 and was sentenced to ten mandatory life sentences with a whole-life tariff.

There are rumours that Fred was introduced to sex by his mother from a young age and allegedly engaged in acts of bestiality with animals in his early teens. When Fred was 17 years old he had a motorcycle accident, from which he received serious head injuries, which left him in a coma for a week. A metal plate was inserted into his head, which may have affected his behaviour and left him with an inability to control impulses.

The story of Fred and Rose West can be read in the book by Howard Sounes called Fred & Rose.

Key term

Whole-life tariff: An order that having been convicted of murder the defendant must serve all of it in prison and not be allowed parole.

Take it further

Research murderers who have been given a whole-life tariff. Discover their names and the names of their victims.

Relevant theories of criminality – Fred West

Social learning theory

If the rumours about Fred's mother introducing him to sex at an early age are true, this may account for the methods and brutality of his crimes later in life. There was a focus on rape and sexual torture, which suggests that he was heavily influenced by his mother who acted as a role model.

Freud's personality theory

It could be argued that Fred was unable to progress from the pleasure-seeking id to the reality principle where the ego is dominant. He continued to need instant gratification from his sexual acts.

Brain damage

Given the brain damage that Fred received as a result of his motorcycle accident, it may be that this provided a biological reason for his criminality. Research has shown that damage to the pre-frontal cortex area of the brain can impact on a person's ability to control their impulsive behaviour. Fred may have been unable to resist the urge for sexual gratification.

CASE STUDY

NICK LEESON

Nick Leeson is known as the man whose fraudulent, unauthorised speculative trading caused the collapse of Barings Bank, the UK's oldest merchant bank. Initially, he was very successful, making large profits for the bank and huge bonuses for himself. However, his luck ran out in 1995 when a secret file, Error Account 88888, showed that he had gambled away £827 million in Baring's name. In his autobiography, Leeson (1997) states, 'We were all driven to make profits, profits, and more profits ... I was the rising star.' It was also said of him that he was a high-flyer who liked to dabble in dare-devil trades.

Nick Leeson

Relevant theories of criminality – Nick Leeson

Eysenck's personality theory

According to this theory, criminals are more likely to be extrovert, impulsive and thrill seeking. It could be argued that Leeson was willing to take chances in financial transactions, running the risk of being caught but enjoying the thrill of making money.

Social structure theory or Marxism

Given the large amount of money that Leeson made, which included bonuses of up to £150,000, it may be that he wanted to avoid falling into the disadvantaged working class in society. Marxists may argue that as the proletariat are heavily policed, white-collar crimes such as fraud are not monitored by the police and this is why he avoided detection for so long.

Tip

Scenarios are written VERY carefully – every single piece of information is there for a reason. Think about why the examiner has given each piece of detail in the scenario – what could it relate to? Mention it in your answer.

Activity

Read the scenario below, from the 2017 Unit 2 exam paper, and consider possible causes of Paul's offending. Discuss your answers with a partner.

> Paul, aged 25, has been unemployed since leaving school at 16. His father and two older brothers have all been to prison, but so far Paul has not been convicted of any crime. His girlfriend is moaning about not having a nice house and holidays like her friends. Paul is very prone to depression as a result of his car accident two years ago, when he received head injuries. Last week, in an attempt to put some excitement into his dull life, Paul took part in an armed robbery of a local post office. However, he was subsequently arrested and is now on remand in prison.

Take it further

Create your own scenarios with behaviour that could relate to the criminological theories. This will help you understand how the criminological theories can apply to situations of criminality.

AC3.2 EVALUATE THE EFFECTIVENESS OF CRIMINOLOGICAL THEORIES TO EXPLAIN CAUSES OF CRIMINALITY

ASSESSMENT CRITERION	CONTENT	AMPLIFICATION
AC3.2 You should be able to … Evaluate the effectiveness of criminological theories to explain causes of criminality	**Criminological theories** • individualistic • biological • sociological	You should evaluate the strengths and weaknesses of criminological theories in terms of explaining crime

Evaluation of individualistic theories

Learning theories – Bandura's social learning theory

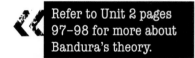

Refer to Unit 2 pages 97–98 for more about Bandura's theory.

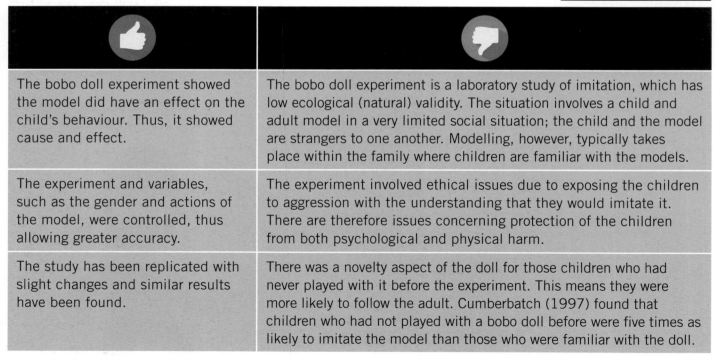

👍	👎
The bobo doll experiment showed the model did have an effect on the child's behaviour. Thus, it showed cause and effect.	The bobo doll experiment is a laboratory study of imitation, which has low ecological (natural) validity. The situation involves a child and adult model in a very limited social situation; the child and the model are strangers to one another. Modelling, however, typically takes place within the family where children are familiar with the models.
The experiment and variables, such as the gender and actions of the model, were controlled, thus allowing greater accuracy.	The experiment involved ethical issues due to exposing the children to aggression with the understanding that they would imitate it. There are therefore issues concerning protection of the children from both psychological and physical harm.
The study has been replicated with slight changes and similar results have been found.	There was a novelty aspect of the doll for those children who had never played with it before the experiment. This means they were more likely to follow the adult. Cumberbatch (1997) found that children who had not played with a bobo doll before were five times as likely to imitate the model than those who were familiar with the doll.

Psychodynamic theories – Freud's theory of the psyche

Refer to Unit 2 pages 101–102 for more about Freud's theory.

👍	👎
Just because Freud's theories are rather odd or unusual it doesn't make them automatically wrong.	Psychodynamic theories of offending are no longer accredited by psychologists due to the difficulty of testing concepts such as the unconscious mind.
Psychodynamic theories have contributed to research about crime and behaviour. In particular, the focus on childhood experiences and the importance of them on future behaviour should not be underestimated.	These theories are very unscientific and lack objective interpretation. It is a very subjective process where different analysts may draw different conclusions.
The id, ego and superego relate to different parts of the brain, and their functions and development. The limbic system is the brain's emotion centre, rather like the id, and the pre-frontal cortex is responsible for rational decision making, just like the ego.	There is a lack of quantitative data from Freud's case studies. He knew his patients and therefore could not be objective. He also psychoanalysed himself, studying his own dreams and childhood memories.

Psychological theories – Eysenck's criminal personality type

Refer to Unit 2 pages 102–103 for more about Eysenck's research.

👍	👎
Eysenck's research on soldiers in hospital supported this theory. He predicted the most traumatised soldiers would score high on neurotic.	There is a lack of reliability, as people may not respond exactly the same to the same questions each day or every time. Alternatively, they may provide an answer that they believe the researcher expects or desires.
If his theory is correct and tendencies towards criminal behaviour are detectable in childhood, then it may be possible to intervene at an early stage and prevent such development. This could lead to interventions based on parenting or early treatment and thus reduce crime.	Research in this area relies on self-report measures about a person's view of their personality. This can result in biased or deliberately false answers (Farrington et al., 1996).
His personality testing has formed the basis of many modern personality tests that try to predict people's behaviour in different situations, for example psychometric tests. DeYoung (2010) suggests there is a link between P, E, N scores and brain processes, such as the release of dopamine being linked to extroversion, and high levels of testosterone to psychoticism.	The theory suggests that personality is genetic and fails to consider that it may change over time.

Take it further

Produce a mind map showing the evaluation of individualistic theories.

Evaluation of biological theories

Lombroso

Do you remember Lombroso's theory?

Introduced the idea of the 'born criminal'.

Criminality is inherited and the way you look will determine if you are a criminal. Criminals have atavistic features (throwbacks).

Refer to Unit 2 pages 93–94 for more about Lombroso's theory.

👍	👎
Lombroso was the first person to give criminology a scientific credibility.	Lack of a control group – so no comparisons can be made.
Charles Goring (1913) did find a low-order intelligence in convicts, which suggests some genetic base to criminality.	Lack of accuracy due to possible disfigurements.
Several pieces of research, for example Bath Spa University (Butcher & Taylor, 2007), suggest that less attractive individuals are more likely to be considered guilty.	Not everyone with atavistic features is a criminal and not all criminals have them.
Lombroso did challenge the idea that criminals are evil or that they choose to be criminal.	Charles Goring (1913) used a non-criminal control group and found no significant differences in terms of behaviour.
Lombroso labelled prisons 'criminal universities' and suggested prisoners came out much worse than when they went in. Given today's recidivism rate this is very perceptive.	Scientific racism – DeLisi (2012) indicated that many of the atavistic features defined are specific to people of African descent.
His work heralded the beginnings of offender profiling.	Extremely deterministic and assumes that we cannot escape destiny.

Key term

Recidivism: The tendency of a convicted criminal to reoffend.

Sheldon

Can you remember Sheldon's theory? It linked body type to criminality. Out of the three somatotypes, a mesomorph, muscular and aggressive, was linked to criminal behaviour.

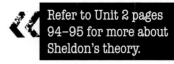

Refer to Unit 2 pages 94–95 for more about Sheldon's theory.

👍	👎
A number of other studies have confirmed that there is a small association between bodily build and criminality (Putwain & Sammons, 2002).	Could not really explain how ectomorphs and endomorphs can also be criminals.
A good-sized sample (200) was used and, importantly, Sheldon had a control condition of non-offenders (students) to compare the results to.	Does not take into account that people's somatotype is not fixed. People's bodies change throughout their lives.
Even though there could be issues surrounding the reliability of Sheldon's study, other researchers have found results that seem to support, at least in part, his initial theory. Glueck and Glueck (1956) found in their research that in a sample of delinquents 60% were mesomorphs, while in a non-delinquent sample there were only 31%.	Consider if mesomorphs get picked upon or invited/dared to do illegal acts? Because of the way people consider mesomorphs, they may be drawn into delinquent activities by peer groups.
Did find that the criminal groups were more mesomorphic.	If a mesomorph's shape is considered criminal, do courts think this too? The judicial system may treat them more harshly, increasing the likelihood that they will officially be labelled as criminal.

XYY theory

Can you remember this genetic theory? Reports identified a large number of criminals imprisoned for violent behaviour as carrying the XYY chromosome.

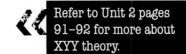

Refer to Unit 2 pages 91–92 for more about XYY theory.

👍	👎
One study by Jacob et al. (1965) found that a significant number of men in prison had XYY sex chromosomes instead of the normal XY.	However, studies have found that genetic abnormalities are widespread throughout the general population and therefore do not explain aggression.
Adler et al. (2007) indicated that it is possible that aggressive and violent behaviour is at least partly determined by genetic factors.	Focusing too heavily on genetics ignores the behaviourist approach.
	Theilgaard (1984) researched the traits of XYY men compared to XY men. He found the characteristic of aggression was not associated with the XYY men.

Twin studies

Refer to Unit 2 page 92 for more about twin studies.

👍	👎
Such studies are natural experiments, as the biological relationships between the twins is a naturally occurring variable.	Early twin studies, such as that of Lange (1929), were inadequately controlled and lacked validity as to whether the twins were DZ or MZ, which was based on appearance and not DNA.
Christiansen (1977) supports the view that criminality does have a genetic component.	The small sample involved in twin studies may not be representative of the general population.
The results of twin studies have helped in prevention of vulnerable disorders.	If twins are brought up in the same environment, criminality could just as easily be related to nurture as to genetics.

Adoption studies

Refer to Unit 2 page 92 for more about adoption studies.

👍	👎
As adopted children are exposed to a different environment to their biological family, it is easier to separate genetic and environmental factors.	The age of adoption may mean the adopted children have already been influenced by either their natural parents or their foster environment.
Studies have concluded that there is a correlation between adopted children and their biological parents.	Information about a biological family is not always available.
	The adoption process is not always random, as often children are placed with parents similar to their biological families.

Tip ✓

Take notice that the evaluation points do not describe the theories. This is not required by this AC. It is important in the exam that you do not waste time by writing descriptions.

Evaluation of sociological theories

Social structure theory or Marxism

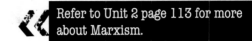 Refer to Unit 2 page 113 for more about Marxism.

👍	👎
Does provide an explanation for crime that covers all social classes and a variety of offences.	Largely ignores other non-class inequalities such as gender or ethnicity.
Highlights the impact of selective law enforcement and how white-collar crime is under-policed.	Overstates the amount of crime in working-class communities. For instance, not all working-class people commit crime. In addition, not all capitalist societies have high crime rates (consider Japan and Switzerland).
Demonstrates how the law reflects differences in power between the social classes. Also, how inequality in society can lead to criminal behaviour.	There are many prosecutions for white-collar or corporate crime. Consider Bernie Madoff and *The Wolf of Wall Street*.

Interactionism – the labelling theory

 Refer to Unit 2 page 107 for more about interactionism.

👍	👎
Shows how law is often enforced in a discriminatory way. It highlights the consequences of labelling.	Fails to explain why deviant behaviour happens in the first place. There is no acceptance that some people may choose deviance.
Highlights weaknesses in official statistics, which allow bias in law enforcement.	Ignores the victim of crime and focuses on the 'criminal'. There is a potential to romanticise crime.
Highlights the role of the media in defining and creating deviance and for producing moral panics.	Criminals do not need a label to know they are doing wrong. Plus, labelling does not always lead to a self-fulfilling prophecy.

Take it further

Read 'Labelling Theory its Strengths and Weaknesses' (2019) found on the LawTeacher website. This will provide you with further information and ideas to help you evalaute this theory of criminality.

Realism – right realism

Refer to Unit 2 page 107 for more about right realism.

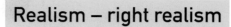	
Has helped produce and shape the government's research into crime. For example, it has stimulated a range of victim surveys and practical measures to combat crime.	Too readily accepts crime statistics. For example, it fails to explain white-collar crime. The focus is on young males and street crime.
Offers a more practical approach to tackling crime than its mainly theoretical predecessors such as Marxism or labelling.	Ignores wider structural causes of crime such as poverty.
Research by Flood-Page et al. (2000) supports the view of the decline of the family. They found children, particularly males, from one-parent backgrounds and step-families were more likely to offend than those who lived with two natural parents.	Ignores the increasing gap between rich and poor, creating resentment (relative deprivation).

Realism – left realism

Refer to Unit 2 page 108 for more about left realism.

Explores the role of the victim of crime, especially the poor or vulnerable, in much more depth than any other criminological theory.	Does not explain why everyone in relative deprivation fails to turn to crime.
Recognises multiple causes of crime.	Arguably made up from a mixture of other theories pulled together.
Left realism avoids the worst excesses of both right- and left-wing approaches by neither glorifying nor attacking the police.	Fails to explain white-collar or corporate crime.

Activity

Divide the class into two: one side in favour of right realism and the other in favour of left realism. Then hold a discussion as to which is the most appropriate realist view for both society as a whole and for explaining criminality.

Handy hints

If, in an exam question, you are asked to evaluate a theory (or theories) you do not need to describe the theory. Often students mistake the two types of questions and fail to provide evaluation when asked to do so.

NOTE

The whole of the following questions can be seen if you go to www.eduqas.co.uk/qualifications/criminology-level-3/#tab_overview, then click on 'Key documents', then 'Past papers'.

Example questions

Exam questions in this area

Unit 2 Exam Summer 2017

Evaluate the effectiveness of a range of individualistic criminological theories to explain causes of criminality. **[8 marks]**

NOTE that from 2020 the changes in the mark bands would mean that this question would be out of 9 marks.

Describe the weakness of the physiological theory described in (a)(i). **[6 marks]**

Unit 2 Exam Summer 2018

Evaluate the effectiveness of the sociological theory described on page 3 in explaining causes of criminality. **[6 marks]**

Evaluate psychodynamic theory in explaining causes of criminality. **[8 marks]**

NOTE that from 2020 the changes in the mark bands would mean that this question would be out of either 4 or 6 marks.

Unit 2 Exam Summer 2019

Evaluate the theory (sociological) described in (a)(i) and (ii). **[6 marks]**

Evaluate the effectiveness of either one physiological or one genetic theory in explaining the causes of criminality. **[6 marks]**

Evaluate the effectiveness of the theory (individualistic) described in (b)(i) in explaining the causes of criminality. **[6 marks]**

Tip

An evaluation question in the external exam could seek consideration of one theory or a range of theories. Be ready to adjust any answer to ensure appropriate use of time.

Exam question Unit 2 Summer 2017

Describe the weakness of the physiological theory described in (a)(i).   **[6 marks]**

These theories refer to the physical shape of someone and at the heart of them is Lombroso. However, his theory that criminals have atavistic features is flawed due to a lack of a control group with which to draw comparisons. Charles Goring (1913) used a non-criminal control group and found no significant differences in terms of behaviour. In addition, this theory can lack accuracy due to facial disfigurements and not everyone with primitive features is a criminal. The theory is far too deterministic. Finally, there is an argument of scientific racism as DeLisi (2012) indicated that many of the atavistic features defined are specific to people of African decent. Sheldon's theory involving somatotypes is weak as it does not explain why endomorphs and ectomorphs can also be criminals. In addition, it does not take into account the fact that a person's somatotype is not fixed; people can change body shape throughout their lives.

Assessment

Mark band 5–6 marks

This answer considers two theories and correctly does not describe what they are about. It is focused on weaknesses. The first part is very detailed with several appropriate comments. It includes other research such as Goring and more modern views including that of DeLisi. The answer could be improved if there was a little further development of Sheldon's theory. Use of specialist terminology is also good.

Literacy skills ⚙⚙

The quality of your written communication is important when writing any answer. To improve your response to a question on this AC, write a series of sentences, each one using one of the words or phrases below:

- explores
- depth
- deterministic
- idealist
- arguably
- theoretic
- this theory is supported by
- however, a limitation is
- fails to explain why
- on the other hand
- fails to give reasons why.

UNDERSTAND CAUSES OF POLICY CHANGE

AC4.1 ASSESS THE USE OF CRIMINOLOGICAL THEORIES IN INFORMING POLICY DEVELOPMENT

ASSESSMENT CRITERION	CONTENT	AMPLIFICATION

AC4.1 You should be able to …
 	
 Assess the use of criminological theories in informing policy development
	Criminological theories
	 • individualistic
	 • biological
	 • sociological
	
	 Policy development
	 • informal policy making
	 • formal policy making
	   • crime control policies
	   • state punishment policies
		You should be able to apply your knowledge of each of the theories and assess their use in informing policy on crime. This could include, for example, penal populism, zero tolerance, CCTV, restorative justice, multi-agency approach

Tip ✔

Think of these assessment criteria as ones that explore methods of crime control that can be linked to the criminological theories discussed in the AC2.1 biological theories, AC2.2 individualistic theories and AC2.3 sociological theories.

Individualistic theories informing policy development

Remember that these are theories linked to the way an individual learns and reacts to life experiences. From this learning experience, crime control policies or measures have developed to prevent or reduce criminality.

Psychoanalysis and treatment for criminal behaviour – linking to psychodynamic theories of criminality

Psychoanalysis, founded by Freud, is a treatment where the patient verbalises their thoughts, through a variety of methods. This method aims to access unconscious, repressed thoughts, which are believed to have led to the criminal activity. The assumptions are that any psychological problems, caused during development or repressed trauma, are embedded

Psychoanalysis treatment

in the unconscious mind. The treatment then tries to bring the repressed thoughts to consciousness where they can be dealt with. The analyst allows free association so the patient talks about whatever enters their mind. This is done with the patient lying down on the couch facing away from the analyst.

Does it work?

- This therapy is probably the least favoured in contemporary approaches to working with offenders. It is very time-consuming and is unlikely to provide quick answers.
- Criticism comes from Blackburn (1993) who points out that there are very few positive evaluations of classic psychoanalysis as a treatment method with offenders.
- Andrews et al. (1990) argue: 'Traditional psychodynamic ... therapies are to be avoided within general samples of offenders' (page 376).
- The nature of psychoanalysis creates a power imbalance between therapist and client that could raise ethical issues.
- A patient could discover very painful memories that were deliberately repressed.
- A study in 2010 concluded that it works as well as, or is at least equivalent to, other psychotherapy treatments, such as cognitive behaviour therapy.

Literacy skills ⚙

Correct the spelling mistakes and explain the concept/study in each of the following:
- pyschoanalysis
- Frued
- Bendura
- free assocision.

Handy hints !

It is important to assess these policies to decide if they work and reduce criminality. It will not be sufficient to just explain them.

There are many negatives concerning psychoanalysis as a treatment.

Behaviour modification – linking to learning theories of criminality

Behaviour modification focuses on techniques to extinguish undesirable behaviours and promote desirable ones. The underpinning principle is that behaviours that are reinforced are strengthened, whereas behaviours that are punished are weakened. With regards criminal behaviour, it is punished in order to weaken the thought-process leading to the illegal behaviour.

The token economy system is one aspect of behaviour modification. This is where a token is given for a desired action, which is later exchanged for a 'treat'. For example, prisoners who follow rules can earn privileges, which is called the 'Incentives and Earned Privileges Scheme'. A prisoner may be able to have more visits from family or friends or be allowed to spend more money each week. The prisoner is simply rewarded for

Token economies illustrate behaviour modification.

desirable behaviour and punished for undesirable behaviour. According to the Prison Reform Trust, a leading charity working in penal reform, the scheme:

promotes conforming behaviour through rational choice. Enabling people to earn benefits in exchange for responsible behaviour encourages prisoners to engage with sentence planning and ensures a more disciplined and controlled environment which is safer for staff and prisoners. **(2017a, page 1)**

Does it work?

Fo and O'Donnell (1975) devised a 'buddy system' in which adult volunteers were assigned to a young offender to provide consistent reinforcement for socially acceptable ways of acting. While this appears to have improved the behaviour of serious offenders, its impact on those who had committed less serious offences was mixed.

Evidence regarding the effectiveness of token economies suggests that they have short-term effectiveness with both young offenders (Hobbs & Holt, 1976) and adult offenders (Allyon & Milan, 1979). However, the improvements tend not to generalise beyond the institution in the longer term.

Other policies or treatments

- Social skills training aims to improve skills in order to avoid offending and become more socially competent. However, once training has stopped, the benefit from it can often be forgotten and even totally disappear in the long term.

- Anger management aims to avoid violent offences taking place by people unable to control their anger. This can be effective if resourced correctly. Novaco (1975) suggests that because offenders cannot deal effectively with their anger, it tends to be expressed in anti-social ways and displaced onto inappropriate targets. In an anger management programme, cognitive behavioural techniques are used to help offenders deal more effectively with their feelings of anger. Research such as Ainsworth (2001) and Howitt (2008) should be quoted.

Take it further ≫

Watch 'Sheldon Shaping Penny in Big Bang Theory' on YouTube, and identify both positive and negative reinforcement in it. Explain the purpose of each by saying what it is that Sheldon is trying to achieve.

The Big Bang Theory *shows both positive and negative enforcement.*

Biological theories informing policy development

Neurochemicals – influencing the brain's chemistry by diet

CASE STUDY

GESCH ET AL. (2002)

In this study, 231 (young, male, adult, prisoner) volunteers agreed to receive either a daily vitamin, mineral and essential fatty acid supplementation or a placebo drug (not real medication). A number of measures were taken before and during the test, including psychological testing, reports of violent acts and reports of disciplinary action.

The result showed the average number of 'disciplinary incidents per 1,000 person-days' dropped from 16 to 10.4 in the group that took the supplement, which is a 35% reduction. Whereas, the placebo group only dropped by 6.7%. Especially violent incidents in the active group dropped by 37%, and in the placebo group only 10.1%.

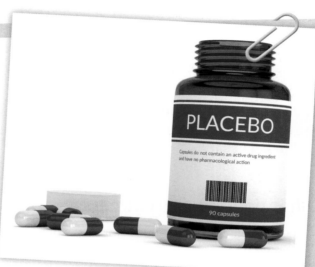

The research shown in the case study above demonstrates that it is possible for diet to positively impact on aggressive behaviour, which in turn may result in less crime. In addition, Virkkunen et al. (1987) found that violent offenders had a lower than average serotonin turnover. This can be treated by a diet with foods that contain serotonin such as salmon and fresh tuna. Also, Schoenthaler (1982) found that a reduced sugar diet reduced anti-social behaviour by 48%. Such research has had an impact on prisons. In general, all prisons have now attempted to embrace the Balance of Good Health model (Edwards et al., 2001) and are providing nutritionally balanced and healthy diets.

In 2012 a pilot scheme provided chemical castration for sex offenders in Her Majesty's Prison (HMP) Whatton, England. Here, volunteers were given a pill, or anti-libidinal psychopharmacological intervention, to reduce their sex drive. Such treatment was positively received by the prisoners who were volunteers.

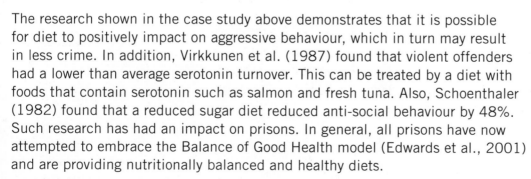

Take it further

Read and summarise the article by Gaby Hinsliff (2003), 'Diet of Fish "Can Prevent" Teen Violence', which can be found on the *Guardian*'s website.

Eugenics

The study of eugenics claimed that:

- Inheritance of genes could explain the presence of simple and complex human behavioural characteristics.
- It reinforces the ideas of biological determinism and claims that biology had contributed towards many of the social problems throughout the late 19th century.

Such a policy has varied over time and in different countries, for example the Nazi sterilisation programme. In essence it advocates higher rates of sexual reproduction for people with desirable traits and higher rates of sterilisation for people with less desired traits. It followed that there were claims that sterilisation laws would prevent incarcerated criminals from giving birth to 'criminal' offspring. Research from Osborn and West in the 1970s provides some support to this theory in that they found 40% of boys whose fathers had criminal records had criminal records themselves, compared with just over 12% of boys whose fathers did not have a criminal record.

While it is extremely unlikely that a widespread policy of eugenics will occur, in 2015, due to moral and ethical reasons, a UK judge gave an order allowing a mother of six with learning disabilities to be sterilised.

Death penalty

Perhaps the most extreme biologically driven policy is that of capital punishment or state execution. According to Amnesty International (2021) 657 people were executed in in 2019 (excluding China). In the UK there was a temporary abolition of the death penalty in 1965. It was shown that the murder rate did not soar as a result of the abolition so a permanent abolition of it for murder took place in 1969.

Does the death penalty work as a crime control method?

Statistics from the USA show that the murder rate is lower in states that do not have the death penalty than those that do. For instance, in 2015 the murder rate was 25% higher in death penalty states then non-death penalty states, according to the Death Penalty Information Center (2017). This suggests the death penalty is not a deterrent at all. Often people kill in the heat of the moment, while under the influence of drugs or alcohol or while suffering from a mental illness. Such people are unlikely to make reasoned and rational decisions based on a fear of future consequences, that is of being given the death sentence.

The death penalty was fully abolished for murder in the UK in 1969.

ONLY *HEALTHY* SEED MUST BE SOWN!

CHECK THE SEEDS OF HEREDITARY DISEASE AND UNFITNESS BY EUGENICS

Eugenics is a biological policy to prevent crime.

Key terms

Biological determinism: A person's personality or behaviour is caused by the genes they've inherited, rather than by social or cultural factors, i.e. by nature rather than nurture.

Incarcerated criminals: People who have been found guilty of a criminal offence and received a term of imprisonment as a punishment.

Tip

Capital punishment can also be considered in AC4.2 'Explain how social changes affect policy development'. However, it is important to understand the context for each criterion. In this AC it is whether or not the death penalty affects state policy, the law or crime control. In other words, is it an effective measure that the state may adopt to control crime? In AC4.2 the focus should be on the changing views of society and how capital punishment has been viewed by people over time.

Sociological theories informing policy development

Penal populism

Penal populism refers to the government's attempts at proposing laws to punish offenders that will be popular with the general public. According to Professor David Wilson (2014) this policy started as a result of the James Bulger case in 1993. When the public became concerned about violent crime in the community. The media fuelled this concern with headlines about the need not to be soft on crime. As a result, there was a consensus between the political parties that they needed to be tough on crime and that offenders needed to be punished. Consequently, this had an impact on the prison population, as so many people were given prison sentences, which means that the UK has more life sentences than the whole of Europe combined, which is still true today.

The media print headlines that add to the public's response for governments to be tough on crime.

HOW CAN THIS BE JUSTICE?

MURDERERS

News of the World hacked Milly Dowler's phone during police hunt

THE REAL TRUTH

The truth about the Cabinet's expenses

NOW YOU PAY FOR PRISON PARTIES

99% DEMAND SARAH'S LAW

A father and son reunited. A secret court forced to open its doors

NOW FOR JUSTICE

Tony Blair, who was Prime Minister from May 1997 to June 2007, in a landmark pledge, when he was Shadow Home Secretary in 1993, was to be 'tough on crime and tough on the causes of crime'. Successive political parties have introduced punitive laws to be tough on crime and this has resulted in punishments, including automatic life sentences, for a second serious offence, and minimum fixed term custodial sentences. For instance, the 'three strikes and you're out' idea within English and Welsh law, where a third class-A drug trafficking offence receives at least seven years imprisonment and a third domestic burglary conviction carries at least three years.

Key terms

Punitive laws: Laws that intend to punish.

Custodial sentence: A punishment of being sent to prison.

Prison

One of the main ways society tries to control crime is by imprisonment. According to Her Majesty's (HM) Prison Service's website (n.d.):

We keep those sentenced to prison in custody, helping them lead law-abiding and useful lives, both while they are in prison and after they are released.

We work with courts, police and local councils, as well as voluntary organisations, to do this.

Prison sentences can be:

- **Concurrent:** where two or more prison sentences are given and ordered to be served at the same time.
- **Consecutively:** served one after the other.
- **Suspended:** served in the community with conditions often relating to unpaid work.
- **Determinate:** of a fixed length.
- **Indeterminate:** of no fixed length.

Prison is a formal sociological-inspired policy.

Does prison work?

This question can be best answered by researching the 'Bromley Briefings – Prison Factfile' found on the Prison Reform Trust website. The following are taken from the Winter 2021 edition:

- The prison population has risen by 70% in the last 30 years.
- Scotland, England and Wales have the highest imprisonment rates in Western Europe.
- Nearly 70,000 people were sent to prison to serve a sentence in the year to June 2020. The majority had committed a non-violent offence (65%).
- Short prison sentences are less effective than community sentences at reducing reoffending.
- Fewer than one in ten people surveyed said that having more people in prison was the most effective way to deal with crime. Early intervention, such as better parenting, discipline in schools and better rehabilitation, were all rated as more effective responses.
- The number of people recalled back to custody has increased, particularly amongst women.
- 8,931 people serving a sentence of less than 12 months were recalled to prison in the year to June 2020.
- Inspectors found that safety was not good enough in more than half of the men's prisons (51%) they visited during the last year. Almost half the people in men's prisons (48%) and women's prisons (49%) said that they had felt unsafe at some point whilst in prison.
- The death rate in prisons has risen by over 50% in the last decade. 282 people died in prison in the year to September 2020.
- The prison system as a whole has been overcrowded every year since 1994.

(adapted from Prison Reform Trust, 2021)

Literacy skills

Write a sentence for each of the following words to explain their use in social control:
- eugenics
- capital punishment
- penal populism
- custodial
- concurrent
- consecutive.

Prison has a poor record for reducing reoffending – 46% of adults are reconvicted within one year of release. For those serving sentences of less than 12 months this increases to 60%.

Zero tolerance

Pioneered by the New York police, this policy demands that all crimes are acted on, no matter how trivial they are. Favoured by right realists, zero tolerance claims to have been very successful in New York. The New York Police Department used computers to analyse crime hot spots street by street and crime by crime before introducing a zero-tolerance approach.

It has been used in the UK in King's Cross (London), Hartlepool, Middlesbrough and Strathclyde. Former Cleveland Police Detective Superintendent Ray Mallon, famously promised to quit if he failed to cut crime on his patch by 20% in 18 months, using zero tolerance, gaining him the nickname 'Robocop'.

The strategy is based on the 'broken windows' theory, developed by George Kelling and James Wilson (1982). This theory suggests a link between disorder and crime, stating that visible signs of decay such as litter, broken windows, graffiti, abandoned housing and so on are signs of public disinterest. Such signs must be acted upon to prevent further crime occurring.

Does it work?

In New York, since 1993, major crime fell by 39% and murder by 49%. The UK has seen similar results: the promise that Detective Superintendent Mallon made, to cut crime by 20% in 18 months, was fulfilled. Figures for the three months to February 1997 showed a 22% fall. These results were also achieved by Mallon in his previous position in Hartlepool, where there was a reduction in crime of 38% in 28 months.

There are negative consequences of aggressive policing, including accusations of heavy-handedness by police.

In addition to zero tolerance, there are other reasons for falling crime in New York. Fewer residents take violence-inducing crack cocaine, while many of those responsible for committing crimes in the 1980s are now in prison. Also, crime has fallen in areas without zero-tolerance policing. Finally, it could be argued that the long-term effects of such a policy are unknown. It works well in heavily populated areas with high policing levels and large amounts of petty crime. But where the population is dispersed or the crime rate is low, it may have little effect. Plus, there is always the possibility of racial tension if people feel victimised, which has been the case in the USA. This has happened on several occasions, including 2020 with the death of George Floyd and the rise again of Black Lives Matter.

Restorative justice

Restorative justice is a voluntary process involving the person who has suffered harm and the person who has caused harm. Trained facilitators work with victims and offenders to talk about what happened, who was affected and how, and what can be done to help repair the harm.

Zero tolerance means that every crime is acted upon.

Key term

Facilitator: Someone who assists in making a task easier or helps someone to find a solution.

Due to legislation, restorative justice can take place at any stage of the criminal justice process, both pre-sentence and after conviction where it can form part of the sentencing procedure. It is used by prisons and police forces and is growing in popularity. Also, government funding has been provided to the police and crime commissioners to make the process available to victims of crime.

RESTORATIVE JUSTICE

The use of restorative justice has grown over recent years.

Activity

Watch 'The Woolf Within' on YouTube and consider the advantages and disadvantages of restorative justice.

Does it work?

Restorative justice does work as it can allow a victim a voice in the criminal justice system and can make offenders accountable for their actions by allowing them to take responsibility for them. According to the Prison Fellowship (2017) website, pilot studies suggest that restorative justice can reduce post-traumatic stress disorder in victims and, in some cases, motivate offenders to turn away from a life of crime. Various studies have been undertaken which suggest that restorative justice reduces reoffending rates and provides value for money government spending. An independent report by the Ministry of Justice in 2001, found that:

- The majority of victims chose to participate in face to face meetings with the offender, when offered by a trained facilitator.
- 85% of victims who took part were satisfied with the process.
- Restorative justice reduced the frequency of reoffending, leading to £9 in savings to the criminal justice system for every £1 spent on restorative justice. (Restorative Justice Council, 2016)

The government's analysis of this research concluded that restorative justice reduces the frequency of reoffending by 14%. A systematic review of the evidence on the effectiveness of restorative justice was published by the Campbell Collaboration in 2013. It concludes that restorative justice both reduces reoffending and improves victim satisfaction.

Take it further

Research the findings and evaluation of the Sycamore Tree victim awareness programme of restorative justice.

CCTV

The use of CCTV (closed-circuit television) in a criminal investigation is an invaluable technique:

- It is one of the first requests made by the police at the start of their enquiries.
- The identification of a potential perpetrator or suspect of a criminal act is very difficult if CCTV footage is not available.
- It has policy implications as a deterrent to prevent crime.

Closed-circuit television

Does it work?

As a deterrent, according to the College of Policing's (2013) breifing, 'The Effects of CCTV on Crime', it can make 'a small, but statistically significant, reduction in crime' (page 2). This is more effective when directed at reducing theft of and from vehicles, while it has no impact on violent crime.

As an investigative technique, it can provide compelling evidence.

It can be used to show the nature and severity of the crime and identify suspects and witnesses. Many infamous cases have been solved thanks to CCTV evidence. For example, many people remember the haunting image of James Bulger being led away by the two ten-year-olds, Robert Thompson and Jon Venables, or the many images of looters during the riots in London in 2011.

CCTV image of James Bulger being lead to his death.

Multi-agency approach

Cooperation between agencies working in the criminal justice system is clearly very important in order to increase the risk of detecting crimes and prevent them happening in the first place. For example, issues such as safeguarding or domestic abuse may be prevented with the aid of numerous agencies working together, so that a full picture of the situation can be seen. In 1984, the Home Office stressed the need for a multi-agency approach with the motto 'Preventing crime is a task for the whole community'. The partnership approach is based on the notion that crime cannot effectively be tackled by the police, or indeed any agency on its own.

Several newspapers published CCTV images of some of the people involved in the 2011 London riots to allow the public to identify suspects.

Section 5 of the Crime and Disorder Act 1998 places a statutory duty on local authorities, the police, health authorities, police authorities and probation committees to work together to tackle problems of crime and disorder in their area.

The multi-agency approach can take several forms, including:

- Involving the police working with the Security Industry Authority, Trading Standards and Environmental Health to reduce alcohol disorder offences.
- Specialist police officers working with resettlement workers, the probation service substance misuse team and drug intervention programme to tackle repeat drug offending.
- Cooperation between the prison service, police, law enforcement agencies and probation services to crackdown on a surge in the number of drones smuggling drugs and mobile phones into prisons in England and Wales.
- The Multi Agency Public Protection Arrangements (MAPPA) assesses and manages the risks posed by sexual and violent offenders, and provides guidance for the police, prison service and probation trusts.

Key term

Safeguarding: Protecting from harm or damage with an appropriate measure.

AC4.2 EXPLAIN HOW SOCIAL CHANGES AFFECT POLICY DEVELOPMENT

ASSESSMENT CRITERION	CONTENT	AMPLIFICATION
AC4.2 You should be able to ... Explain how social changes affect policy development	**Social changes** • social values, norms and mores • public perception of crime • structure of society • demographic changes • cultural changes	You should have an understanding of social changes and how they have affected policy development

Tip

This assessment criterion requires you to explain how changes in society and views of people result in changes in law or policy. This is quite broad and is not prescriptive, so allows you to select areas of choice to study for the exam. For example, the social changes could be due to the structure of society, for example religion, women's rights, disability rights or racism. Alternatively, social changes could be due to a change in society's culture, for example changes to the views about smoking of tobacco, homosexuality, domestic abuse, assisted dying, etc. It is acceptable for you to touch on campaigns; however, the AC is not about campaigns but society.

Social values, norms and mores

Social values

Social values are rules that are shared by most people in a culture or the ideas that they hold in value. They are more general guidelines than norms. For example:

- Most people feel that the elderly should be respected and that seats should be given up for the older people to sit on.
- The phrase 'women and children first' related to the social value of letting women and children leave a sinking ship in priority to men.

Norms

These are social expectations that guide behaviour, and explain people's behaviour and why they act in the way they do. They keep in check deviant behaviour. Social expectation is expected behaviour but could vary from one culture to another. For instance, in the UK people often wear dark sombre colours to a funeral but in China the colour of mourning is white.

Mores

These are morals or good ways of behaving. Norms that a culture would think of as too serious to break, for example murder or sexual offences against children.

Social values, norms and mores have all changed over time, resulting in changes to law or policy.

Society's changing views regarding smoking

In the 1930s it was a social norm to smoke cigarettes and such behaviour was acceptable. However, as the health implications of smoking were understood, people's views changed and it is now not only frowned upon but in certain circumstances is also illegal.

In the 1930s, smoking was glamorised and encouraged, even by doctors. Film stars would be seen smoking cigarettes in movies and it was acceptable to smoke indoors, in restaurants, in cars and beside children. However, from the mid-1950s several pieces of research were published that confirmed a link between tobacco products and lung cancer. The public had growing concerns about the dangers of smoking cigarettes, which meant the eventual disappearance of doctors from cigarette advertisements.

Cigarette advertisements were originally endorsed by doctors.

CASE STUDY

In 1964 the Surgeon General (in the USA) concluded that there was a link between lung cancer and chronic bronchitis and cigarette smoking. By the end of 1965, the tobacco industry was required to put warning labels on its products and advertisements to warn the public of the health risks associated with smoking. Society's attitudes changed and smoking became less glamorous and not as accessible. Health warnings started to appear on cigarette packets, which developed into warnings with graphic images.

Warnings about smoking developed into graphic images on cigarette packets.

There are now many campaign groups that encourage people to stop smoking, for example ASH (Action on Smoking and Health).

See Unit 1 and Unit 2 AC4.3 for more on campaigns.

Over recent years, campaigning against the smoking of cigarettes has resulted in numerous pieces of restrictive legislation. For instance, the Tobacco Advertising and Promotion Act 2002 comprehensively banned the advertising and promotion of tobacco products, including the use of brand-sharing and sponsorship of cultural and sports events. The Health Act 2006 prohibits smoking in enclosed and substantially enclosed work and public places. Also, the Children and Families Act 2014 enabled the government to implement regulations to prohibit smoking in vehicles when children are present.

Activity

Watch 'Unbelievable: Doctors Recommend Smoking! 60 Years Ago ...' and 'Changing Social Norms to Reduce the Acceptability of Smoking' on YouTube. This will help you to appreciate the changing views of society with regards to smoking.

Society's changing views of homosexuality

From the previous section on smoking, it is clear that a change to social values and attitudes can have a significant impact on policy development. Homosexuality is now socially acceptable in the UK and the fight for equality has represented one of the most dramatic cultural changes in public opinion.

In the 16th century, homosexual acts were punishable by death. This penalty was removed in the 19th century but the law prohibited any sexual activity between males. Oscar Wilde was convicted under this law and sentenced to two years in prison. Views continued to change and in 1967 homosexuality was decriminalised. However, it was to take several decades before homosexuals received the same rights as heterosexuals.

Homosexuality was a criminal offence and serious societal taboo in Britain during Oscar Wilde's time.

- **1950s:** there were several high-profile arrests for acts of homosexual indecency. This allowed the open discussion for a change in the law.
- **1957:** the Wolfenden Report was published, which concluded that the laws were an impingement on civil liberty and that the law should not intrude into matters of personal morality.
- **1967:** homosexuality was decriminalised in England and Wales, with the age of consent for homosexuals set as 21 years old.
- **1994:** the age of consent was lowered to 18 years old by the Criminal Justice and Public Order Act 1994.
- **2000:** the age was lowered to 16 years old by the Sexual Offences (Amendment) Act 2000. This brought the practice of homosexuality to be on equal terms with heterosexual sex.

However, many rights under the law were still different, for instance homosexuals could not legally marry. A further decade of campaigning would be needed before this was to happen.

- **2000:** various groups such as Stonewall campaigned for equal rights for same-sex couples.
- **2004:** civil partnerships were permitted as a result of the Civil Partnership Act 2004.
- **2014:** the law allowed the first same-sex marriage under the Marriage (Same Sex Couples) Act 2013.

In addition, in stark contrast to the times when homosexuality was punishable by death, there are now laws that make it a criminal offence to discriminate against someone on the grounds of their sexual orientation, which resulted from the Equality Act 2010.

Homophobic crime is one of the strands of hate crime that allows the CPS to apply for an uplift in sentence against an offender.

There are several reasons why the views of society have changed, including:

- The cultural changes or even the structure of society changing.
- Society is less religious now than at any time in its history.
- The teachings of many religions suggest that homosexuality is wrong.
- People generally do not fear or even believe in God.

This has meant that ideologies from the Bible, for example, are no longer followed and a more tolerant or relaxed attitude ensues. In addition, age is important, as each new generation develops an enhanced tolerance, which moves forward with them. Hence, an ever-growing proportion of society is accepting of homosexuality.

Society's changing views on women's rights

At the beginning of the 20th century, women had very few legal and political rights. The stereotype of a married woman would be one that stayed at home to look after the children, while the husband went out to work. Unmarried women were often employed in a service such as teaching, waitressing or cooking.

However, as the Suffragette movement fought for the right to vote, women rebelled against marriage, seeking education and equality. Society slowly started to change its views about women, as witnessed by the passage of legislation.

- **1928:** support for equality from both women and men meant that women received the right to vote.
- **World War II:** with the advent of war, women had to fill many roles traditionally occupied by men.

The Suffragette movement championed the campaign for the right of women to vote.

- **1960s:** the Women's Liberation movement helped many changes come about through their policies and radical thinking. Policies concerning equality continued to be introduced by numerous governments and touched upon education, discrimination and employment.
- **1970:** the Equal Pay Act 1970 made it illegal to pay women lower rates than men for the same work.
- **1975:** the Sex Discrimination Act 1975 made it illegal to discriminate against women in work, education and training.

Society's changing views

Other areas that could be considered about the changing attitudes in society include:

- domestic abuse
- racism
- death penalty
- seat belts in cars
- abortion

- disability rights
- employment rights
- religion
- assisted suicide.

A Right to Independent Living delegation marched to the House of Commons and on to Downing Street in 2016 to protest about discrimination against disability.

Activity

Research recent attempts in Parliament to change the law on assisted suicide.

Structure of society – demographic changes

Criminologists use demographics to understand the reasons why people commit crime. Such information includes location of the crime and details of the person who offends. Hence, aspects of demographics such as age, race, gender and social class can be studied to provide information on criminality. Such information can help us understand why crime occurs and so can provide ways of combating and tackling those issues. This information is recorded in both the Crime Survey for England and Wales and the records maintained by the police on recorded crime.

Activity

Go to the Office for National Statistics (ONS) and look at some of the annual trends and demographic tables. Make a note of what the information is saying about who is committing crime and the location of it.

AC4.3 DISCUSS HOW CAMPAIGNS AFFECT POLICY MAKING

ASSESSMENT CRITERION	CONTENT
AC4.3 You should be able to … Discuss how campaigns affect policy making	**Campaigns** • newspaper campaigns • individual campaigns • pressure group campaigns

Synoptic links

You need to refer to campaigns considered in Unit 1, and others, to identify the policies that they introduced. Also, try to include a range of campaigns such as:

- Newspaper campaigns about, for instance, Sarah's law.
- Individual campaigns such as that of Ann Ming's fight for the abolition of the law against double jeopardy or Bobby Turnbull's campaign to amend the gun laws.
- Pressure group campaigns such as those run by ASH, Greenpeace, the Howard League for Penal Reform and so on.

Points to cover

Points to cover for each campaign include:

- Explain what the campaign was about or how/why it was started.
- Key parties involved.
- How it tried to change policies/laws (examples of campaign methods).
- How it changed people's views or altered thoughts.
- The actual law or policies it introduced, if successful. This is arguably the most important aspect of your answer so ensure you are aware of the impact of the changes and can state the name of the law/policy.

The Greenpeace ship 'Arctic Sunrise' helps to promote its work.

Newspaper campaign

Sarah's law

Explain what the campaign was about/or how/why it was started

In 2000, Sarah Payne was only eight years old when she was abducted and murdered by Roy Whiting. He had been jailed in 1995 for kidnapping and indecently assaulting a nine-year-old girl. His name was also placed on the Sex Offenders Register. On a trip to visit family members, Sarah's parents allowed her and her siblings to play by themselves, which was when she was abducted. However, the family were adamant that if they had known about Whiting being in the area they would have taken steps to protect her.

Key parties involved

Sarah's parents started a campaign to have information about known sex offenders made available to the public. The former Sunday newspaper, the *News of the World*, supported the campaign for a change in the law. The paper published the names and pictures of 50 people who they claimed to be sex offenders. Unfortunately, this produced a vigilante effect and the government refused to agree to the demands.

How it changed people's views or altered thoughts

However, the newspaper and Sarah's parents continued with their campaign, and when another young girl was kidnapped and sexually assaulted the government began to change its mind. A minister was sent to the USA to see the workings of Megan's law, a US policy that allows parents access to information on paedophiles living in their community.

The actual law or policies it introduced

In 2008 a pilot scheme was introduced in four areas of the UK to allow parents to make enquiries about named individuals. Police would then reveal details confidentially to the person most able to protect the child, usually a parent, if it was thought in the best interests of the child. In 2011, after the pilot proved successful, the scheme was extended to cover the whole of England and Wales. It is known as the Child Sex Offender Disclosure Scheme.

> **Key term**
>
> **Sex Offenders Register:** Contains the details of anyone convicted, cautioned or released from prison for sexual offences against children or adults since September 1997. It is kept by the police and has around 9,000 people on it.

> **Key term**
>
> **Pilot scheme:** Used to test an idea before deciding whether to introduce it on a large scale.

The News of the World's *last edition was in July 2011.*

Other newspaper campaigns that helped change the law

Key parties involved

The *Bradford Telegraph & Argus* campaigned to improve road safety.

The Bradford Telegraph & Argus *front pages showing the results of dangerous driving.*

How it tried to change policies/laws

It encouraged readers to send in dash-cam videos of examples of dangerous driving.

How it changed people's views or altered thoughts

As a result of this the police began 'Operation Steerside', to crack down on dangerous driving, which to date has led to almost 8,000 drivers being caught breaking the law by the roads policing team. Police say that this operation is now embedded in local force culture.

The actual law or policies it introduced

Towards the end of 2016, the campaign was highlighted in Parliament by Bradford MPs and used by them as part of a national consultation about the toughening up of dangerous driving legislation.

> **Take it further** »
>
> Research the 'Beyond the Blade' project, launched by the *Guardian* in 2017. How did it try and change policies/laws?

Individual campaigns

Ann Ming's campaign to abolish the double jeopardy law

What the campaign was about

'Mother's Devotion Makes History' was the headline of the *Journal* newspaper when Billy Dunlop was given a life sentence for the murder of Julie Hogg.

Key parties involved

Julie's mother, Ann Ming, vowed to bring her daughter's killer to justice, having to ensure the abolition of an 800-year-old law to do so.

Explain what the campaign was about

The double jeorpardy law prevents a second prosecution for the same offence after an acquittal or conviction. Julie was killed in her Billingham, Teesside, home in 1989 and Dunlop was put on trial for the murder. However, in 1991 a jury at Newcastle Crown Court failed to reach a verdict. A second trial took place later that year but, after a different jury failed to reach a verdict, Dunlop was formally cleared.

However, he later confessed to killing Julie in the belief that the double jeopardy law prevented him from going back on trial for the murder. He was convicted of perjury, which is lying in court under oath, but no action could be taken in connection with the murder.

How it tried to change policies/laws

Ann Ming began her campagn to have the double jeopardy law abolished. She took her campaign to newspapers, radio and television stations, and many politicians.

The actual law or policies

Eventually, the government backed changes to the law and as a result of the Criminal Justice Act 2003 double jeopardy was abolished for 30 serious offences, including murder. The law was retrospective and Dunlop became the first person to be convicted of murder under the new law. He is currently serving life for Julie's murder.

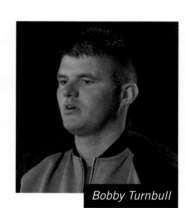

Billy Dunlop was finally convicted of Julie Hogg's murder 19 years after her death.

Bobby Turnbull's anti-gun campaign

What the campaign was about

On New Year's Day in 2012, Bobby Turnbull's mother, Alison, sister Tanya and aunt Susan were killed at their Horden home in County Durham by Michael Atherton. Michael Atherton, Susan's partner, legally owned six weapons including three shotguns, despite having a history of domestic violence. After the triple murder he went on to kill himself. Atherton had the guns removed from him after the previous domestic violence but they were later returned to him.

Key parties involved

Bobby Turnbull started a camapign to change the gun laws and also sought to have a gun hotline established for people to report concerns.

Bobby Turnbull

How he tried to change policies/laws

He launched a petition, which gained 20,000 signatures, regularly appeared in the media seeking support and lobbied MPs for the changes.

The actual law or policies

As a result of the campaign, amendments to the Firearms Act 1968 came into effect, preventing any person who receives a suspended sentence of three months or more, for any offence, from purchasing or possessing a firearm. In addition, every incident of domestic violence, whether or not firearms are involved, should prompt a police review of whether a firearms certificate should continue.

However, funds for a hotline have never been available for it to be launched.

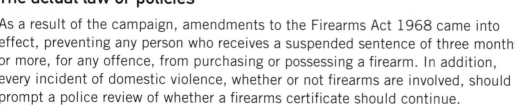

Activity

Search the internet for articles to read and clips to watch about Bobby Turnbull's campaign.

Other individual campaigns

Clare's law

Clare's law was a campaign to create a scheme that allows people to find out, from the police, if their partner has a history of domestic violence. After Clare Wood was killed by her violent partner, a campaign was championed by her father, Michael Brown. He was convinced that Clare would still be alive had she known the full extent of her partner's previous violent behaviour.

The campaign introduced the 'Domestic Abuse Disclosure Scheme'. The aim of this scheme is to give members of the public a formal mechanism to make enquires about an individual they are in a relationship with or who is in a relationship with a person they know, and there is a possiblity that the individual may be abusive towards their partner.

Lillian's law

Lillian's law campaign sought to introduce roadside drugs testing devices, make it a criminal offence to drive under the influence of drugs, have random drug spot checks and give tougher sentences on those found guilty of drug driving. The campaign was started after 14-year-old Lillian Groves was killed outside her home by a speeding motorist who had been smoking cannabis. Her family, in particular Lillian's mother and father Natasha and Gary Groves, collected more than 22,000 signatures on a petition and met the Prime Minister, David Cameron, at Downing Street. Natasha Groves also wrote to every MP encouraging them to back the changes in Parliament. As a result of the campaign, in March 2015, the changes to the law were introduced by the Drug Driving (Specified Limits) (England and Wales) Regulations 2014.

Activity

Research the campaign known as Helen's law. Discover:

(i) the aim of the campaign

(ii) what happened to the killer of Helen McCourt.

Take it further

Research and present your findings to the class on the campaign by the widow of PC Harper. She is campaigning for killers of emergency service workers to be given whole-life sentences.

Pressure group campaigns

British Lung Foundation (BLF)

What the campaign was about and key parties involved

The British Lung Foundation (BLF) aims to prevent lung disease by campaigning for positive change in the UK's lung health. It raises awareness about lung disease, the dangers that cause it, and how to look after your lungs. One of their recent campaigns involved changing the law on smoking in cars with children. BLF secured 50,000 signatures on a petition in 2011 and presented it to 10 Downing Street. It also produced research about the effects of second-hand smoke and the lasting damage it can do. The research also showed that more than 430,000 children were exposed to second-hand smoke in family cars each week. As a result of this campaigning, a ban on smoking in cars with children came into force in England and Wales in October 2014. It was introduced by the Children and Families Act 2014.

The BLF, together with other pressure groups such as ASH, campaigned for plain packaging of cigarettes. The packets are now drab and standardised instead of the colourful branded packs of previous years. Their research showed that one of the reasons young people started to smoke was the attraction of the colourful, cleverly designed packaging. Again, the Children and Families Act 2014 introduced the changes.

Activity

Research the charity Catch 22 and discover from the 'Justice' link the work they are carrying out with young people and adults in custody.

In addition you can find out about the work of Catch 22 in your local area, which can be found at www.catch-22.org.uk/our-services/.
Use the postcode tool on its website to do this.

The Howard League for Penal Reform

What the campaign was about and key parties involved

The Howard League for Penal Reform campaigns for change in the criminal justice system. Its aim is for less crime, safer communities and fewer people in prison. It has campaigned for over 150 years and has had many successes. One of its more recent successes is the 'UR Boss' campaign, which aimed to improve young people's experiences in the criminal justice system. It was supported by young people both in custody and the community by involving them in campaigning for change.

'UR Boss' has changed the policy concerning young people in several areas, including:

- Ending routine use of strip searching on arrival at a Youth Offenders Institution, which was a key policy success.
- Extending the Prisons and Probation Ombudsman's remit to young people detained in Secure Training Centres, giving the young people an independent external complaints system.
- Closing all Young Offenders Institution units for girls. Girls are now only held in secure units or residential care in cities such as Sheffield, Leeds and Manchester.
- A change to remand legislation so that 17-year-olds are now treated as children.

> **Key term**
>
> **Young Offenders Institution:** A type of prison for 18- to 20-year-olds.

Activity

Research other success stories achieved by the Howard League for Penal Reform at http://howardleague.org/what-we-have-achieved. This will provide you with further details of success by this group.

UNIT SUMMARY

By working through this unit:

- You will have gained the skills to evaluate some criminological theories and know there are debates within the different theories.
- You will understand how changes in criminological theory have influenced the law and policy.
- You will also have gained the skills to apply the theories to a specific crime or criminal in order to understand both the behaviour and the theory.

UNIT 3
CRIME SCENE TO COURT ROOM

In this unit you will develop the understanding and skills needed to examine information in order to review the justice of verdicts in criminal cases.

- You will follow a crime from the initial crime scene to the investigation by the police and other personnel involved in criminal investigations.

- You will discover some of the techniques used by the police and follow the criminal justice process through the various stages.

- You will learn all about the rules of evidence and the role of juries and magistrates.

- There will also be a focus on the validity of information, including court cases, verdicts and sentencing.

- Finally, miscarriages of justice will be considered by exploring real-life situations.

Assessment: 8-hour controlled assessment

From September 2020 the assignment brief for Unit 3 will be released at the start of the controlled assessment and no earlier. This brings it in line with Unit 1. No textbooks or previously prepared material may be taken into the assessment.

However, please note there is no time allocated for the use of the internet. Therefore, there should be no images or hyperlinks in your work.

AC1.1 EVALUATE THE EFFECTIVENESS OF THE ROLES OF PERSONNEL INVOLVED IN CRIMINAL INVESTIGATIONS

ASSESSMENT CRITERION	MARK BAND 1	MARK BAND 2	MARK BAND 3
AC1.1 Evaluate the effectiveness of the roles of personnel involved in criminal investigations	Limited evaluation of the effectiveness of the relevant roles	Some evaluation of the effectiveness of relevant roles	Clear and detailed evaluation of the effectiveness of roles
	Response is largely descriptive and may only be a list of personnel involved	Description of the roles of personnel involved is also evident	The personnel involved are clearly discussed in terms of potential limitations
	(1–3)	(4–7)	(8–10)

CONTENT	AMPLIFICATION
Personnel	You should have an understanding of the roles of the personnel involved and be able to evaluate their effectiveness in criminal investigations. The effectiveness should be considered in the context of potential limitations:
• crime scene investigators	
• forensic specialists	
• forensic scientists	
• police officers/detectives	• cost
• Crown Prosecution Service (CPS)	• expertise
• pathologists	• availability
• other investigative agencies, for example Serious and Organised Crime Agency (now National Crime Agency), HM Revenue & Customs	

Handy hints !

Try to cover cost, expertise and availability in as many roles as possible. However, it may not always be appropriate to do so for some roles.

Handy hints !

This AC requires an evaluation of the roles of personnel in criminal investigations. If you merely describe the area of work, you will not reach the top mark band. A better answer will evaluate the role by considering positive points and focus on limitations, with case examples in support.

Who are the personnel involved in criminal investigations? Think of all the people who are involved in criminal investigations from the commission of a crime until a suspect is charged. Such roles include:

- Crime scene investigators or, as they are called in the UK, scenes of crime officers (SOCOs) who collect the evidence.
- Forensic scientists who interpret the evidence.
- Forensic specialists with expertise in different areas.
- Police officers/detectives who investigate the crime.
- The Crown Prosecution Service (CPS), which decides if a suspect is charged.
- A pathologist who determines the cause and means of death, which can provide vital investigative evidence.
- There are also other agencies, for example the National Crime Agency, which is responsible for leading the UK's fight to cut serious and organised crime, and HM Revenue & Customs.

Scenes of crime officers (SOCOs)

These roles are often depicted on television as CSIs or crime scene investigators and are employed by the police service to preserve and protect a crime scene and recover evidence. Clearly, such evidence can be vital in criminal investigations.

It is essential that evidence at a crime scene remains uncontaminated and is collected as soon as possible to provide reliable evidence in a criminal investigation. SOCOs typically search for trace evidence such as gunshot residue, fingerprints, and hairs and fibres. Should contamination occur, the evidence will be inadmissible in court. However, such a risk is minimised as SOCOs are trained and qualified in this area. They usually operate on an on-call system and are therefore always available to assist in criminal investigations.

Scenes of crime officers can also be known as forensic scene investigators.

Limitations

However, there are times when the role produces limitations to solving a crime:

- SOCOs may be exposed to hazardous substances in the course of their role, such as contaminants contacting the skin or airborne substances that could enter the mouth.
- Such risks are minimised by the wearing of protective clothing, including masks and glasses.

Activity

Join in an interactive crime scene from West Midlands Police. You're the first responding officer. Interact with evidence room by room and discover how it happened, at

www.west-midlands.police.uk/27stationroad.

CASE STUDY

AMANDA KNOX

There are cases where contamination of evidence at a crime scene has occurred, such as in the murder of Meredith Kercher, for which Amanda Knox was held to trial. Here detectives outside of the house wore shoe covers, while others failed to have any protective clothing on inside the house. This was used in court to suggest that the evidence collected was unreliable.

Amanda Knox

Forensic scientists

Forensic scientists review evidence from a crime scene and produce information for a court. Evidence such as blood and other body fluids are analysed in a laboratory and interpreted. This information can assist a court in making a decision and producing a just result.

One of the advantages of forensics is that it includes many specialist areas with expertise such as:

- computers
- toxicology (drugs)
- dentistry
- fire
- psychology.

Limitations

However, there are limitations of this role:

- Some people believe that DNA analysis of a person can be against human ethics as it reveals private information.
- It can be very expensive and time-consuming.
- If care and attention are not present a miscarriage of justice could occur. For example, in the case of Adam Scott, a plastic tray that contained his DNA had not been disposed of and was re-used in a rape case. This mistake resulted in him being in custody for five months.

Police officers

The police play a key role in the investigation of criminal cases:

- They are the first personnel called to a crime scene and their initial action is very important.
- While their first job is to preserve life, they will also secure the crime scene in an attempt to conserve evidence.
- They are trained professionals who investigate crime and attempt to reduce it and the fear of it.

Handy hints !

Remember that the evaluation of roles of personnel should be linked to their part in the investigation of criminal cases and not of the role itself. For example, it is not about the positives of being a police officer but of having police investigate crime.

There are specialist units within the police service, including the Criminal Investigation Department (CID). CID officers are trained to investigate a wide range of crimes and can call upon the assistance of various specialist sections such as firearms or underwater teams.

Activity

Research the various specialist roles within the police service, such as the drug agency, mounted police, etc., and consider how they contribute to the evaluation of the police in criminal investigations.

Limitations

The limitations of the police service can be seen in several cases, including:

- The Stephen Lawrence case: the Macpherson Report (1999), issued as a result of the Lawrence case, said the police had institutional racism and made 70 recommendations to improve the service.
- The Hillsborough disaster also shows that the police can act inappropriately in criminal investigations. The inquest in 2016 concluded that blunders by the police caused or contributed to the disaster and that victims had been unlawfully killed.

Crown Prosecution Service (CPS)

This department was set up in 1986 to be an independent prosecution agency to take over from the police. Clearly, there is a risk of bias if the same agency investigates and prosecutes a criminal case. However, the CPS works with the police to review cases and decide if it is appropriate to prosecute. The CPS is effectively a law firm and their 2,000+ crown prosecutors are fully qualified barristers and solicitors. Consistency is provided by the tests they apply, which consider the evidence collected by the police and whether or not it is in the public interest to prosecute. Advice regarding how to support the police in their investigations and as to whether or not there could be a criminal charge brought against a suspect is available 24 hours a day from CPS Direct.

The CPS logo

Limitations

However, there are limitations to the CPS:

- In the past it has been criticised for the number of cases that have collapsed due to lack of evidence.
- Its relationship with the police has sometimes been difficult, for example in the case of the hate preacher, Abu Hamza, who was found guilty of inciting murder. However, prior to this the police had put evidence to them on more than one occasion but the CPS refused to prosecute.

Take it further

Research the case of the murder of Damilola Taylor, making a timeline of events, including the second trial in 2006 that finally resulted in a conviction. Also watch *Our Loved Boy*, a BBC drama about the death of Damilola Taylor.

CASE STUDY

DAMILOLA TAYLOR

The reputation of the CPS was damaged as a result of the case of Damilola Taylor, where there was a heavy reliance on the evidence from a 14-year-old girl. The girl's evidence was thrown out of court when it was shown she had lied. The CPS was widely condemned as it was said that the lies were extremely obvious and the CPS should have known they would be exposed. There were criticisms that little time had been spent cross-checking her evidence against known facts and videotaped interviews with her.

Damilola Taylor

Pathologists

Pathologists are medical doctors who perform autopsies to establish cause of death. Such information is vital in a criminal investigation, providing clues for the other roles within an investigation. Pathologists are experienced and well-qualified practitioners with knowledge of many areas such as pathology, crime scene evaluation, anatomy and anthropology.

Limitations

- Pathologists are very limited in numbers and might have to work on several cases at any one time.
- The cost of a pathologist is very high; in the public sector a consultant can earn £100,000 per year and potentially more within the private sector.

CASE STUDY

ANTHONY HARDY

Limitations of the role of a pathologist in criminal investigations can be seen in the case of Anthony Hardy, also known as the Camden Ripper. Here, the pathologist, Freddy Patel, decided that a victim had died from natural causes despite the way her body was found in a locked room in Hardy's flat. There were blood stains on her clothes, the bedding and on the wall. As the police had no crime to investigate nothing further could be done and Hardy went on to kill two other women. He was later convicted of the murder of all three women and Patel was suspended from his role following comments by the General Medical Council Disciplinary Panel, which said his actions were irresponsible and not of the standard expected of a competent pathologist.

Freddy Patel

AC1.2 ASSESS THE USEFULNESS OF INVESTIGATIVE TECHNIQUES IN CRIMINAL INVESTIGATIONS

ASSESSMENT CRITERION	MARK BAND 1	MARK BAND 2	MARK BAND 3	MARK BAND 4
AC1.2 You should be able to … Assess the usefulness of investigative techniques in criminal investigations	A largely descriptive response with very limited, basic/ simple assessment At the lower end, investigative techniques may be simply listed **(1–5)**	Limited evidence of relevant assessment of the use of investigative techniques At the lower end, some investigative techniques are described **(6–10)**	A range of investigative techniques are used to make some assessment of their usefulness in criminal investigations **(11–15)**	Clear and detailed assessment is made of the required range of investigative techniques **(16–20)**

CONTENT	AMPLIFICATION

Techniques
 • forensic
 • surveillance techniques
 • profiling techniques
 • use of intelligence databases, for example National DNA Database
 • interview techniques, for example eyewitness interviews, expert interviews
 	
 Criminal investigations
 • situations
    • crime scene
    • laboratory
    • police station
    • 'street'
 • types of crime
    • violent crime
    • e-crime
    • property crime
	You should have an understanding of the range of investigative techniques and assess their usefulness in a range of different types of criminal investigations, considering situations and types of crime
	
	 You are expected to include all the 5 techniques stated in the content section

NOTE

From 2020 the wording of AC1. has been changed slightly to provide greater clarity of what a moderator wants to see in the answer and to better reflect the wording of the AC. For example, the amplification section, the wo effectiveness has been changed usefulness. The change is show red in the table on the left.

Investigative techniques

Use of intelligence databases to investigate crime

The police use many databases to help them store and access information to help in the fight against crime. Examples include the UK National DNA Database and Police National Computer or PNC, which holds extensive information on people, vehicles, crimes and property. Crimint, run by the Metropolitan Police Service of Greater London, stores information on criminals, suspected criminals and protesters. Also, there are databases that contain information from witnesses, informants and agents.

Forensics

Today's world of forensic science is very different from 100 years ago. In the past, when police had to attend a crime scene they would be alone until a doctor arrived to confirm death and carry out a very quick review of the body. In today's world of forensic science:

- The police are accompanied by a range of forensic experts to help in the investigations.
- The police discuss actions and usefulness of various forms of evidence with the other experts.
- There is limited access to a crime scene and protective clothing is required to be worn, to avoid contamination.
- The police recover evidence scientifically, which is then considered by a range of experts in many different fields.

Key term

DNA or deoxyribonucleic acid: The chemical that carries genetic information and is contained in chromosomes found in the nucleus of most cells. Sometimes called our genetic code as it determines all our characteristics.

CASE STUDY

COLIN PITCHFORK

One of the most useful forensic techniques is that of the use of DNA or deoxyribonucleic acid. The first criminal conviction using DNA evidence was that of Colin Pitchfork in 1986. Pitchfork was found guilty of the 1983 murder of Lynda Mann and of the 1986 murder of Dawn Ashworth.

At the time of the second murder, Alec Jefferys, a British geneticist, was pioneering profiling techniques by using DNA and was able to use his work to confirm that the two girls had been killed by the same man. He was also able to show that Robert Buckland, who had confessed to Dawn Ashworth's murder, was not the Mann killer. When the police obtained blood samples from all the men in the area, Pitchfork had persuaded a friend to impersonate him and provide the sample. This was eventually discovered by the police who arrested Pitchfork and were able to use Jeffreys' DNA profiling technique to confirm him as the double killer.

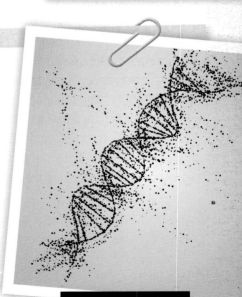

Deoxyribonucleic acid

DNA can be seen as a useful investigative technique for the following reasons:

- It is found in virtually every cell of the human body.
- Everybody's DNA is unique, which allows for very high reliability.
- It gives the chance to solve old murders.
- It can help prove innocence as well as guilt.
- It can help identify victims when other methods do not work.
- DNA from closely related relatives, such as siblings, have many similarities in common. See the Colette Aram murder investigation (below).

However, DNA can produce limitations in an investigative technique. For example:

- Cross-contamination of evidence is possible.
- To secure a match with a sample from a crime scene the perpetrator must be on the National DNA Database.
- Such a technique may infringe civil liberties, especially when DNA profiles are stored from people who are innocent.
- It is possible that trace amounts of DNA can falsely implicate a person. See the Case Study on David Butler on page 155.
- The financial cost of DNA testing.

Take it further

Research the murder case of Melanie Road and find out how DNA collected in 1984 solved a 32-year-old case.

CASE STUDY

COLETTE ARAM

Colette Aram was murdered in 1983, before DNA was established as an investigative technique. However, as forensics developed, scientists were able to build up a DNA sample taken from the murder scene and from a local pub the murderer had visited after he killed Colette. Familial DNA profiling enabled the conviction of Paul Hutchinson, when a close relative had a sample taken following a driving offence. Despite Hutchinson's sample not being on the National DNA Database, the family link was made and a conviction was secured 26 years after Colette's murder.

Colette Aram

CASE STUDY

DAVID BUTLER

David Butler was charged with the murder of a prostitute, Anne Marie Foy, as a result of a partial DNA match. His DNA was found under the victim's fingernails. However, despite being in custody for eight months, at trial Butler's lawyers were able to show the jury that the procedures used to obtain the DNA were unreliable and the evidence was of poor quality. In addition, Butler suffered from a dry skin condition which meant he shed large flakes of skin, so his DNA was easily transferred. As he worked as a taxi driver it is possible that he had taken a passenger to the red light district, where the victim worked, and DNA was passed on in the change given to a passenger and then to the victim. This meant that Butler was acquitted of the murder.

David Butler

DNA evidence can be particularly useful in violent and sexual offences. In such cases evidence is usually left at the scene in the form of blood, hairs or semen. This allows a DNA profile of the potential defendant to be constructed.

Surveillance

In modern policing surveillance, CCTV is a major investigative technique that is used. It is one of the first things an investigating officer asks for following a crime, as it can provide permanent images of the crime taking place and pictures of the criminals.

Surveillance: Keeping a close watch over something or someone.

CCTV plays a large role in everyday life and there are cameras on the streets of many towns and cities as well as business premises and inside shops. State-of-the-art technology can trace a suspect's movements and be used to both incriminate someone or show their innocence. An example of the use of CCTV as evidence is shown in the London riots of August 2011, when recordings of the crimes taking place and photographs of the alleged offenders regularly appeared in the media and people were able to identify some of them.

CCTV evidence can be particularly useful in cases involving street crime, such as robbery, as all busy areas of a city are nowadays covered by cameras. Also, thefts from commercial premises are likely to be filmed on CCTV.

CCTV is a type of surveillance.

Another type of surveillance used by the police in their investigations is covert surveillance. Covert human intelligence sources (CHISs) applies to information obtained by a person who establishes or maintains a personal or other relationship with a person for the covert purpose of using it to obtain or provide access to any information. This covers use of informants and undercover officers. Due to possible infringements of civil liberties there are strict rules that govern undercover police work. However, this technique can be useful in combating serious crimes such as terrorism and major drug dealings.

CASE STUDY

COLIN STAGG

Following the murder of Rachel Nickell in 1992, Colin Stagg was arrested but there was no evidence to link him to the crime. Police therefore established a 'honey-trap', involving a female officer, known as 'Lizzie', who pretended to be interested in forming a relationship with Stagg. Despite trying to entice him into a murder confession, Stagg maintained his innocence. However, information gained as a result of this covert operation was put before the court. The trial judge described the undercover operation as 'misconceived' and 'not merely an excess of zeal, but a blatant attempt to incriminate a suspect by positive and deceptive conduct of the grossest kind'. All the covert evidence was ruled inadmissible and the case against Stagg was dropped. Robert Napper later pleaded guilty to Nickell's murder.

Colin Stagg was awarded £706,000 after being wrongly identified as Rachel Nickell's killer.

Activity

Ask your teacher to invite a police officer into your centre. There should be one that is responsible for the community area in which your place of education is located. They will be able to help you with many of the ACs in this unit and Unit 4.

Profiling techniques

Activity

Find and watch on YouTube 'Offender Profiling' to hear a summary of criminal profiling.

Offender profiling is grounded in the belief that it is possible to work out the characteristics of an offender by examining the characteristics of their offences. As Ainsworth (2001, page 7) puts it:

profiling generally refers to the process of using all the available information about a crime, a crime scene, and a victim in order to compose a profile of the (as yet) unknown perpetrator.

Geographical profiling, also known as a bottom-up approach, uses information to provide suggestions about potential offenders. It relies on data and statistics, and, while it cannot solve a crime, the suggestions provided may mean that resources can be used to maximum effect. In particular it looks at patterns in the location and timing of offences to allow judgements to be made about connections between the crimes, which may provide ideas about where the offender lives or works.

In 1986 the psychologist David Canter assisted the police in their investigation of a series of rapes and murders in London. Using the information on the crimes and details of how the offender interacts with their surroundings, Canter applied psychological principles to suggest where the offender was living, their type of employment and their social life. This allowed the police to prioritse resources and narrow down a list of suspects. Surveillance was placed on John Duffy who was later arrested and convicted of the crimes.

David Canter

Investigative psychology is an approach that grew out of geographical profiling and provides support in criminal investigations. Pioneered by Professor David Canter, this approach has been developed and enhanced so that it is now a structured approach to provide investigative support for suspect identification and crime linking to evidence. Investigative psychology does not focus on why the offender commits the crime but instead it infers the characteristics of the offender from the known actions taken by them during the crime. It uses offender profiling research together with extensive database and specialist software to predict objective offender characteristics from offending behaviour. It analyses a large volume of data and breaks down crime scene information into component parts. In other words, dominant themes can be suggested from which inferences about the offences can be derived. Such research is also subjected to peer review and is therefore objective. Arguably the large amount of data used allows for certainty in determining how often particular types of behaviour are seen in particular crimes.

Typological profiling, also known as a **top-down approach**, was developed by the Federal Bureau of Investigations (FBI) in the USA during the late 1970s. It produces a profile of a suspect, often using intuition, and is used to narrow down potential leads. Crimes are categorised into organised or disorganised crimes, the characteristics of each are shown in the following table.

Key terms

Geographical profiling: Considers patterns revealed in the location and timing of offences to make judgements about where the offender lives (circle theory).

Investigative psychology: A profiling technique based on psychological theory and research to provide support for suspect identification and crime linking to evidence.

Typological profiling: Considers characteristics of the offender by analysing the crime scene and crimes.

ORGANISED CRIMES	DISORGANISED CRIMES
Planned, selected victim, violent fantasies carried out on victim, weapon brought to crime scene, an intelligent offender who likes to control victim, offender is socially and sexually competent.	Impulsive, unplanned crime with randomly selected victim, use of an improvised weapon with evidence left at scene, little engagement with victim and sexual activity likely to occur after death. Offender likely to be socially and sexually inept.

From this a profile is created, including suggestions about the offender's age, gender, occupational background, IQ, and social and family links. It is this profile that the police would use to investigate the crime.

This investigative technique has been very influential in helping to identify a suspect and has been adopted by many countries. It can help narrow down a list of suspects, for example the Yorkshire Riper inquiry generated 268,000 named suspects but profiling can reduce this and save on time and costs.

However, many of the characteristics have been developed from interviewing serial killers who are clearly not the most reliable and honest of people. Plus, offenders are not always neatly divided into the categories of organised and disorganised crimes and can have aspects of both or move between them. Finally, profiles are unscientific and can often be vague and apply to a large number of individuals, known as the Barnum effect.

Criminal profiling can be particularly useful in cases that are linked such as rapes, murders, arson, robbery and bombings.

Key term

Barnum effect: When individuals give high accuracy ratings to descriptions of themselves. However, the descriptions are in fact vague and very general, capable of being applied to a wide range of people.

CASE STUDY

COLIN STAGG

Returning to the case of Colin Stagg (see page 156), this case can show the error of relying too heavily on criminal profiling. The psychologist Paul Britton was asked to produce a profile of the killer of Rachel Nickell. This led to the police obsessively pursuing Stagg, as he fitted Britton's profile. Britton played a central role in the investigation and was instrumental in the covert surveillance and honey-trap with 'Lizzie'.

Take it further

Read the article 'Psychological Profiling "Worse than Useless"' (Sample, 2010) on the *Guardian* website, which will help you appreciate some of the issues involved in profiling.

Identification parade

Interview – eyewitness testimony

Eyewitness testimony (EWT) is evidence given by someone who has witnessed a crime. As such, the expectation of reliability is high and juries are often content to believe such testimony. The Devlin Committee (Report) in 1976 looked at the identification of suspects by witnesses and found that in 1973 there were 850 cases where suspects were identified in a line-up, with an 82% conviction rate. In addition, 347 of these were prosecuted where EWT was the only evidence of guilt. Of them, 74% were found guilty by a jury. Clearly, juries rely on such identification and, on the face of it, EWT is good solid evidence.

However, some research doubts the accuracy of EWT on the basis that factors can affect the strength of it. For instance, it can be affected by anxiety and stress in a positive way.

CASE STUDY

RONALD COTTON

Ronald Cotton spent ten years in prison for a crime he did not commit. He was convicted of rape after the jury believed the eyewitness evidence of the victim Jennifer Thompson-Cannino. When she was being raped she was determined to recall her attacker to help secure his conviction. Jennifer picked Cotton out of a photo line-up and then also out of an ID parade. A jury believed this EWT and convicted Cotton. He tried to appeal the conviction on several occasions, but was never successful until the development of DNA. A positive match was made between the victim and a fellow prisoner who had confessed to committing the crime to another prisoner. Cotton was accordingly cleared and became good friends with Jennifer. They both campaign for reform of EWT and try to prevent other wrongful convictions.

Ronald Cotton and Jennifer Thompson-Cannino

...rts

...ew an expert witness to gain specialist knowledge ...n investigation. For example, medical experts can prov... ...bout cause of death or cause of injury. Other expert witnesses includ... ...ose who can provide alcohol back-calculations to discover if the suspect was driving under the influence of alcohol in road traffic accidents. In other words, the expert can use the concentration of alcohol in a sample of blood to calculate the alcohol concentration at an earlier time. This will show that, for example, a suspect was over the prescribed limit of alcohol consumption for driving.

There are experts in blood pattern analysis to determine factors such as movement during an attack or force and nature of an assault. Such evidence can help the police and Crown Prosecution Service to decide whether or not to pursue a case.

In an investigation, if it is important to show the location of a suspect or a connection between suspects: an expert telephone witness can provide an analysis of usage of telephone equipment such as mobile phones. Specialists can utilise software programs to access and extract relevant data such as contact lists, deleted texts, deleted voice messages and deleted usage histories. This was used in the investigation of the death of Alice Ruggles by her former boyfriend Trimaan Dhillon.

Entomology expert witnesses can help in cases of suspicious deaths or murders by commenting on such matters as moving the body after death and whether a body has been in an exposed or concealed environment. They use information from insects to establish time of death and location. Such a technique was used to solve the murder of Leanne Tiernan.

Blood pattern analysis can provide clues as to how an offence took place.

Key term

Entomology: The scientific study of insects.

Insects are attracted to a corpse and can help determine the time and place of death.

AC1.3 EXPLAIN HOW EVIDENCE IS PROCESSED

ASSESSMENT CRITERION	MARK BAND 1	MARK BAND 2
AC1.3 Explain how evidence is processed	Basic response that may only list procedures or mention case studies **(1–3)**	Clear and detailed explanation of how evidence is processed using relevant examples **(4–6)**

CONTENT	AMPLIFICATION
Types of evidence • physical evidence • testimonial evidence **Process** • collection • transfer • storage • analysis • personnel involved	You should have an understanding of the different types of evidence and how they are collected and processed You should explore how different types of evidence were processed through a range of case studies, for example Barry George, Sally Clark, Angela Cannings, Amanda Knox

Types of evidence

Evidence can be divided into two categories:

- **Physical:** also referred to as real evidence, consists of tangible articles such as hairs, fibres, fingerprints and biological material.
- **Testimonial:** statements or the spoken word from the defendant, a victim or witness.

Physical evidence

The concept known as the Locard's exchange principle states that every time someone enters an environment, something is added to and removed from it. The principle is sometimes stated as 'every contact leaves a trace', and applies to contact between individuals as well as between an individual and a physical environment. Scenes of crime officers always work on the principle that physical evidence is left behind at every scene.

Key term

Locard's exchange principle: Dr Edmond Locard was a French forensic scientist, often informally referred to as the 'Sherlock Holmes of France'. He was a pioneer in forensic science techniques, including the exchange principle that something is added to and removed from an environment every time someone enters it.

An outdoor crime scene is the most vulnerable to loss or contamination of evidence. Individuals with access to the scene can potentially alter, destroy or contaminate evidence. The risk is greatest when investigators fail to secure the crime scene properly. Weather conditions, such as heat, cold, snow and rain, can destroy or ruin evidence.

Activity

Ask your teacher to invite the course leader of a forensic science course, at a local university, to come and talk about the course they teach – its demands and entry requirements.

Testimonial evidence

Testimonial evidence is the spoken word of the witnesses, which could include either the victim or defendant. Evidence must be admissible, which means complying with the rules of evidence. For instance, in the Colin Stagg case all the evidence relating to 'Lizzie' was excluded by the trial judge.

Statements of witnesses will have been taken by each side and disclosed prior to the court case. In court the testimonial evidence is usually given in the witness box, with the opportunity for the opposing side to cross-examine or question the witnesses' evidence. Occasionally, evidence can be agreed by the defence and prosecution, in which case it is simply read out without the witness attending. It is up to the jury/magistrate to decide how much reliance is placed on a witness. Vulnerable witnesses may give evidence by video link. Defendants cannot be forced to give evidence and may refuse to enter the witness box if they choose not to do so.

Process of physical evidence collection

- **Blood stains** can be collected on sterile material, if still in a liquid form, and left to dry at room temperature. Within 28 hours they should be transferred to the laboratory for the forensic scientists to examine. If the blood has already dried on material, the article should be placed in a container, sealed and labelled.

- **Semen stains** are often found on clothing or bedding and should be allowed to dry on the material, then wrapped in paper and placed in paper bags. It is important in offences of a sexual nature that evidence is secured and that the victim is examined by a doctor. All relevant clothing and other exhibits should be packaged separately.

Key terms

Rules of evidence: Legal rules that explain when evidence, as in a court case, is admissible and when it will be disallowed or ruled inadmissible.

Vulnerable witness: Anyone under the age of 17, or a victim of a sexual offence, or a person whose evidence or ability to give evidence is likely to be diminished by reason of mental disorder, significant intelligence or physical impariment.

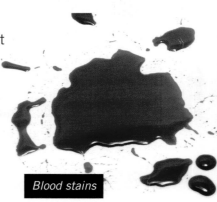
Blood stains

- **Hair samples** are likely to be on clothing and if so the clothing should be wrapped in paper and submitted to the laboratory for examination. Any small fragments of hair should be placed in paper, which can be marked and sealed. Occasionally, examination of hairs can reveal the possible race of the individual from whom they came and the part of the body from which they originated.

- **Fibres and threads** are often found on other items or caught in torn materials. Examination can normally be conducted to determine the type or colour of the fabric they are from. Forensic scientists can sometimes indicate the type of garment or fabric from which they originated. Comparisons can also be made with a suspect's clothing. Fibres and threads can be picked up with gloved fingers or tweezers and wrapped in paper, then put in an envelope, which is then sealed and marked.

A fingerprint

- **Fingerprints** can be patent and may be left in a liquid such as blood. Photographs can be taken as a lasting record. Fingerprints may be latent, but may become more identifiable with the use of powder or a chemical agent. An ultra-violet light may be used if prints are ones where they would not normally be easily visible. Prints can be collected by brushing over with a magnesium powder often mixed with a superglue-type substance. Finally, prints can be impressed, which means they are made in soft material or tissue by pressing down with the finger or hand. These prints can be photographed or in certain circumstances a mould made if they are very fragile.

- **Shoeprints** can often let police know what type of shoes to look for when searching a suspect's home. Photographs should be taken using a tripod, ruler and level to show scale. Casts can be made of impressions and, once hardened, they can be packaged in paper and submitted to the laboratory. This allows a match to a suspect's shoes.

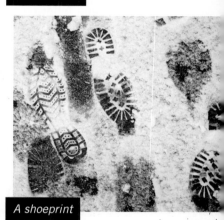

A shoeprint

- **Bite marks** are common in sexual assaults and can be matched back to the individual concerned. They should be photographed and a cast can be made. Casts and photographs of the suspect's teeth and perhaps the victim's teeth will be needed for comparison. A specialist forensic odontologist could be consulted.

Key terms

Patent: Clearly visible to the naked eye.

Latent: Not visible to the naked eye.

Forensic odontologist: Someone who can present dental knowledge in legal cases.

Activity

Research fingerprinting, including:

(i) the different types

(ii) the likely percentage of each type of fingerprint occurring in the population

(iii) when fingerprinting was first used.

You could even join in with friends and raise money to purchase a simple ink fingerprinting kit to work out your type of fingerprint.

CASE STUDY

Amanda Knox

AMANDA KNOX

Numerous pieces of evidence were discovered in the Amanda Knox case, when she and her boyfriend Raffaele Sollecito were charged with the murder of Meredith Kercher. The main evidence centred around DNA found on the murder weapon of a knife and the clasp on the victim's bra, found seven weeks after the murder. The knife was recovered from Sollecito's apartment and had the victim's DNA on the blade, and Amanda Knox's DNA on the handle. However, Knox's lawyers argued that the correct procedures had not been followed and contamination could have occurred.

Raffaele's DNA was found on the bra clasp of the victim. The defence team relied on the delay in discovering this evidence and argued that it was unreliable. According to the police evidence, footprints of both Knox and Sollecito were found near the murder scene. One of the footprints, which was found in Kercher's bedroom, was said to match Knox's footprint. In addition, another two footprints were found on the bath mat and in the corridor, which were said to be compatible with Sollecito. However, another forensic expert argued that the prints did not match Sollectio's feet.

CASE STUDY

Barry George was originally convicted of the murder of TV star Jill Dando.

BARRY GEORGE

George was convicted of the murder of television star Jill Dando in 1999. However, his conviction was quashed seven years later, when the appeal centred around a single speck of gunshot residue in the pocket of his coat, which was invisible to the naked eye and measured one-ten-thousandth of a centimetre. However, George maintained that the police took firearms into his flat when they first searched it. The jacket's pockets were opened inside the flat while particles of gunshot residue could have been in the air as a result of the presence of armed officers.

Literacy skills

Add in the missing words.

1. Evidence comes in two forms: physical and _____ .

2. Locard's theory basically states 'every _____ leaves a trace'.

3. If a crime scene is not appropriately secured the evidence can be _____ .

4. A _____ witness could be someone under the age of 17 years.

5. Fingerprints can be either latent or _____ .

Handy hints

In the controlled assessment, explain the two types of evidence and then select relevant examples of evidence from the scenario to explain in detail (collection, analysis, etc.). Include cases explaining the evidence and issues surrounding it.

AC1.4 EXAMINE THE RIGHTS OF INDIVIDUALS IN CRIMINAL INVESTIGATIONS

ASSESSMENT CRITERION	MARK BAND 1	MARK BAND 2
AC1.4 Examine the rights of individuals in criminal investigations	The rights of individuals in criminal investigations are simply listed or may have limited description **(1–3)**	The rights of individuals in criminal investigations are clearly examined from investigation through to appeal **(4–6)**

CONTENT	AMPLIFICATION
Individuals • suspects • victims • witnesses	You should consider the rights of all individuals from investigation through to appeal

Handy hints !

To achieve maximum marks you need to consider the rights of all individuals; namely the suspect, including appeal rights, victims and witnesses.

The rights of a suspect

A police officer can arrest a suspect, without a warrant, if they have reasonable grounds to believe that a person is committing, has committed or is about to commit an offence and, importantly, that an arrest is necessary.

A police officer must inform the person that they are being arrested, and what they are being arrested for, even if this is obvious, and why it is necessary to arrest them. So, a PC might say, '*I am arresting you for assault* and *to prevent you causing injury to any other person.*' This power comes from section 24, the Police & Criminal Evidence Act 1984 (PACE) as amended by the Serious Organised Crime and Police Act 2005 (SOCAPA).

Unless impossible to do so, the police must then caution the arrested person. See the following page about the right to silence.

An arrested person must be cautioned.

At the police station a suspect is handed over to the custody officer who ensures the person is treated in accordance with the law and is given all their legal rights. The custody officer also reviews the length of detention to ensure time limits are complied with. Generally, a person must be released within 24 hours of their arrival at the police station but in the case of indictable offences a further 12 hours (so, up to 36 hours) can be authorised. After 36 hours any further detention requires approval from the magistrates who can grant up to 96 hours of detention.

There are basically three main rights under PACE for the detainee:

- **S. 56 PACE:** a right to have someone informed of their arrest.
- **S. 58 PACE:** a right to consult privately with a solicitor.
- A right to consult the Codes of Practice.

At the police station, fingerprints and DNA in the form of a mouth swab can be taken from a suspect, with reasonable force if necessary. So the police will have the suspect's DNA as evidence.

Anyone detained at a police station may be questioned by the police. Suspects have certain rights and safeguards to protect them. For instance, all interviews must be tape recorded, in some areas of the UK the police video-record interviews. Detainees are also entitled to have a solicitor present during the interview.

During interviews suspects do not have to give any form of reply, these are often known as 'no comment' interviews. This 'right to silence' is given in the caution by the police:

You do not have to say anything. But it may harm your defence if you do not mention when questioned something which you later rely on in court. Anything you do say may be given in evidence.

This means a suspect cannot be forced to speak, they can still remain silent, and at any trial the judge may comment on the defendant's failure to mention something that is crucial to their defence. This failure to mention something, which they now wish to rely on in court, can form part of the evidence against them. A defendant's silence is not enough for a conviction on its own and the prosecution must still have other evidence in order to prove their case.

If tried in a magistrates' court, a defendant has the right to appeal against conviction, if they pleaded not guilty, and also to appeal against sentence, to the Crown Court. The case would be reheard by a judge and two magistrates. Any further appeal must be given leave (permission) and must be on a point of law.

If a defendant was tried in a Crown Court an appeal is not automatic as leave must be sought within 28 days of the decision. An appeal against sentence and/ or conviction is possible. The only ground to appeal against a conviction is that it is unsafe. The grounds of appeal would be heard, although not as a full retrial and only about the grounds of appeal, in the Court of Appeal, Criminal Division by three judges. Only cases involving a point of law of general public importance would be able to appeal further, with leave, to the Supreme Court.

Key terms

Custody officer: The police officer, of at least the rank of sergeant, who is responsible for the care and welfare of an arrested person.

Indictable offence: A serious offence that must be dealt with at a Crown Court.

A major right of a suspect is a right to silence.

Activity

Draw a diagram of the appeal routes a defendant has available, indicating courts, if leave is required, and including who hears the appeal and the form of hearing the appeal takes.

The rights of a victim

The rights of a victim are contained in the Victim's Code or the Code of Practice for Victims of Crime, established by the Domestic Violence, Crime and Victims Act 2004. The rights include to:

- be kept informed about the progress of your case by the police
- hear when a suspect is arrested, charged, bailed or sentenced
- apply for extra help when giving evidence in court (called 'special measures') if you are vulnerable, intimidated, or a child or young person
- apply for compensation
- make a Victim Personal Statement to explain the impact of the crime, and to have it read out in court, with the permission of the court. (Victim Support, 2006)

Independent Victim Support provides emotional and practical help to victims of all crimes.

Compensation can be awarded to a victim of crime by the court, for example in cases such as personal injury or damage to property. In addition, if you have been the victim of a violent crime it is possible to apply to the Criminal Injuries Compensation Authority (CICA), a government-sponsored agency, for compensation.

The rights of a witness

There is also a Witness Charter containing the standard of service a witness can expect in a court case. The standards include:

- having a main point of contact for information about the case
- being able to claim expenses for travel and for loss of earnings incurred due to the court case
- receiving special measures if you are a vulnerable or intimidated witness. For example, giving evidence by video link or the removal of wigs and gowns by the judge and lawyers.

Activity

Ask your teacher to contact your local Victim Support office and ask if someone could visit your centre to give a talk about their work.

There is also a complaints procedure if the standards are not followed, which eventually would be dealt with by the Parliamentary Ombudsman.

The Crown Prosecution Service (CPS) also provides information, assistance and support to victims and prosecution witnesses.

AC2.1 EXPLAIN THE REQUIREMENTS OF THE CROWN PROSECUTION SERVICE (CPS) FOR PROSECUTING SUSPECTS

ASSESSMENT CRITERION	MARK BAND 1	MARK BAND 2
AC2.1 Explain the requirements of the Crown Prosecution Service (CPS) for prosecuting suspects	A simple/basic explanation of the CPS with little or no reference to the prosecution of suspects **(1–2)**	Detailed explanation including clear and relevant examples of the requirements (tests) of the CPS in prosecuting suspects **(3–4)**

CONTENT	AMPLIFICATION
Requirements • charging role – Criminal Justice Act 2003 • Prosecution of Offences Act 1985 • Full Code Test	You should have an understanding of the role of the CPS You should explain the evidential and public interest tests in the decision to prosecute

The Crown Prosecution Service, CPS, was established in 1986 by the Prosecution of Offences Act 1985. Prior to this date the police both investigated and prosecuted crimes. However, it was felt that a more independent organisation and one separate from the police was needed to prosecute. The CPS therefore:

• advises the police in the early stages of an investigation
• decides which cases to prosecute
• determines the appropriate charge
• prepares cases for court
• presents cases in court.

The CPS, while being independent, works closely with the police. There is also a 24-hour advice service for the police through CPS Direct.

The CPS makes the decision whether or not to prosecute in all but very minor offences.

Full Code Test

To help produce fairness and consistency in prosecuting, the CPS uses a two-stage test to decide whether or not to prosecute. The two stages are the:

(i) evidential test

(ii) public interest test.

The evidential test

The evidential test asks if there is enough evidence to gain a 'realistic prospect of conviction'. The CPS must consider what the defence case may be, and how that is likely to affect the prosecution case. A realistic prospect of conviction is an objective test, which means that a jury or bench of magistrates or judge hearing a case alone, with the correct advice about the law, is more likely than not to find the defendant guilty. If the answer is yes then the evidential test is made out.

To help the CPS decide if there is sufficient evidence it must consider if the evidence can be used in court. If you recall the case of Colin Stagg, the 'Lizzie' evidence was held by the judge to be inadmissible (see page 156). The CPS must also consider if the evidence is reliable, including deciding upon the integrity of witnesses and whether or not the evidence, in particular the witnesses and their evidence, is credible or believable. If the case fails this test it does not proceed any further and there will be no prosecution. However, if it does pass the evidential test then the second test can be considered – the public interest test.

The public interest test

The CPS must consider whether or not it is in the public interest to prosecute. It may be that the public interest is better served with an out of court disposal. To help it decide the public interest test there is a list of questions to consider. The list is not exhaustive and not all questions might be relevant or a different weight may be attached to each answer in different cases. The questions are viewed more by way of guidance and are as follows:

- How serious is the offence committed? The more serious the offence, the more likely there will be a prosecution.
- What is the level of culpability (responsibility) of the suspect? The greater the level, the more likely there will be a prosecution.

- What are the circumstances of and the harm caused to the victim? If the victim is vulnerable or the defendant held a position of trust over them, or if the offence is motivated by discrimination, a prosecution is more likely.
- Was the suspect under the age of 18 at the time of the offence? This is because the interest and welfare of a child must be considered.
- What is the impact on the community? The greater the impact, the more likely there will be a prosecution.
- Is prosecution a proportionate response? This may be best explained by considering a case involving multiple suspects; prosecution might be reserved for the main participants in order to avoid excessively long and complex proceedings.

The threshold test

The threshold test allows an immediate charging decision despite not all the evidence being available, hence the Full Code Test cannot be used. This is obviously an infringement of liberty, as the evidence would not suggest a court is likely to convict, and is made on reasonable suspicion rather than evidence. However, it can only be applied where the suspect presents a substantial bail risk and not all the evidence is available at the time the suspect is to be released from custody. The questions to be answered in the threshold test are:

(i) Is there reasonable suspicion that the person to be charged has committed the offence?

(ii) Are there reasonable grounds for believing that the continuing investigation will provide further evidence, within a reasonable period of time? A decision to apply the threshold test, in these circumstances, must be kept under review.

Activity

Go to the official website of the CPS, www.cps.gov.uk/.

You will find a large amount of information useful for this AC and others in Units 3 and 4.

If you study A Level law or BTEC law it is also useful for those courses.

CASE STUDY

DAMILOLA TAYLOR

Remember the case of Damilola Taylor (see AC1.1, page 151)? The CPS was widely condemned, as it was said that the lies of a main prosecution witness were extremely obvious and the CPS should have known they would be exposed. There were criticisms that little time had been spent cross-checking her evidence against known facts and videotaped interviews with her.

CASE STUDY

ABU HAMZA

Abu Hamza, a radical Muslim cleric, was convicted in 2006 of several offences including soliciting murder and inciting racial hatred. However, this case threw controversy over the CPS and its application of the Full Code Test, as police had twice previously (in 1999 and 2000) formally asked prosecutors to consider terrorist charges against him in the seven years prior to his conviction. The CPS decided there was insufficient evidence to prosecute him. However, they finally decided to prosecute in 2006.

Abu Hamza

CASE STUDY

JOAN FRANCISCO

Joan Francisco's murder, in 1994, saw the CPS refuse to prosecute due to a lack of evidence. However, four years later her family sued her former boyfriend in a civil court and won. This was the first time someone had been sued for a murder for which they had never been charged. Again, the CPS refused to prosecute, citing a lack of evidence. However, a review of the evidence was ordered and evidence that was originally missed came to light that tied the former boyfriend to the murder. If it wasn't for the civil case the CPS may never have prosecuted.

Handy hints !

Improve your answer by including Acts of Parliament that relate to the CPS. For example, the Prosecution of Offences Act 1985, which established the CPS. Or the Criminal Justice Act 2003, which confirmed it was the CPS, rather than the police, that must make the decision on whether or not to charge an accused person.

AC2.2 DESCRIBE TRIAL PROCESSES

ASSESSMENT CRITERION	MARK BAND 1	MARK BAND 2
AC2.2 Describe trial processes	A simple/basic description of trial processes and/or personnel involved. May only be a list (1–2)	Describe in some detail the stages of the trial process, including the personnel involved (3–4)

CONTENT	AMPLIFICATION
Processes • pre-trial • bail • roles • plea bargaining • courts • appeals	You should have knowledge of each of the stages of the trial process including the roles of the personnel involved

Pre-trial

Types of criminal offences

There are three types of criminal offences:
• indictable
• triable either way (hybrid)
• summary.

Indictable offences

Indictable offences are the most serious and, although they start in a magistrates' court, they must be tried in a Crown Court. Examples of indictable offences include murder, manslaughter, rape and robbery.

Triable either way offences

Triable either way offences can be tried in either the magistrates' court or Crown Court. The judge in a Crown Court has higher sentencing powers but the chance of being acquitted by a jury is higher than that of a trial in a magistrates' court. Examples of either way offences include theft, burglary and assault occasioning actual bodily harm.

Summary offences

Summary offences are the least serious and include minor offences such as assault, battery and most motoring offences. They must stay in the magistrates' court.

Bail

A person can be released on bail at any point after being arrested by the police. Being on bail means that the person is allowed to be free until the next stage in the case. Bail is granted by the police and the courts. It can be unconditional or contain conditions such as curfew, reporting, residence and not to contact witnesses. The reasons for these conditions are to ensure that the person:

- surrenders to bail
- does not commit an offence while on bail
- does not interfere with witnesses.

 **Activity**

It is possible to take an online 360-degree virtual tour of the Supreme Court at www.supremecourt.uk/visiting/360-degree-virtual-tour.html.

With regards to police bail, both before and after a charge, a custody officer can refuse to grant it if:

- the suspect's name and address cannot be ascertained
- there are doubts about whether the suspect's name and address are genuine.

A magistrate's powers to grant bail are contained in the Bail Act 1976. This Act starts with the assumption that an accused person should be granted bail. Section 4 of the Bail Act 1976 gives a general right to bail. However, a court (that is, the magistrate) will not grant bail if it is satisfied that there are substantial grounds for believing that the defendant, if released on bail, would:

- fail to surrender to bail
- commit an offence when on bail

Bail is a release from custody.

- interfere with witnesses or otherwise obstruct the course of justice.

The court can also refuse bail if it is satisfied that the defendant should be kept in custody for their own protection.

The factors a court considers when deciding bail are:

- the nature and seriousness of the offence
- the character, antecedents, associations and community ties of the defendant
- the defendant's record of previous bail
- the strength of the evidence.

However, for murder charges bail can only be granted by a judge and reasons for the decision must be given.

Roles

In a criminal case the prosecution will be represented by a representative from the Crown Prosecution Service. Their role is to present the facts of the case to the court in a fair way. This lawyer may either be employed by the CPS or acting as their agent for the court case.

The defendant, especially in serious offences, will have legal representation. Generally, a solicitor will provide representation in a magistrates' court and a barrister in a Crown Court. Their role is to cast doubt on the prosecution's evidence. They do not have to prove innocence. A defendant cannot be compelled to give evidence.

In a magistrates' court the role of the magistrates is to decide liability, whether the case is proved by the CPS, and pass the appropriate sentence. In a Crown Court a jury decides guilt or innocence and a judge determines the appropriate sentence.

Plea bargaining

Plea bargaining is an arrangement agreed by the prosecution and defence or the judge as an incentive for the defendant to plead guilty. It could concern the actual charge, when the defendant pleads guilty to a lesser charge or only to some of the charges that are filed against them, for example manslaughter instead of murder. Or it might relate to the sentence, when the defendant is told in advance what their sentence will be if they plead guilty. This can help the prosecutor obtain a conviction, particularly in cases where the defendant is facing serious charges.

Criminal courts

Magistrates' court

All criminal cases are first heard in a magistrates' court and the vast majority, approximately 95%, stay there. Only a small percentage proceed to a Crown Court. Generally, there are three magistrates who decide both guilt and an appropriate sentence. They are laypeople, meaning that they are unqualified in the law. They

are assisted by a legally qualified clerk. Their sentencing powers are limited to six months and/or a £5,000 fine for one offence, this is doubled for two or more offences.

If they feel their sentencing powers are inadequate they can send a case to Crown Court for sentencing. Defendants are usually represented by a solicitor, often with the assistance of legal funding. A representative from the CPS will present the case for the prosecution.

Crown Court

All indictable offences, those cases where trial by jury has been selected by a defendant, in triable either way offences and cases where the magistrates have refused jurisdiction, are heard in a Crown Court. Refusing jurisdiction means the magistrates believed the case to be far too serious for them to hear and ordered the triable either way offence to proceed to a Crown Court. If the defendant pleads not guilty, a jury trial will be arranged. The jury must listen to the evidence from both prosecution and defence, including the witnesses. They are entitled to consider any exhibits such as photographs, make notes if they wish to do so and ask any questions via the judge. They must then retire and consider, in secret, a verdict.

Initially, a judge will request a unanimous verdict, where all members of the jury agree, but a majority verdict of 10/12 is acceptable, when so ordered by a judge. Defendants are usually represented by barristers and a member of the CPS presents the case for the Crown.

A judge's role is to advise the jury on the law and ensure that a trial is fair and human rights compliant. The criminal system is adversarial, which means that the parties – the prosecution and defence – run their cases, with the judge acting as referee. The judge will advise the jury on procedure and explain their duties. The judge will deal with any points of law that have to be decided and advise the jury on how to apply the law to whatever facts they find. A judge will also pass sentence if the defendant is found guilty. Under the Criminal Justice Act 2003, it is possible for a judge to sit alone, without a jury, to determine a verdict.

A Crown Court judge will wear a wig and gown.

Court of Appeal Criminal Division

The Court of Appeal Criminal Division is an appeal court that decides if the Crown Court's verdict is safe. Permission, or leave, is required for this to happen. It does not hold a retrial but can direct that one takes place or dismiss the verdict (quash it) and vary a sentence, making it longer or shorter. Cases are heard by judges, there is no jury.

Supreme Court

Formally known as the House of Lords, a case may proceed to the Supreme Court – top court in the hierarchy – if it concerns a point of law of general public importance. Leave is required for this to happen. Twelve Law Lords sit in this court and make rulings that bind all courts beneath it.

> ### Key term
>
> **Law Lords:** Also known as the 12 Lords of Appeal in Ordinary, are judges who hear cases in the Supreme Court.

Appeals

Appeals from a magistrates' court

The defendant can appeal against their conviction or sentence received from a magistrates' court to have their case heard at a Crown Court. Here the case is heard as a retrial by a judge and two magistrates. The conviction can be confirmed, quashed (dismissed) or varied, perhaps to a lower charge. As regards sentence, it can be reduced or increased. The right to appeal is automatic and no leave or permission is needed. If a point of law is involved there is a right to appeal to the High Court by way of 'Case Stated'.

Appeals from a Crown Court

The defendant could seek leave to appeal, to the Court of Appeal Criminal Division, against their conviction and/or sentence. The only ground to appeal against a guilty verdict is that the conviction is unsafe. The Court of Appeal has the power to order a retrial, vary the conviction, decrease the sentence – although not increase it – on a defendant's appeal. Any further appeal by either the defence or prosecution would be to the Supreme Court, with leave, or permission, if the case involved a point of law that was of general public importance.

 **Activity**

> Using the information given here about appeals, draw diagrams to show the appeal routes by both the defence and prosecution.

The prosecution has limited rights to appeal but appeal would be allowed if:

- an error in law by a judge led to a dismissal
- the prosecution believes an acquittal was as a result of the jury being nobbled (bribed or intimidated)
- there is new and compelling evidence of the defendant's guilt, in a serious case.

The prosecution and defence also have a right to appeal to the Court of Appeal if the judge has erred in law or if the sentence was unduly lenient.

Activity

> Arrange a visit to your local Crown Court to see law in action.

Key terms

Nobbled: Bribed or intimidated.

Lenient: Not as harsh in punishment as would be expected.

AC2.3 UNDERSTAND RULES IN RELATION TO THE USE OF EVIDENCE IN CRIMINAL CASES

ASSESSMENT CRITERION	MARK BAND 1	MARK BAND 2
AC2.3 Understand rules in relation to the use of evidence in criminal cases	A simple/basic understanding of the rules in relation to the use of evidence in criminal cases **(1–2)**	Detailed understanding of the rules in relation to the use of evidence in criminal cases **(3–4)**

CONTENT	AMPLIFICATION
Rules of evidence • relevance and admissibility • disclosure of evidence • hearsay rule and exceptions • legislation and case law	You should have an understanding of how evidence is used in court

Handy hints !

Make sure that you include examples of legislation or Acts of Parliament covering various rules of evidence.

Relevance and admissibility

Evidence should always be relevant, reliable and admissible. However, this is not always the case. There have been many cases where these simple rules have not been followed.

Improperly obtained evidence – entrapment

If the police are finding it difficult to secure evidence that will be admissible in court, they can consider a technique where they act as 'agent provocateurs'. In other words, they induce others to break the law so that they can secure a conviction. English law does not allow a defence of entrapment but in principle such evidence may be excluded under s. 78 Police & Criminal Evidence Act 1984 (PACE). A good example of this is the case of Colin Stagg and the 'Lizzie' evidence (page 156).

There is no rule requiring the exclusion of evidence simply because it has been improperly obtained. The judge has discretion to exclude such prosecution evidence under both common law, which is law not contained in an Act of Parliament, and under statute. One of the main statutory provisions is under section 78 PACE 1984. There is also the European Convention on Human Rights (ECHR) where Article 6 provides the right to a fair trial. The defendant would argue an entrapment was not fair.

Evidence must be relevant and admissible.

The common test for exclusion is whether the probative value of the evidence is less than its prejudicial effect. In other words, is the evidence proven to be more helpful in establishing the truth than be harmful, unnecessary, to the case?

Section 78 PACE gives a discretionary power to judges and magistrates to exclude evidence on which the prosecution proposes to rely on, if it appears that 'having regard to all the circumstances, including the circumstances in which the evidence was obtained, the admission of the evidence would have an adverse effect on the fairness of the proceedings that the court ought not to admit it'.

Key term

Probative value: How useful evidence is to prove something important in a trial.

Handy hints !

In the controlled assessment try to indicate which rules of evidence are relevant to the brief you are given.

Pre-trial silence

A suspect's failure to give an explanation when questioned by the police under caution may allow the jury at the trial to draw an inference of guilt under the Criminal Justice & Public Order Act 1994 (CJPOA). This applies even if the suspect has received legal advice. Inferences alone cannot establish guilt, other evidence is needed.

Key term

Inference of guilt: It is possible to decide, on the evidence given, that the person is guilty.

Handy hints !

In this section do not explain evidence, as this has already been covered in AC1.3. Instead, make sure that there is a focus on the law or rules that govern the admissibility of evidence in a criminal case.

Character evidence and past convictions

Under the Criminal Justice Act (CJA) 2003, previous convictions are not automatically allowed as evidence but there are occasions when they will be allowed to be given to the court. The CJA provides several rules or 'gateways' to allow this to happen. One of the 'gateways' or ways of introducing a defendant's previous convictions is under section 103 and includes matters relating to the question whether the defendant has a propensity to commit offences of the kind with which they are charged. This means they have a tendency to commit offences of the same description or offences of the same category.

Activity

Hold a class debate over the issue of whether previous convictions are relevant to guilt in a criminal case and whether they should be disclosed to a jury.

Disclosure in criminal cases

Disclosure is one of the most important aspects in the criminal justice system. It ensures that there is a fair trial. The prosecution must disclose all the documents it is going to use at the trial. The rule to ensure a fair trial is that full disclosure should be made of all material held by the prosecution, even if it weakens its own case or strengthens the case of the defence. The rules are in the Criminal Procedure and Investigations Act 1996 (CPIA) amended by the Criminal Justice Act 2003.

The defence will make a statement that requires the prosecution to disclose evidence. The statement made by the defence must be in writing and contain the following:

- the nature of the defence
- the matters of fact that the defence will challenge and why they are being challenged
- the matters of fact that the defence will rely on
- any relevant points of law.

Take it further

Conduct an internet search about the collapsed court case involving Samson Makele. His trial was stopped when it was discovered the Crown Prosecution Service failed to disclose relevant evidence.

CASE STUDY

SALLY CLARK

The Sally Clark case is considered in greater detail in AC3.1 (page 193). However, it is relevant to note that the miscarriage of justice was caused by the prosecution failing to disclose medical evidence of a microbiological report that suggested the second of her sons had died of natural causes. This case shows the danger of not disclosing documents.

Hearsay evidence

Hearsay evidence refers to a statement that has been made out of court and a witness wishes to rely on this statement (made by another person) being used in court. For example, witness X is giving evidence in court and states: '*witness Y told me that he saw the defendant commit the crime ...*'

Hearsay is defined in section 114 (1) Criminal Justice Act 2003 as a:

statement not made in oral evidence in the proceedings that is evidence of any matter stated.

It is generally not admitted as evidence, as the maker of the statement should attend court to give evidence. This is so they can be cross-examined about their evidence. There are exceptions, for instance if the witness is not available or if they have died. Alternatively, the parties can also agree to admit hearsay evidence or it can be admitted if the court is satisfied it is in the interests of justice for it to be used as evidence.

Hearsay evidence is generally not admissible.

AC2.4 ASSESS KEY INFLUENCES AFFECTING THE OUTCOMES OF CRIMINAL CASES

ASSESSMENT CRITERION	MARK BAND 1	MARK BAND 2	MARK BAND 3
AC2.4 Assess key influences affecting the outcomes of criminal cases	Key influences affecting the outcomes of criminal cases are largely described **(1–3)**	Some understanding of the key influences affecting the outcomes of criminal cases is shown and some assessment made of their impact **(4–7)**	Assesses the required range of key influences affecting the outcomes of criminal cases There is clear and detailed understanding of their impact **(8–10)**

CONTENT	AMPLIFICATION
Influences • evidence • media • witnesses • experts • politics • judiciary • barristers and legal teams	You should have an understanding of the many factors that can influence the outcome of a trial and be able to assess their impact

Handy hints !

For full marks you should include reference to all the influences in the content section. However, they are not all expected to be in the same detail.

Activity

Match the effect of the influence to the correct influence in the table below:

	INFLUENCE		HOW IT COULD AFFECT THE OUTCOME OF A TRIAL
1	EVIDENCE	A	People who give evidence in court and need to be believed to affect the outcome.
2	MEDIA	B	Personnel in charge of the court room and interpreter of the law. How the law is explained or interpreted can have an influence on the outcome.
3	WITNESSES	C	The group of people responsible for advocacy in court. They will have a major impact on the presentation of evidence.
4	EXPERTS	D	A means of communicating to the public what is happening at trial. However, biased reporting or the way stories are written could have a major influence on the outcome.
5	POLITICS	E	Witnesses with specialised knowledge may seem impressive and believable to the jury and therefore have a major impact on the outcome of a case.
6	JUDICIARY	F	Key to an outcome as it is presented by both sides during a trial. The jury must only take this into account when deciding a verdict.
7	LEGAL TEAMS	G	Activities associated with the government. Laws are established in this way and certain areas can be promoted and encouraged to be prosecuted.

Answers: 1 – F, 2 – D, 3 – A, 4 – E, 5 – G, 6 – B, 7 – C.

Evidence

The evidence in a trial should have the main impact on the outcome. Each jury member takes an oath (or affirmation), traditionally as follows:

I swear by almighty God that I will faithfully try the defendant and give a true verdict according to the evidence.

The evidence must be only that presented in court in the form of physical or testimonial evidence. It is up to each jury member or each magistrate to attach whatever weight they consider appropriate to each piece of evidence.

The usual witness oath is 'I swear by ... [according to religious belief] that the evidence I shall give shall be the truth the whole truth and nothing but the truth.'
An alternative to the oath is: 'I do solemnly, sincerely and truly declare and affirm that the evidence I shall give shall be the truth, the whole truth and nothing but the truth.'

It is important to note that in the law of England and Wales the prosecution must bring evidence to prove the claim they are making, this is known as the burden of proof. The standard of proof, in criminal matters, is beyond reasonable doubt or until the jury or magistrate are sure of the verdict. If there is any doubt there must be an acquittal. The defence do not have to prove anything, although in practice they will try to cast as much doubt as possible on the evidence.

Key term

Burden of proof: The duty of proving the charge.

Media

The media can affect the outcome of a criminal case. If a story is published, the public will read it and could believe that the material printed is true, even if it is not. This may mean that a suspect does not get a fair trial. Under English law a person is innocent until proven guilty, but if a jury has a preconceived idea from media reports this could affect the outcome of a trial. This is what is meant by 'trial by media' rather than a trial by jury on the evidence presented on the court room.

CASE STUDY

CHRISTOPHER JEFFERIES

Christopher Jefferies was arrested and interviewed by the police in connection with the murder of Joanna Yeates in 2010. However, he found himself the subject of a media frenzy, appearing on the front page of the national newspapers. He was was described as 'weird', 'lewd', 'strange', 'creepy', 'angry', 'odd', 'disturbing', 'eccentric', 'a loner' and 'unusual' in just one article. Jefferies was, however, innocent and Vincent Tabak, Yeates' neighbour, was jailed for life in October 2011 after being convicted of her murder. The newspapers were forced to issue a public apology and paid substantial libel damages to Jefferies.

MYSTERY PAIR AT JO FLAT

OBSESSED BY DEATH

WAS JO'S BODY HIDDEN NEXT TO HER FLAT?

JO SUSPECT IS PEEPING TOM

The Strange Mr Jefferies

Christopher Jefferies' trial by media newspaper headlines

Take it further

Read the article by Boris Johnson (2006), called 'Colin Stagg Shows Why Trial by Judge, Not by Media, is Right', which can be found on the *Daily Telegraph*'s website. This will provide you with information about how a court case can be affected by the media.

Activity

Watch the drama series called *The Lost Honour of Christopher Jefferies*.

Witnesses

Both the prosecution and defence are entitled to call witnesses in support of their case. If the witness evidence can be agreed, and is not in dispute, it can be read out in court in the form of a statement. This prevents the witness from having to attend the court and give evidence. However, if the witness evidence is contested the witness must appear in court to give their side of the story, which is called examination-in-chief. Witnesses can also be asked questions by the other side, or cross-examined. The jury are entitled to give as much weight as they consider appropriate to witness evidence. So, if the witness is believable this could influence the jury towards whichever side the witness represents. Similarly, if the witness appears to be unreliable they may adversely affect the outcome of a case.

Key term

Examination-in-chief: The questioning of a witness by the party who has called that witness to give evidence, in support of the case being made.

Experts

A witness with specialist knowledge is known as an expert. Expert evidence can have a major influence on the outcome of a case, especially when that evidence is very technical or relies heavily on statistics. In such a situation the typical jury is likely to be swayed by the expert knowledge and specialist qualifications of the witness. Juries are ordinary people who are unlikely to have any expert knowledge of the subject in question. It is human nature to be influenced by experience and credentials; almost a case of being 'blinded by science'.

However, where such evidence is incorrect or misleading, miscarriages of justice can occur. This happened in the case of Sally Clark (see AC3.1, page 193) and Angela Cannings, when Sir Roy Meadow gave incorrect evidence on the statistical chances of sudden infant death syndrome.

Even if instructed by one party, an expert witness should remain independent.

Politics

There are certain activities associated with the government and political areas that can influence the outcome of a case. Obviously, all statutory laws are produced by parliament, and the politicians debate, vote and produce amendments to the proposals. In other words, politics influences the laws that legislatures enact. For instance, if the mood of the country is to get tough on crime then laws increasing sentencing can be passed. If a particular crime is identified as a major problem then sentencing could reflect a discouragement of such a crime. For example, following the London riots in 2011 sentencing was noticeably tougher. Also, the law on bail has substantially changed in recent years, with an increased focus on denying bail in certain circumstances. This is the political response to defendants committing crimes, sometimes serious ones, while on bail.

Judiciary

The judges provide clarification on the law and explain the way it is to be applied. Such interpretation is given to the jury and hence this and any summary of evidence from the case can influence the decision making. If a judge appears to be biased and favour one side, the jury may be inclined to follow such an opinion. Judges are experienced and highly qualified, which may result in others following their views.

In addition, since the Criminal Justice Act 2003, judges can hear a case without a jury if they believe that the case will be long/complex or that jury tampering could occur or is occurring. This happened in the case of Twomey, 2009, where this right was exercised following allegations of jury tampering (for more on Twomey see page 188).

Activity

Research the cases of *R. v Ponting* (1985) and *R. v Wang* (2005) and decide if you would have given the same decision as the jury provided for these cases.

Barristers and legal teams

Legal teams can influence the outcome of a court case. For instance, it is possible for a jury to be swayed by a particularly charismatic barrister. Or they may be misled by a barrister's techniques and ability to present the evidence. There have also been occasions when a juror has become infatuated with a barrister, which could affect the outcome.

The style of criminal proceedings, namely adversarial, also tends to enable the barrister to be influential upon a jury. The adversarial system is when a jury decides on guilt having heard defence and prosecution presentations of the case. Such a system therefore relies on the skill of the advocates representing their respective party's interests and not on a neutral party, usually the judge, trying to ascertain the truth of the case.

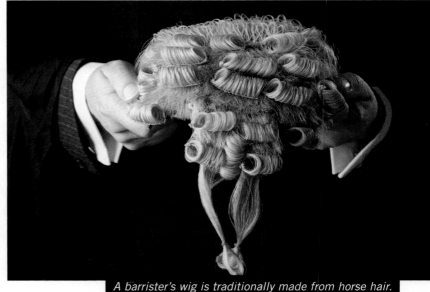

A barrister's wig is traditionally made from horse hair.

AC2.5 DISCUSS THE USE OF LAYPEOPLE IN CRIMINAL CASES

ASSESSMENT CRITERION	MARK BAND 1	MARK BAND 2
AC2.5 Discuss the use of laypeople in criminal cases	A basic/simple description of juries and magistrates **(1–3)**	The uses of laypeople (juries and magistrates) are discussed fully in relation to their strengths and weaknesses in criminal cases **(4–6)**

CONTENT	AMPLIFICATION
Laypeople • juries • magistrates	You should be able to discuss the strengths and weaknesses of both juries and lay magistrates

Juries

Jurors are ordinary members of the public, or laypeople, without legal knowledge, who decide the outcome of criminal cases. The eligibility for jury selection and qualification is contained in the Jury Act 1974 and the Criminal Justice Act 2003. Jurors:

- are randomly selected from the names on the electoral register
- are between the ages of 18 and 75
- have a residency requirement of five years or more in the UK, Channel Islands or Isle of Mann
- have no recent criminal convictions.

Take it further »

Find out about jury duty from the Gov.uk website.

A jury trial only takes place in around 1% of criminal cases.

A jury's role is to listen to the evidence and then decide the guilt or innocence of the defendant. They are advised on the law by the judge and can take notes and ask questions, via the judge, if so desired. The decision they make cannot be questioned.

Jury duty is compulsory but there is a possibility of it being deferred for good reasons such as a holiday, medical appointment, etc. Lawyers, judges and other legal personnel are now able to carry out jury service as a result of the Criminal Justice Act 2003.

Strengths

Jurors (members of the jury) are ordinary people who, as such, can bring their own 'justice' or fairness to a case (sometimes called jury equity).

Even if a judge explains the law and how it should be applied, the jury can still reach a verdict contrary to the evidence.

Key term

Jury equity: A jury can bring in a verdict that is morally right rather than one that complies with the law and previous cases.

CASE STUDY

R v OWEN

Jury equity can be shown in the case of R v Owen where the defendant's son was killed by a careless driver who was given a 12-month prison sentence. The driver knocked Owen's son off his bicycle with a 30-ton truck, which was not insured and was not roadworthy. In addition, the driver had never passed a driving test and was blind in one eye. Owen felt the sentence was insufficient and decided to take his own justice for the loss of his son. He therefore shot the driver in the back and arm with a sawn-off shotgun. Charged with attempted murder, Owen was plainly guilty as he had deliberately shot the man. However, the jury understood why he had done this and decided to acquit him. Later, some members of the jury congratulated him. This was the jury's verdict and nothing could be done about it.

Take it further

Research the case of R v Ponting to see jury equity in action.

The jury system is popular with the public, who have confidence in the system as they are aware it is ordinary members of the public playing such an important role in the criminal justice system. This right to be tried by your peers is enshrined in our history and is seen as a democratic right. Moves to withdraw it for minor offences of theft were met with great resistance. It is the 'lamp which shows that freedom lives' (Lord Devlin).

There are 12 people on a jury, which means no one individual is responsible, it allows for numerous opinions to be discussed and taken into account. In addition, jury deliberations are held in secret and members of the jury cannot be called upon to explain their verdict. This allows them to reach a decision even if it is not popular with the public.

The jury is impartial as members cannot be connected to anyone in the case. They only sit for two weeks, unless agreed that the case may take longer, so do not become case hardened.

STRENGTH   WEAKNESS

Weaknesses

As the jury do not give reasons for their decision, perverse verdicts or ones that go against the evidence can be delivered. A judge or magistrate must always give reasons for their decisions but a jury does not. In the case of *R* v *Kronlid and Others*, the jury acquitted the defendants despite the clear-cut evidence against them. They caused over a million pounds worth of damage to an aeroplane to prevent it being sent to Indonesia, where it was to have been used in an attack against people from East Timor.

In recent years a growing weakness of the jury system is the use of the internet and social media during the trial. Despite the jury being told by the judge not to research or look on the internet about the case, it still happens. It is now a criminal offence for a juror to intentionally search the internet for relevant information. Theodora Dallas was a juror who was jailed for researching online a case in which she was sitting, and then brought outside media information into the court. This made the trial process unfair and unjust, as it meant all the jurors could have stereotyped the offender and decided they were guilty regardless of the evidence presented in the trial.

As jurors are ordinary people they may also bring their prejudices to the case. Racial bias was seen in the case of *Sander* v *United Kingdom*. Here a juror sent a note to the judge stating that other members had been making openly racist remarks and jokes. Despite this the judge allowed the case to proceed. It was later held that the judge should have discharged the jury as there was obvious risk of racial bias.

There is no intelligence test to be a juror and it is possible that with complex areas of law some people may find cases difficult to understand. In particular, fraud cases can be very long and complex.

Finally, jurors can be open to 'jury nobbling' or tampering. In other words, jurors could be bribed or intimidated to bring in a desired verdict. To prevent this from happening, judge-alone trials are now possible. Despite such a concept going against the ancient democratic right of trial by peers, the case of *R* v *Twomey* was decided by a judge alone in 2009. Three previous jury trials had collapsed due to serious attempts at jury tampering. The judge found the defendants guilty.

Take it further

Research the case of *R* v *Randle and Pottle*, and consider why the jury may have refused to convict the defendants, despite the fact that the evidence clearly showed they were guilty.

Handy hints !

Many of the strengths of the jury system can be turned around and considered as weaknesses.

Take it further

Research the 'special arrangements' courts made during the Covid 19 pandemic. Do you think the special arrangements produced justice?

For help go to: https://justice.org.uk/our-work/justice-covid-19-response/.

Magistrates

Also known as Justices of the Peace, magistrates are laypeople aged between 18 and 65 on appointment. However, they differ from juries as they apply to sit in a magistrates' court and decide if a case has been proved by the prosecution and, if so, also pass the appropriate sentence.

Magistrates are unpaid but receive training and continued support. They have a legally qualified clerk to ensure they are aware of the law and comply with all rules.

Strengths

Magistrates are volunteers and only receive expenses, which means the lack of cost is a major advantage to the criminal justice system. To pay professional judges to carry out the work would cost millions of pounds.

As magistrates are laypeople, the system again allows ordinary people to take part in the administration of justice. Magistrates come from all walks of life and therefore bring a cross-section of the public to the job. They are more representative of the public than professional judges. This is particularly true of women, as approximately half of magistrates are female, compared to around 30% of the judiciary.

Magistrates sit in their neighbourhood and therefore have local knowledge that can be applied to cases. This allows community issues and concerns to be acknowledged. In addition, as magistrates usually sit in threes, a balanced view is more likely. If all three fail to agree, the majority view prevails.

All criminal cases start in the magistrates' court and around 95% of cases are dealt with by these unpaid volunteers. This is a very large number of cases every year. Given this, there is a surprisingly small number of appeals from the magistrates' decisions.

Activity

Learn about the history of magistrates by reading 'History of the Magistracy',

www.magistrates-association.org.uk/About-Magistrates/History-of-the-magistracy.

There is a magistrates' court in most cities.

Weaknesses

One of the main weaknesses is the inconsistency in sentencing. Magistrates can pass varying sentences in different areas of the country for the same offences. According to Jacqueline Martin, in her book *English Legal System* (2016), in 2010 Bristol magistrates imposed custodial sentences on 11.1% of defendants, while Dinefwr magistrates imposed a custodial sentence on only 0.1% of defendants. In addition, Bristol magistrates imposed 32.2% community sentences compared to Dinefwr where it was only 6.6%.

Magistrates are also criticised as being middle aged and middle class, as a large majority of magistrates are retired or from a professional or managerial background. However, given the fact that this is an unpaid role and employees must take time away from employment to carry out their duties, this is not an unsurprising weakness. There have been numerous campaigns to increase the cross-section of magistrates and some younger people have been recruited. However, the age inequality still applies.

Despite training to prevent this happening, Magistrates have also been accused of being prosecution-biased with a tendency to believe police evidence. Magistrates may see the same prosecutors on a regular basis and this could affect their judgment. If they sit on a regular basis they may also become case hardened.

Take it further

Watch 'The Work of Magistrates in England and Wales' by the Sentencing Council at

www.youtube.com/ watch?v=fCybrBaKj8s

to discover the work of magistrates in England and Wales.

LEARNING OUTCOME 3
BE ABLE TO REVIEW CRIMINAL CASES

AC3.1 EXAMINE INFORMATION FOR VALIDITY

ASSESSMENT CRITERION	MARK BAND 1	MARK BAND 2	MARK BAND 3
AC3.1 Examine information for validity cases	Limited information sources are described (listed at the lower end) At the top end, some information sources are discussed in relation to validity **(1–5)**	A range of information sources are examined and reviewed in terms of their validity At the bottom end, the range of information sources and/or the review will be limited **(6–10)**	Detailed examination of a relevant range of information sources (including reference to the brief) There is a clear review of their suitability in terms of validity **(11–15)**

CONTENT	AMPLIFICATION
Examine for • bias • opinion • circumstances • currency • accuracy **Information** • evidence • trial transcripts • media reports • judgements • Law Reports	You should develop the ability to review information and make judgements on the suitability of the content they provide against a number of criteria In your controlled assessment response, you should make reference to the assignment brief and other examples you have studied

NOTE

Changes to the assessment criterion AC3.1 and AC3.2 have been slightly amended to place a greate emphasis on a reference being made to the brief. Th amplification column in AC3.1 has been amended a shown in red in the above table.

Activity

Watch the following two clips on YouTube. Can you trust everything you see?

- 'Flying Penguins / World Penguin Day/ BBC', www.youtube.com/watch?ank&v=9dfWzp7rYR4.
- 'BBC: Spaghetti-Harvest in Ticino', www.youtube.com/watch?v=tVo_wkxH9dU.

Handy hints !

In this section you should examine a range of different information sources and show you appreciate that not everything is accurate or valid. An item may, for instance, be very biased, such as newspaper reporting being politically biased. The author may be expressing their opinion only and failing to take into account all sides of the argument.

Sometimes an information source may be factually wrong or outdated and reliance on such information can be dangerous, especially in criminal cases. Always consider who has written the source and why it was written. This can influence the validity and legitimacy of the information provided. Also consider when the source was created. Policy and the views of society change and information sources may be written to reflect the time.

Key term

Biased: Unfairly prejudiced for or against someone or something.

Handy hints !

When looking for validity consider the following questions:

- What is the purpose of the resource?
- Is it a one-sided view?
- Is negative language used?
- Is it neutral on controversial issues?
- What is the source of the information?
- What is the purpose of the document?

Always examine sources for bias.

Evidence

While evidence in a criminal case is generally reliable, there are occasions where it has been shown that evidence is not valid. An example of this is the case of Sally Clark and the expert evidence of Sir Roy Meadow.

CASE STUDY

SALLY CLARK

Sally Clark was convicted of the murder of her first two children in 1999. The death of her first child, aged just under three months, was originally treated as natural causes or sudden infant death syndrome (SIDS). Her second child died over a year later at the age of two months. However, this time the death was treated as suspicious. Indeed, the Home Office pathologist revisited the first death and then claimed that was suspicious too.

Sir Roy Meadow made 'simply astonishing' mistakes with regards to the statistical evidence. The professor claimed there was a '1 in 73 million' chance of two children dying of SIDS in a household where no risk factors were present. However, this statistical evidence was unreliable. The medical evidence was extremely complicated and debated by many specialists, who often reached contradictory conclusions. He likened it to the probability of backing a winning horse that is an outsider (a horse unlikely to win) in the Grand National four years running: 1 in 73 million. The statistical evidence did not acknowledge that the risk may be greater if the condition was inherited. The jury accepted his evidence as he was a medical expert. Sally Clark was released after spending three years in prison, following an appeal hearing that deemed her conviction to be unsafe. Clearly, the evidence was not valid in this situation.

Sir Roy Meadow stated in his book (1997), 'one sudden infant death is a tragedy, two is suspicious and three is murder, until proved otherwise'. This was later shown to be invalid.

Trial verdicts

CASE STUDY

BARRY GEORGE

Barry George

Barry George was found guilty of murdering Jill Dando, who was shot in the head outside her home in London in 1999. She was a very famous news presenter for the BBC and also presented the television programme *Crimewatch*. There was intense public pressure for the murder to be solved; however, as there was no forensic evidence, the police struggled to find a suspect.

While looking at local people the police came across Barry George, who had an obsession with guns. They found out that he liked to follow women and take photos of them. The police looked around his house and found old newspapers, some with stories about Jill Dando, and over 480 photos of different women. But none of them connected him with Jill Dando. Throughout his life George had used several pseudonyms, different names, such as Paul Gadd (Gary Glitter's real name) and after the death of Freddy Mercury the name Barry Bulsara (Mercury's real surname). The police seized one of his jackets and found some gun discharge in the pocket that matched the bullet at the crime scene. A fibre discovered at the crime scene matched the fibres from a pair of George's trousers. A jury found him guilty and he spent eight years in prison.

However, the validity of the conviction was questioned. Clearly, George was a loner with a bizarre personality. However, this is certainly not evidence against him for this crime and cannot prove he is a murderer. The gunshot residue was very small, less than a half of a thousandth of an inch. In addition, the jacket in which it was found was not recovered until a year after the shooting. It could be argued, therefore, that such evidence is unreliable and inconclusive. George's defence team argued it could have appeared as a result of contamination of the jacket when it was placed on a mannequin to be photographed as police evidence. Following a successful appeal, George's conviction was quashed and he won a retrial, when a jury found him not guilty. This shows that the original trial and jury verdict lacked validity.

Activity

Research the case of Jeremy Bamber, who was convicted of killing five members of his family in 1985. Make a table showing the points that suggest the verdict is not valid. Much information can be found at www.jeremy-bamber.co.uk/. However, remember to always consider information for validity and bias.

Jeremy Bamber

Media reports

The media play a major role in the way the public perceive crime. However, media reports should always be examined for the sources used, the political viewpoint of the article, whether stereotypes appear, and whether all people are held to account or if there are double standards.

News reports should remain objective and impartial so as to produce validity. However, at times reporting may have compromised impartiality and by providing subjective political commentary. This lack of objectivity could mean the reporting lacks accuracy and is not valid.

Activity

Read the 'BBC Accused of Political Bias – on the Right not the Left' (Burrell, 2014) on the *Independent*'s website and provide a brief summary showing that media reporting can be biased.

Judgment from official inquiry

Hillsborough disaster inquiry

On 15 April 1989 at the start of an FA Cup semi-final match between Liverpool and Nottingham Forest at Sheffield Wednesday's Hillsborough stadium, a crush against the steel terraces led to the death of 96 Liverpool fans and left hundreds more injured.

It was suggested by the media that drunken Liverpool fans were to blame. The police also blamed fans for being late and drunk. Despite an interim report by Lord Justice Taylor, criticising the police, the Director of Public Prosecutions ruled there was insufficient evidence to bring any criminal charges against the police. Inquests into the deaths returned verdicts of accidental death for the victims and ruled they were all dead by 3.15pm. However, this meant that the response of the police and ambulance services after 3.15pm could not be properly examined.

After a lengthy campaign, the Hillsborough Independent Panel was set up to examine papers surrounding the case. The Panel eventually found that the police orchestrated a cover-up, falsified documents and blamed innocent supporters. Sadly it found 41 fans could have been saved and the report clears supporters of any wrongdoing or blame for the disaster.

A new inquest was ordered and, after two years of evidence, it found that all 96 fans were unlawfully killed. This time fans were not to blame for their behaviour but police failures, stadium design faults and a delayed response from the ambulance services instead were all blamed. Clearly, the first findings were not accurate.

Activity

Produce a timeline of the Hillsborough Inquiry. Make sure you include the criminal charges brought against the police match commander, David Duckenfield, in June 2017.

Key term

Accidental death: A verdict at an inquest given where a death is considered to be as a result of an accident.

The Sun's reporting of the disaster.

Law reports

With so many cases being heard every year, there has to be some way that the lawyers/judges can find out which decisions they must follow. To make sure that this is achieved, a comprehensive system of law reporting has been established. In cases decided in the superior courts, the judgment is written down and published in law reports, for example the All England Law Reports and the Weekly Law Reports. There is also an online database of law reports called Lexis.

You can find these in a university law library and consider them for their validity.

AC3.2 DRAW CONCLUSIONS FROM INFORMATION

ASSESSMENT CRITERION	MARK BAND 1	MARK BAND 2	MARK BAND 3
AC3.2 You should be able to … Draw conclusions from information	Draws conclusions on criminal cases Conclusions may be mainly subjective, with limited evidence used in support **(1–5)**	Draws some objective conclusions on criminal cases, using some evidence and reasoning in support of conclusions **(6–10)**	Draws objective conclusions on criminal cases (including reference to the brief), using evidence and clear reasoning/argument in support of conclusions **(11–15)**

CONTENT	AMPLIFICATION
Conclusions • just verdicts • miscarriage • safe verdict • just sentencing	You should develop skills to analyse information, in order to draw conclusions based on reasoned evidence In your controlled assessment response, you should make reference to the assignment brief and other examples you have studied

Handy hints !

Make sure you consider a range of information. A common mistake is to rely solely on the brief and draw conclusions only from that. However, you should also include other case verdicts and miscarriages of justice. To ensure the top mark band being awarded also include conclusions about sentencing.

Just verdicts

There are approximately 130,000 criminal cases held before the Crown Court every year, and the vast majority are decided appropriately and in accordance with the legal rules and evidence available at that time. Sometimes justice is swift but on other occasions it can takes years for defendants to be brought to justice. The case of Stephen Lawrence took over 18 years for a conviction to take place, he was murdered on 22 April 1993 and two defendants were convicted of his murder on 3 January 2012.

CASE STUDY

STEPHEN LAWRENCE

The murder of this young man and the subsequent police investigation revealed many conclusions suggesting that the police were both racist and incompetent. The following points are noteworthy:

The case of Stephen Lawrence took over 18 years to secure justice.

- There was a lack of first aid at the scene by the five police officers.
- Full information was never given to his family.
- The Macpherson Report (1999) said there was institutional racism in the police force.
- The HOLMES computer system was inadequate, with a lack of trained officers who could use the system and this resulted in a loss of information.
- Internal police review supported the initial enquiry and was considered to be a 'whitewash'.
- The initial officer in charge was temporary; he lacked urgency and was often inactive on the case.
- During a 'no comment' interview of a suspect only seven questions were asked about the murder.
- Information on weapons being under the floorboards of a suspect's house was not given to the search team.
- The initial investigation was again reviewed and 28 failings of the police were found.
- Police received 22 firm leads about the suspects being a group of five white men but no prosecution followed from them.
- A video showing four out of the five suspects being racist and violent with a knife was played to the Stephen Lawrence Public Inquiry in 1998. The video was shot with a secret police surveillance camera and shows the youths brandishing a variety of long-bladed knives. One of the men is seen acting out the same over-arm bowling, stabbing movement used to inflict one of the wounds on Stephen Lawrence.

As a result of the family's campaign for justice and the critical Macpherson Report (1999), the Race Relations Amendment Act 2000 was passed, which imposed a duty on public bodies, such as the police, to promote equality. In addition, this case also helped bring about the abolition of the double jeopardy law, in the Criminal Justice Act 2003, which enables suspects to be charged twice for the same crime.

Miscarriage of justice

A miscarriage of justice involves the conviction and subsequent punishment of a person for a crime that they did not commit. The most notorious cases often involve the person having served a lengthy jail sentence.

There have been numerous miscarriages of justice within our legal system; thankfully, the following are examples of cases that have resulted in the quashing of a wrongful conviction. Can you draw conclusions from these examples?

Stefan Kiszko

Stefan Kiszko spent 16 years in prison after he was arrested and convicted of a sex attack and murder of a young girl. He did sign a confession, without a lawyer being present, as he believed he would then be allowed to return to his mother. The confession was later withdrawn and he stated that the police had bullied him into signing it. His mother campaigned for his release for many years and eventually, at an appeal hearing, three appeal court judges heard scientific evidence to the effect that he was physically unable to produce semen. His conviction was quashed in 1992. Sadly, he died a year after his release from prison due to a heart attack.

Six months after Stefan Kiszko passed away, his mother also died.

Timothy Evans

Timothy Evans was a tenant at 10 Rillington Place, along with John Christie. Despite Christie killing both Evans' wife and child, it was Evans who was hung for the murders in 1950. However, Christie's killings were later discovered and he confessed to killing seven people. He was hanged in 1953. This was one of the cases that helped change the policy on capital punishment.

Stephen Downing

Stephen Downing spent 27 years in prison for a murder he did not commit. He worked at a cemetery and, in 1973, found Wendy Sewell who had been sexually assaulted and beaten with a pickaxe handle. She died two days later and after being interviewed by the police, without a solicitor, Stephen confessed to the murder. However, he had a reading age of only 11 years and later retracted the confession. He protested his innocence throughout his time in prison. A campaign to seek his release was headed by a local journalist and, in 2001, Downing was released pending an appeal case. He was later cleared of the murder in 2002 with the Court of Appeal stating that his conviction was unsafe.

Sean Hodgson

Sean Hodgson was wrongly jailed, in 1979, for a murder he did not commit and spent 27 years in prison. While he confessed to the murder it was known that he had mental health issues and was a pathological liar. However, his conviction was quashed in 2009 after advances in DNA testing showed he was innocent. He died three years after his release.

Handy hints !

Make sure that you consider case verdicts other than the case in the brief, otherwise your mark will be restricted to mark band 1.

Handy hints !

What conclusions did you draw? Perhaps that miscarriages of justice do still happen, and that at times they can take a very long time to put right. Try to develop these conclusions in the controlled assessment.

Just sentencing

As with the number of convictions in criminal cases, the vast majority of the sentences provided are appropriate and bring about justice. However, there are times when sentencing appears to be unfair or unduly lenient. In such a situation it is possible for anyone to ask the Attorney General to seek an appeal against this type of sentence. Introduced by the Criminal Justice Act 1988, the scheme covers offences such as:

• murder

• rape

• robbery

• serious drug offences

• a range of terrorist offences (introduced in July 2017).

The scheme operates if the sentence 'falls outside the range of sentences which the judge, applying his mind to all the relevant factors, could reasonably consider appropriate'.

In 2016, 41 prison sentences were increased in England and Wales under the Unduly Lenient Sentence scheme. This represents a 17% rise from the previous year.

Examples of unduly lenient sentences include:

• In 2017, Ian Paterson, the surgeon who performed unnecessary breast operations and made healthy patients believe they had cancer, had his sentence increased from 15 to 20 years.

• Rhys Hobbs had his prison sentence increased from eight years to 12 and a half years, for killing his former girlfriend, in 2016, in a 'violent and protracted way'.

• Stuart Hall, a former BBC presenter, was jailed for 15 months following the conviction of a series of sexual assaults. However, in 2013 his sentence almost doubled to 30 months when the judge confirmed the original sentence was unduly lenient given the impact on the victims.

Handy hints

In the controlled assessment consider whether a miscarriage of justice may have occurred. Consider all the ACs and whether the law and procedures may been fairly applied. For example:

(i) Has any evidence been contaminated?

(ii) Have all the personnel, including the jury, involved in the investigation acted with integrity and by the rules?

(iii) Has there been a trial by media?

Take it further

Are sentences too lenient? You be the judge by deciding the sentences for yourself. Look at the 'You be the Judge' website and compare your sentence with what was actually given: http://ybtj.justice.gov.uk.

UNIT SUMMARY

By working through this unit:

• You will be able to assess the use of laypeople in determining the fate of a suspect, and evaluate the criminal trial process from crime scene to court room.

• You will have gained the skills to review criminal cases, evaluating the evidence in the cases to determine whether the verdict is safe and just.

UNIT 4
CRIME AND PUNISHMENT

In this unit you will develop skills in order to evaluate the effectiveness of the process of social control in delivering policy in practice. There is a focus on agencies in the criminal justice system such as the police, Crown Prosecution Service, probation and prisons.

You will focus on their role, limitations and effectiveness. There will also be the opportunity to consider pressure groups and charities and the role they play in achieving social control. You will discover the way our laws are made as well as studying the methods used by society to bring about social control.

Assessment: 1 hour 30 minutes external exam

Synoptic links: Units 1, 2 and 3

LEARNING OUTCOME 1
UNDERSTANDING THE CRIMINAL JUSTICE SYSTEM IN ENGLAND AND WALES

AC1.1 DESCRIBE PROCESSES USED FOR LAW MAKING

ASSESSMENT CRITERION	CONTENT	AMPLIFICATION
AC1.1 You should be able to … Describe processes used for law making	**Processes** • government processes • judicial processes	You should have knowledge of the legislative process and the role of judges in making criminal law

Synoptic links

You should relate this AC to the review of verdicts in criminal cases in Unit 3 and campaigns and changes in policy learned in Unit 1. In Unit 1 you learned that campaigns can result in changes in the law by parliament passing acts that bring in new laws. For example, the campaign fronted by Ann Ming to abolish the double jeopardy law for serious offences resulted in the passing of the Criminal Justice Act 2003.

In Unit 3 you learned that if cases are appealed, especially on a point of law, it is possible for judicial law making to take place. For instance, in the case of *R* v *R* the judicial ruling ensured that marital rape was a criminal offence.

The Houses of Parliament are also known as the Palace of Westminster.

Government processes

The majority of the law in England and Wales is made in Parliament by a process of consultation, debate and voting.

When a new law is considered, there is public consultation in the form of a Green Paper. From this a White Paper with formal proposals for reform is produced. This allows a draft act called a Bill to be presented to Parliament.

It begins its journey in one of the houses – it can be either of the houses unless it is a finance bill, which must start in the House of Commons – and follows a number of stages:

- **First reading:** where the name of the Bill and its main aims are read out and a formal vote is taken.
- **Second reading:** the main debate takes place followed by another vote.
- **Committee stage:** a chosen group of representatives look closely at the Bill to address any issues and suggest appropriate amendments.
- **Report stage:** the Committee report back to the full House who then vote on the proposed amendments.
- **Third reading:** the final vote on the Bill.
- All of the above stages are repeated in the other house.
- **Royal assent:** the Monarch signs the Bill. She cannot refuse as it is now only a symbolic stage as the Head of State.
- The Bill then becomes an **Act of Parliament** and the commencement date is given.

Key term

Parliament: Made up of three parts. Firstly, the House of Commons, the elected representatives, or members of Parliament, voted by the people in an election. Secondly, the House of Lords, which still contains some hereditary peers (Lords) and now many lifetime appointed peers who do not pass on their title after death. For example, Sir Alan Sugar, Baroness Doreen Lawrence (Stephen Lawrence's mother) and Sir John Prescott. Lastly, the Monarch, who provides approval to the finalised Bill.

Exam question Unit 4 2017

Outline the process used by the government for making
laws such as the Theft Act 1968. **[3 marks]**

The public's response to a change in the law is collected through a Green Paper followed by firm proposals in a White Paper. A Bill is then presented to Parliament and it follows a series of stages such as the first and second readings in both the House of Commons and House of Lords. The Bill may be amended before it is voted upon by Parliament and then given the Royal Assent by the Monarch.

Assessment

Up to 3 marks could be awarded to this answer.

This answer correctly explains the procedure for government law making and uses technical terms such as White Paper and House of Commons. In addition, it doesn't go into unnecessary detail of all the stages, as only 3 marks are available and the question asks for a brief outline of the process.

Judicial processes

Judicial precedent

Judicial law making or judicial precedent is law made by judges in the courts. When a case appears before them they must make a judgment and this forms the law. It must be followed in future similar cases. This can be seen in the following examples:

A judge can make law.

Donoghue v *Stevenson* (1932)

Two friends visited a cafe and one drank a bottle of ginger beer that had the remains of a decomposing snail in it. The woman fell ill and sued the manufacturer. She won her case. The court decided a duty of care was owed by the manufacturer to the woman. Known as the 'neighbour principle', this case founded the modern-day law of negligence.

Daniels v *White* (1938)

The claimant bought a bottle of lemonade and when it was drunk he felt a burning reaction in his throat. The lemonade was found to have corrosive metal in it. The case of *Donoghue* v *Stevenson* was used when suing for compensation even though the facts were slightly different. It was sufficiently similar for the purpose of precedent.

Judges need to apply the law consistently and use the same principles in similar cases. The law must be common in all cases and hence it became known as common law; that is, judge-made law. As there are several courts there is a hierarchy and lower courts must abide by the decisions from higher courts.

There are several options for not following a past decision if deemed appropriate, such as distinguishing or overruling. However, this is only permitted by the very senior courts such as the Supreme Court. When there is no precedent the judge must make a decision and give an original precedent.

Statutory interpretation

An alternative way a judge can make law is through statutory interpretation. This is where judges in the superior courts such as the Court of Appeal and Supreme Court are sometimes called upon to interpret words and phrases within a statute. They have various rules and aids to help them do this and have the ability to interpret in the way they see fit. Once again this could be seen as creating laws by the judiciary. For example, in the case of *Whiteley* v *Chappell* (1868) the defendant was charged with an offence of impersonating any person entitled to vote. The defendant had pretended to be a person who was on the voters' list, but that person had died. The court held the defendant was not guilty since a dead person is not 'entitled to vote'.

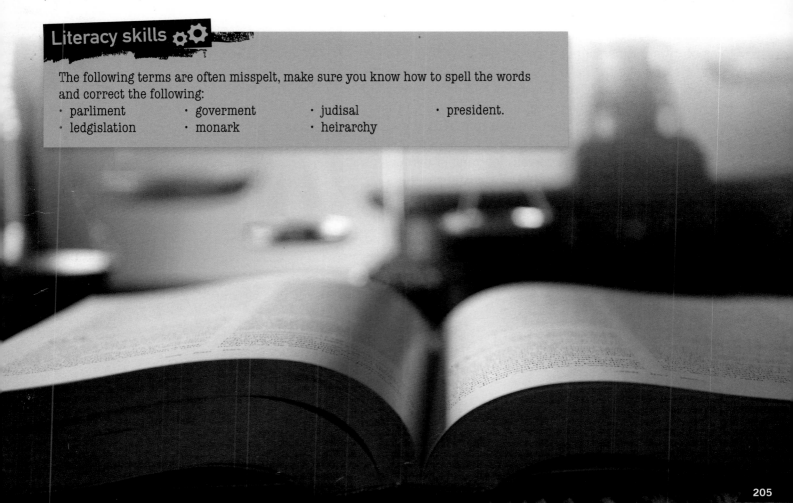

Literacy skills ⚙️⚙️

The following terms are often misspelt, make sure you know how to spell the words and correct the following:

- parliment
- goverment
- judisal
- president.
- ledgislation
- monark
- heirarchy

AC1.2 DESCRIBE THE ORGANISATION OF THE CRIMINAL JUSTICE SYSTEM IN ENGLAND AND WALES

ASSESSMENT CRITERION	CONTENT	AMPLIFICATION
AC1.2 You should be able to … Describe the organisation of the criminal justice system in England and Wales	**Criminal justice system** • police • law creation • courts • formal punishment • relationships	You should have knowledge of the organisation and role of the agencies involved in criminal justice You should also consider the relationships between different agencies and the extent of cooperation that exists

Synoptic links

You should draw on your learning in Unit 3 regarding the process taken to obtain verdicts in criminal cases, and the roles of different personnel and agencies involved. Start at the arrest stage by the police and reflect on the process through investigation to the court proceedings and beyond to a conviction and management of an offender. All these agencies have a connection and a role to play in the justice system. Think about where they connect and work together. You can also draw on your learning of campaigns and changes in policy from Unit 1. For instance, the police played a key role in the campaign for Sarah's law, working with probation services and the prison service to manage the list of child sex offenders.

The relationship between the agencies in the criminal justice system

AREA OF CRIMINAL JUSTICE SYSTEM	RELATIONSHIP WITH OTHER ORGANISATIONS
Police	Work with the courts to ensure defendants, in custody, are brought before them.
	Often give evidence in court.
	Work with probation in the management of an offender.
	Work closely with the CPS in the charging and prosecution of offenders.
Ministry of Justice	Oversees the work of: • HM Courts and Tribunals Service • probation services • prison systems.
HM Courts and Tribunals Service	Contributes, by the judiciary, to law creation through judicial precedent and statutory interpretation.
	Liaison with the police/independent security firms and prisons to ensure safe delivery of prisoners to court.
	Arrangements of video links if a prisoner is not to attend court for a hearing.
	Prisoners held in court cells pending their court hearing and return to prison.
Crown Prosecution Service	Advise the police on charging a suspect.
	Appear in the courts to conduct the advocacy of a case.
HM Prison Service	Lawyers may seek visits to prisons for legal consultations.
	It is the judge who sets a term of imprisonment, including the length, type and whether it is concurrent or consecutive.
	Those defendants who have been denied bail by the police or courts will be remanded to prison.
	Work with probation services when a prisoner is to be released.
National Probation Service	Police will arrest a prisoner recalled while on probation and ensure return to prison.
	Liaison and preparation between agencies when prisoners are released.
	Overseeing prisoner once released if on licence or parole.
	Liaison with police should there be any issues and recall to prison if appropriate.
	Overseeing all prisoners who have served a sentence of up to two years, and released on licence for a minimum of 12 months.

AREA OF CRIMINAL JUSTICE SYSTEM	RELATIONSHIP WITH OTHER ORGANISATIONS
Sentencing Council	Works with the judiciary and other legal professionals to produce guidelines on sentencing.
Campaigns for change	Can liaise with various agencies for support to enable change to be effective.
	Sarah's law: worked with police on child sex offender disclosure scheme.
	Bobby Turnbull's campaign for a change in the gun licensing laws also liaised with the police.
	The Prison Reform Trust works with prisons and other agencies to improve the penal system.

Summary of the criminal justice system procedure

Law creation: criminal law is made in parliament.

▼

Police enforce the law that is made by investigating breaches of the criminal law. They will arrest a suspect and use their powers of detention and interview.

▼

Crown Prosecution Service: will advise the police on the appropriate charge.

▼

Suspect brought before the court: all cases start in the magistrates' court and around 5% go to the Crown Court.

▼

Defendant released on bail or remanded into custody.

▼

A guilty plea results in sentencing or a plea of not guilty results in a trial. A trial will include witnesses giving evidence. A bench of magistrates or a jury decide the verdict.

▼

If convicted, formal punishment is given by the magistrates or a judge. The Sentencing Council provides guidelines to assist the courts. If a custodial sentence is given the defendant is sent to prison.

▼

HM Prison Service oversees the welfare of prisoners. HM Inspectorate of Prisons is an independent body that reports on the conditions and treatment of those in prisons.

▼

When released from prison a prisoner is usually on licence and is subject to supervision by the probation service. Any breach may result in a return to prison.

Activity

Plan a visit to your local magistrates' court. Consider contacting the local branch of the Magistrates' Association which may provide a tour and talk to enhance your visit, as part of their project 'Magistrates in the Community'.

Example questions

Questions in this area are as follows:

Unit 4 2017
Describe the relationship of the prison service with other agencies in the criminal justice system. **[7 marks]**

NOTE that from 2020 the changes in the mark bands would mean that this question would be out of either 6 or 9 marks.

Unit 4 2018
Describe relationships between the police, the Crown Prosecution Service and the courts as a case proceeds through the criminal justice system. **[6 marks]**

Unit 4 2019
Analyse the relationship between the Probation Service and other agencies in the criminal justice system. **[8 marks]**

NOTE that from 2020 the changes in the mark bands would mean that this question would be out of either 6 or 9 marks.

Exam question Unit 4 2017

Describe the relationship of the prison service with other agencies in the criminal justice system. **[7 marks]**

NOTE that from 2020 the changes in the mark bands would mean that this question would be out of either 6 or 9 marks.

The prison service has a relationship with many other agencies in the criminal justice system. One of these is the police, as prisons hold people who have been remanded into custody and denied bail by the police and the courts. The CPS liaise with prisons to request a prisoner's appearance in court or over video link. The judiciary are the ones that send people to prison and keep prison as a sentencing option. Probation services have a relationship, as if a person fails to keep their conditions, for example not turning up for appointments, the person may be sent to prison to serve the remainder of their sentence. The government creates legislation regarding prisons and often inspects them ensuring all rights, etc. are maintained.

Assessment

If out of 6 marks (the new mark band) this answer would be in mark band 5–6 because there is a clear and detailed focus on the question, with mainly accurate support and an effective use of specialist vocabulary. The demands of the question are fully addressed.

The positive points in this answer are that several agencies are mentioned in it, with an attempt at explaining the connection between them and the prison service. The answer maintains the focus of the prison service throughout and uses some technical language such as judiciary, legislation and remanded into custody.

The answer could be improved with further detail, for instance: all prisoners who have served up to two years and are released on licence will be subject to a minimum of 12 months' supervision by the National Probation Service. If there are breaches of probation the police will arrest and return the person to court where they face a return to prison. It is the HM Inspectorate of Prisons who reports on conditions and treatment of those in prisons.

The prison service has a professional relationship with many other organisations in the criminal justice system.

Activity

Take a virtual tour of HMP Holloway, http://hollowayprisonconsultation.co.uk/site-visit-virtual-tour/.

Activity

In pairs spend three minutes creating a poster of relationships between different agencies in the criminal justice system. After this time, pass the poster on to the next pair for them to increase the detail. Continue in this fashion until all the posters are complete.

AC1.3 DESCRIBE MODELS OF CRIMINAL JUSTICE

ASSESSMENT CRITERION	CONTENT	AMPLIFICATION
AC1.3 You should be able to … Describe models of criminal justice	**Models of criminal justice** • due process • crime control	You should be able to describe the theories of the two models of criminal justice

Synoptic links

You will draw on your understanding of criminological theories in Unit 2 and on the review of criminal verdicts in Unit 3 to gain awareness of the application of these models. For instance, you should be able to apply right and left realism approaches to explaining crime to the two models. In addition, you can consider which cases are dealt with using the principles in each of the models. Consider the case of Colin Stagg; it could be argued that the most important aspect of the police investigation was to secure a conviction of Stagg. Even when the case against him was dismissed, the police indicated that they would not be looking for any other person. This comment and the 'Lizzie' honey-trap are arguably evidence of the crime control method.

Herbert Packer (1968), a Stanford University law professor, constructed two models to represent the two competing systems of values operating within criminal justice. These models are:

• crime control

• due process.

Both are ways of applying justice, as they see it, to deal with crime.

CRIMINAL JUSTICE

Due process model

This model is the opposite of crime control. It focuses on the presumption of innocence and the necessity of producing fairness by protecting the defendant's legal rights. Rather than an increase in police powers, it asserts that police should be limited to prevent official oppression of the individual. The justice system should safeguard all the rights of an individual to provide against a wrongful conviction. Justice should involve a thorough investigation, where there is protection of the innocent by legislative obstacles to overcome before a conviction can occur. This helps to ensure a correct and just verdict can be reached. It relates to the left realism approach to criminality, with a focus on the inequalities created by a capitalist society. A more equal and caring society would eventually eliminate crime.

Examples of areas of law that support the due process model

- The acknowledgement of the need for police procedural safeguards by the introduction of the Police and Criminal Evidence Act (PACE) 1984.
- All interviews are now recorded and suspects have the right to legal representation.
- The Human Rights Act 1998 allows for criminal justice practices to be thoroughly looked at from a human rights perspective.

Examples of cases investigated using the due process model

- Siôn Jenkins
- Garry Weddell
- *Thompson* v *UK*
- *Venables* v *UK*.

The above cases are examples of where the defendant has been given their statutory legal rights. For instance, that of the right to appeal against a conviction thus allowing a retrial (Siôn Jenkins). Or the exercise of the presumption of bail, even to a charge of murder, prior to conviction (Garry Weddell). Also, to ensure a trial was fair, the use of human rights using the European Convention on Human Rights (Thompson and Venables, the killers of James Bulger).

The due process model uses principles that are opposite to the crime control model and promotes the presumption of innocent until proven guilty.

Crime control model

The crime control model seeks a quick and efficient disposal of criminal cases, similar to an assembly line or conveyor belt. The aim is to punish criminals and stop them committing further crimes. The focus of protecting rights falls on the rights of victims rather than defendants. It would also include the assertion that the police should have enhanced powers to ensure a conviction is achieved. It can link to the zero tolerance approach found in right realism. It does not address the causes of crime nor that crime can be deterred through detection and conviction.

Examples of areas of law that support the crime control model

- Allowing the introduction of 'bad character' evidence and previous convictions information for the courts to consider when deliberating a verdict.
- The removal of the 'double jeopardy' rule for murder and other serious offences.
- The extended pre-charge detention time for terrorist offences.

Examples of cases investigated using the crime control model

Colin Stagg and Barry George

Arguably, the key focus in both these cases is on securing a conviction at any cost. Each victim's murder provoked strong public reaction and a demand for the case to be solved as quickly as possible. In both cases the police felt sure that the suspect was guilty and used all measures available, including undercover police surveillance, to produce evidence of guilt.

The focus of crime control justice is to produce a swift verdict.

Example questions

Exam questions in this area:

Unit 4 2017
Describe two models of criminal justice. [4 marks]

Unit 4 2018
Describe how one model of criminal justice could apply
to Colin's case. [6 marks]

Unit 4 2019
Describe the crime control model of criminal justice referred
to by Sarah's lawyer. [4 marks]

Exam question Unit 4 2017

Describe two models of justice. [4 marks]

The crime control model promotes justice within the system and can be described as a conveyor belt as it wants cases to get through quickly and convict offenders at the first possible opportunity. It promotes victims' rights and takes a right realist zero tolerance approach.

The due process model can also be described as an obstacle course. It prioritises the rights of the defendant to ensure that innocent people are acquitted and only the guilty are convicted. It has hoops that must be jumped through before a verdict is reached. The subject is innocent until proven guilty. It links to a left realist's approach to justice.

Assessment

Mark band 3–4.

This answer accurately explains each model, showing the differences between the two. It also uses some specialist terminology such as right and left realism. It could be enhanced with examples of both areas of law and relevant cases.

Tip

Always try to include examples to help describe the two models of justice. This could be details of an area of law or a criminal case.

Take it further

Can you create two different scenarios, each one focusing on one of the models? Consider how the police and courts system could behave in each scenario.

UNDERSTAND THE ROLE OF PUNISHMENT IN A CRIMINAL JUSTICE SYSTEM

AC2.1 EXPLAIN FORMS OF SOCIAL CONTROL

ASSESSMENT CRITERION	CONTENT	AMPLIFICATION
AC2.1 You should be able to … Explain forms of social control	**Forms of social control** Internal forms • rational ideology • tradition • internalisation of social rules and morality External forms • coercion • fear of punishment Control theory • reasons for abiding by the law	You should have an understanding of different forms of social control with reference to theory

Synoptic links

You will need to relate your understanding to theoretical knowledge acquired through Unit 2. You should also be able to apply your understanding to situations studied in Units 1, 2 and 3.

Key terms

Forms: Types, ideas, theories, ways of, methods.

Social: Society, public, community, collective, common, shared, group.

Control: Regulate, govern, manage, organise.

The term social control refers to any strategies for preventing deviant human behaviour. We encourage everyone in society to conform to the law and any course of action that helps to achieve this is a form of social control. It is action that tries to persuade or compel members of society to conform to the rules.

Internal forms of social control

Ask yourself why do you not steal things?

You will probably respond by saying things such as 'because it is wrong', or 'I have been brought up not to'. It is your conscience telling you it is wrong. We conform to rules because our sense of self-respect demands it, this process of social control is internal.

Internal forms of social control regulate our own behaviour in accordance with the accepted form.

Your conscience is a form of internal control.

Rational ideology

This is an idea or belief to achieve social control. Your conscience, with feelings of guilt, anxiety or worry from within, guides you to reach a solution or follow laws and rules.

Tradition

It may be you own traditions, customs or norms that ensure you conform to the rules. Sometimes religion or culture or purely your upbringing ensures that you do not break the law, for instance not eating red meat on Good Friday.

 **Activity**

Discuss in pairs the traditions in your families. How do they differ?

Internalisation of social rules and morality

The internalisation of social rules and morality is working out what is the right thing to do and therefore knowing what is right or wrong based upon social values. For example, not eating all the biscuits but leaving some for others. Or not queue jumping but waiting in line for your turn and not cheating in an exam.

Cheating in an exam is not the right thing to do.

External forms of social control

External pressures persuade or compel members of society to conform to the rules. For example, your teachers may set detention or extra work if you fail to hand in homework. They are trying to ensure you do not do it again.

Have your parents or guardian ever grounded you or taken your mobile phone away from you when you have broken their rules? This would be an example of external control to make you follow the rules.

Police presence alone can ensure people conform.

The most obvious and visible form of external social control is exercised by people and organisations specifically empowered to enforce conformity to society's laws. Police officers, judges and prisons are the most evident agents of external social control. The mere presence of the police may ensure the vast majority of people behave. However, those who commit crimes are arrested by the police. Under the Police and Criminal Evidence Act (PACE) 1984 the police have powers of detention and interview. If you face charges then other organisations such as the courts and ultimately prisons will try to bring about control. They will use both coercion and fear of punishment as methods to ensure people abide by the law.

Key term

Coercion: The use of force to achieve a desired end.

Coercion

Coercion may be physical or non-violent. Physical coercion may take the form of bodily injury, imprisonment and in some countries the death penalty. Non-violent coercion consists of a strike, boycott and non-cooperation. Prisons clearly use coercion and the threat of loss of liberty. This can be seen in a suspended sentence with the continued threat of custody for future breaking of the law.

Coercion is used by external agencies to seek social control.

Fear of punishment

The use of punishment as a threat to stop people from offending is called deterrence. Deterrence has two key assumptions:

- individual deterrence
- general deterrence.

Fear of imprisonment can be a deterrence.

Individual deterrence

Individual deterrence is punishment imposed on offenders in order to deter or prevent them from committing further crimes. For example, a suspended prison sentence or conditional discharge, where there are other, more serious, consequences for further offending.

General deterrence

General deterrence is the fear of punishment that prevents others from committing similar crimes. For example, a lengthy prison sentence or heavy financial penalty allows others to see the potential consequence and are deterred from committing the same action. There are policies that promote this that are known as 'getting tough on crime'. These policies include:

- **'mandatory minimums':** a life sentence for murder; seven years for a third drug offence; three years for a third burglary
- **'three strikes and you're out':** third conviction for a violent crime, likely to be life sentence (the USA).

Control theory

Control theories try to explain why people do not commit crimes. They support the view that people require nurturing in order to develop attachments or bonds that are key in producing internal controls, such as conscience. According to this view, crime is the result of insufficient attachment and commitment to others.

Think theory

WALTER C. RECKLESS

Reckless developed one version of control theory, known as containment. He argued that we can resist committing crimes due to inner and outer containment:
- Inner containment comes from our upbringing and particularly the influence from our family.
- Outer containment refers to the influence of social groups, including the laws of the society in which we live.
- A combination of internal psychological containments and external social containments prevents people from deviating from social norms and committing crimes.

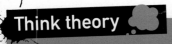

Think theory

TRAVIS HIRSCHI

Hirschi believed that people must form social bonds to prevent criminal behaviour. He stated there are four bonds, namely attachment, commitment, involvement and belief, and these must be properly formed to prevent a person having a propensity to commit crime.

Hirschi's research claimed that positive attachment to parents, school and a peer group was important to promote pro-social behaviour. In addition, commitment to accomplishing future positive goals such as a good job and nice house, etc. was needed. Alongside these an involvement with some social activity such as playing in a sports team or belonging to a community group is needed to prevent criminal activity. Finally, what is also needed to ensure people conform to society's rules is a belief in society's values such as honesty and believing committing crime is wrong.

Exam question Unit 4 2017

Using examples, explain what is meant by internal social control.

[4 marks]

Internal forms of social control are what motivate us not to commit crimes. But these are not written rules but things that we believe because of the way we have been brought up. For example, family ties help people not to commit crimes as they are attachments. Also, if you have many interests you concentrate on them and therefore not crime. For example, you may belong to a community group. Belief is another example.

Assessment

Mark band 3–4.

This response demonstrates the idea of internal control by linking it to family influence. It touches upon the control theory by using terminology such as attachments, interests and beliefs. However, to achieve full marks there needs to be a development of the examples. For instance, our parents may tell us it is wrong to steal and punish us if we do. Or a conscious belief that it is wrong to steal and that we should abide by society's rules.

AC2.2 DISCUSS THE AIMS OF PUNISHMENT

ASSESSMENT CRITERION	CONTENT	AMPLIFICATION

AC2.2 You should be able to …
 	
 Discuss the aims of punishment
	Aims of punishment
	 • retribution
	 • rehabilitation
	 • deterrence
	   • prevention of reoffending
	   • deterrence of others from committing similar crimes
	 • public protection
	 • reparation
		You should be able to explain each of the aims of punishment

Synoptic links

You should be able to consider these aims in the context of the criminological theories learned in Unit 1. We will consider this connection under each of the aims.

Aims of sentencing

The aims of sentencing are contained in section 42 of the Criminal Justice Act 2003, which defines the purposes of sentencing as:

a. the punishment of offenders

b. the reduction of crime (including by deterrence)

c. the reform and rehabilitation of offenders

d. the protection of the public, and

e. the making of reparation by offenders to persons affected by their offences.

Retribution

Retribution is a major aim of punishment:

- Based on the idea that the offender deserves punishment.
- The punishment can be seen as a display of public revulsion for the offence.
- Contains an element of revenge, in that society and the victim are being avenged for the wrong done. For instance, the death penalty can be seen to fulfil the biblical expression of 'an eye for an eye, a tooth for a tooth, a life for a life'.
- Provides a compensating measure of justice to someone who has committed murder.
- Does not seek to alter future behaviour, merely to inflict punishment in proportion to the offence.
- Provides an appropriate punishment to provide justice for both the defendant and the victim.
- Can be expressed as a defendant getting their 'just desserts', which defines justice in terms of fairness and proportionality.
- Supported by the Sentencing Council, which provides guidelines for the courts on the range of appropriate punishments that are available.

According to the Coroners and Justice Act 2009, a court must follow guidelines unless it is against the interests of justice to do so.

> **Key term**
>
> **Retribution:** Aiming to punish an offender to the level that is deserved.

Activity

Research cases dealt with in your local court. Consider the aim of the sentences provided.

The guidelines for an offence of theft are as in the following table:

HARM	CULPABILITY A	CULPABILITY B	CULPABILITY C
Category 1 Very high-value goods stolen (above £100,000) or high value with significant additional harm to the victim or others	Starting point three years six months' custody Category range two years six months'–six years' custody	Starting point two years' custody Category range one–three years six months' custody	Starting point one year's custody Category range 26 weeks'–two years' custody
Category 2 High-value goods stolen (£10,000 to £100,000) with no significant additional harm, or medium value with significant additional harm to the victim or other people	Starting point two years' custody Category range one–three years six months' custody	Starting point one year's custody Category range 26 weeks'–two years' custody	Starting point high-level community order Category range low-level community order–36 weeks' custody
Category 3 Medium-value goods stolen (£500 to £10,000) and no significant additional harm or low-value with significant additional harm to the victim or others	Starting point one year's custody Category range 26 weeks'–two years' custody	Starting point high-level community order Category range low-level community order–36 weeks' custody	Starting point Band C fine Category range Band B fine–low-level community order
Category 4 Low-value goods stolen (up to £500) and little or no significant additional harm to the victim or others	Starting point high-level community order Category range medium-level community order–36 weeks' custody	Starting point low-level community order Category range Band C fine–medium-level community order	Starting point Band B fine Category range discharge Band C fine

Retribution is a backwards-looking theory of punishment. It looks to the past to determine what to do in the present. Examples of punishments that clearly contain retribution include the mandatory life sentence for murder and increased punishment for crimes with a hate motive.

LIFE SENTENCE

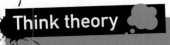

Think theory

A right realist approach would consider retribution as a fitting method of punishment. This is because it ensures the defendant is being punished to an appropriate level without consideration of the reasoning behind the crime or prevention of future offending.

Rehabilitation

The aim of rehabilitation is to reform offenders and reintroduce them into society. Unlike retribution it is a forwards-looking aim with a hope that the offenders' behaviour will be altered and they will not reoffend. Also known as reformation, this aim presumes that criminal behaviour is a result of free will and rational choice. In other words, it is caused by factors that the defendant can actually do something about.

The aim of rehabilitation can be seen in community sentences. Probation orders, for instance, could involve unpaid work or completion of an education or training course, and treatment for addictions such as alcohol or drugs. This may aid rehabilitation. The abuse of drugs causes many crimes and there have been punishments introduced to help rehabilitate the offenders. For example, the Drug Treatment and Testing Order, which provides supervision on work on drug use.

Think theory

Individualistic theories of criminality would support rehabilitation as an aim of punishment. For instance, behaviour modifications treatment such as anger management courses focus on techniques to extinguish undesirable behaviours and promote desirable ones.

Key terms

Rehabilitation: Aiming to alter the offender's mindset so that future reoffending can be prevented.

Reformation: To reform or rehabilitate.

Community sentence: A punishment from a court that involves activities carried out in the community.

Probation order: A punishment from a court where you serve your sentence in the community. While on probation, you may have to do unpaid work, complete an education or training course, get treatment for additions, such as drugs or alcohol, and have regular meetings with an 'offender manager'.

Rehabilitation may reduce crime.

Deterrence

Deterrence can be either individual in respect of the offender, or general with regards to society as a whole.

Key term

Deterrence: Aims to dissuade the offender, or anyone in society, from committing crime by a fear of punishment.

Individual deterrence

The aim of individual deterrence is to ensure that the offender does not reoffend. A suspended sentence is clearly an example of individual deterrence, as the term of imprisonment will only activate if further offending occurs. If there is no reoffending the offender will not go to prison. Hence, the expectation that the impact of losing your liberty will prevent future offending.

However, the recidivism rate would suggest that many prisoners are not deterred from committing crimes by the possibility of a term of imprisonment. According to the Bromley Briefings Prison Factfile Autumn 2017:

prison has a poor record for reducing reoffending as 46% of adults are reconvicted within one year of release. For those serving sentences of less than 12 months this increases to 59%. **(Prison Reform Trust, 2017b, page 14)**

Think theory

The above statistic may suggest that the social learning theory could account for criminality. Prisons are often classed as universities of crime so it may be that some offenders are learning how to commit more crime from fellow prisoners. The prevalent sub-culture such as a peer group is one of the main ways observational learning takes place.

General deterrence

The aim of general deterrence is to prevent potential offenders from committing a crime. However, often the impact of a sentence with a deterrent element is weakened by the fact that it relates to someone else. In addition, people are not always aware of the punishment that has been given by a court unless it is so severe that it is published by the media. This was seen in the harsh punishments given out during the 2011 London riot cases.

For example, two men, aged 21 and 22 years, were jailed for four years each after admitting using Facebook to incite disorder. However, no disorder took place as a result of their posts. Also a 23-year-old man was sentenced to six months in prison for stealing £3.50 worth of water.

Think theory

Marxists are likely to view criminality and the above punishments as inevitable given the capitalist society in which we live. The sentences given are a means to control the working class who are heavily policed in comparison to the upper classes.

Public protection or incapacitation

This is the idea that punishment must serve a useful purpose for society as a whole by protecting us from dangerous criminals. Sometimes it is referred to as incapacitation as the offender is prevented from exercising their freedom. A long prison sentence is an obvious example of incapacitation. However, other punishments will restrict an offender. Curfew orders restrict when people can leave their home. Sometimes these are supported by electronic tagging, which provides both incapacitation for the criminal and protection for society. Some states in the USA carry out castration of sex offenders and right hands have been cut off at the wrist as punishment for theft in Sharia-controlled areas of Nigeria and in Saudi Arabia.

Key term

Incapacitation: A sentence of the court to prevent further offending. This could include a term of imprisonment.

An electronic tag provides incapacitation.

Think theory

A right realist viewpoint may see the need to impose a sentence to protect the public, as social constraints on behaviour are weak. Stricter social control is needed to reduce crime and punishment, which restrict liberty and will help to achieve this.

Reparation

Reparation often involves compensating the victim of the crime, usually by ordering the offender to pay a sum of money to the victim. This concept also includes making reparation to society as a whole, for example doing unpaid work in the community through a community order.

There is also an increasing number of schemes that bring offenders and victims together, so offenders can make direct reparation. It can include writing a letter of apology, repairing any damage caused or meeting face to face to discuss the issues. This is known as restorative justice.

Reparation means paying back.

Think theory

The left realist approach may see such punishments as a way of providing practical measures to reduce crime and produce a long-term change to a more equal, caring society.

Key term

Reparation: Aims to ensure the defendant pays back to the victim or society for the wrongdoing.

Denunciation

Denunciation helps to reinforce the moral and ethical codes or boundary maintenance. These may have changed over time to what is acceptable within society. For example, smoking cigarettes was once acceptable and even encouraged by the medical profession. Now it is illegal in the workplace and in a motor vehicle with a child passenger.

Key term

Denunciation: Aims to show offenders that society disapproves of their behaviour and that it is unacceptable conduct.

Think theory

A functionalist approach to criminality would see social control as a means of achieving solidarity in society. The setting of boundaries of acceptability towards crime strengthens social cohesion or the willingness of members of society to cooperate with one another.

In addition, it could be argued that by labelling offenders as criminal it produces further crime, as they start to view themselves as criminals. This can lead to a self-fulfilling prophecy, which means that they start to internalise the label and start acting and behaving in a way that mirrors the label.

Tip

In the exam you may be asked to explain the aim(s) of a punishment referred to in a question scenario. You should consider all the aims that are appropriate. Make sure you make reference to:
- the defendant's situation
- type of offence
- how serious of its type it is.

Literacy skills

Correct the following spelling mistakes:
- dinnuncination
- retrobution
- repairation
- deterence
- residacism.

Activity

Research the case of the abduction of Shannon Matthews. The estate where she lived, The Moorside, saw the community come together and carry out searches and marches to show the boundaries that they felt to be appropriate in the case.

Take it further

Can you write your own scenario with an appropriate sentence given out by a court? Then swap with a friend and see if they can explain why the sentence was given and the aims that may be relevant.

AC2.3 ASSESS HOW FORMS OF PUNISHMENT MEET THE AIMS OF PUNISHMENT

ASSESSMENT CRITERION	CONTENT	AMPLIFICATION
AC2.3 You should be able to … Assess how forms of punishment meet the aims of punishment	**Forms of punishment** • imprisonment • community • financial • discharge	You should be able to assess how different forms of punishment meet the aims of punishment

Synoptic links

You should be able to draw on your learning developed in Units 1, 2 and 3 in order to make objective evidence based conclusions. In other words, make a decision on whether or not punishments work or achieve their aims.

A summary of punishments available:

Imprisonment	Mandatory and discretionary life sentences, fixed-term and indeterminate sentences, suspended sentences
Community sentences	Combination order, for example: • unpaid work • curfew • drug treatment and testing • supervision (probation)
Fines	Depend on financial circumstances of the offenders and seriousness of offences
Discharges	Conditional, where the defendant reoffends during a set period of time (up to three years), the courts can impose a different sentence Absolute, where no penalty is imposed as the defendant is guilty but morally blameless

Handy hints !

Read the Bromley Briefings Prison Factfile produced through the Prison Reform Trust (2016). It contains a great deal of information and statistics on prisons, the inmates and success of our penal system. It will help you make judgements about the system of social control.

All the data mentioned in this assessment criterion, unless otherwise stated, are from the Bromley Briefings Factfile (Prison Reform Trust, 2016).

Does imprisonment meet the aims of punishment?

A life sentence is the most serious punishment available to our courts. A mandatory life sentence applies to a murder conviction. However, other serious offences such as manslaughter, robbery and rape carry a discretionary life sentence.

People serving mandatory life sentences are spending more of their sentence in prison. On average, they spend 16 years in custody – up from 13 years in 2001. When released, 'lifers' continue to serve their sentence for the rest of their lives. They are subject to monitoring and restrictions and can be returned to custody at any point if they break the terms of their licence. From this it could be argued that retribution takes place with an offender being given their just desserts.

Prison is a form of external social control.

Activity

Research people who have been released from a mandatory life sentence only to commit murder again and be sent back to prison. Then make a judgement about the effectiveness of prison.

There is also a number of prisoners serving an indeterminate sentence to protect the public from them. These are sentences where there is no release date. These are for dangerous offenders and the Parole Board decides when they should be released. This might suggest that prison is achieving the aim of the protection of society. Indeterminate sentences can no longer be given as they were abolished in 2012. However, there are still many people serving such a sentence currently in prison. In January 2018, it was announced that the convicted rapist John Worboys, who was serving an indeterminate sentence, was to be released. This provoked a public outcry.

The majority of people sent to prison are given fixed term sentences and therefore know the amount of time they have to serve. Anyone given a sentence of between two days but less than two years will be released on licence half-way through their sentence. They are then on licence until the end of their sentence, with an additional post-sentence supervision of at least 12 months. Prisoners serving over two years will serve half of the sentence in prison and the reminder in the community, subject to supervision and including conditions. This could point to the aim of rehabilitation being achieved or at least an attempt at rehabilitation.

The changes to the post-sentence supervision may account for the increase in the number of people recalled to custody. The recall population has increased by nearly 1,000 people since the changes were introduced in February 2015. There were 6,554 people in prison on recall at the end of March 2017. This would suggest that prison does not rehabilitate people.

Key term

Parole Board: An independent body that carries out risk assessments on prisoners to determine if they can be safely released into the community.

Activity

Research the release of John Worboys, who was given a determinate sentence and was initially granted release by the Parole Board after 10 years imprisonment. However, the controversial decision was overturned and he continues to serve a custodial sentence.

Do community sentences meet their aims?

According to the Sentencing Council, a community sentence combines punishment with activities carried out in the community. It can include a requirement such as carrying out up to 300 hours of unpaid work, which might include tasks such as removing graffiti or cleaning overgrown areas. It could also involve the offender undergoing alcohol or drug treatment to tackle causes of offending. Overall, this aims to try to not only punish offenders but to change their behaviour and prevent further offending.

According to the Bromley Briefings (Prison Reform Trust, 2016), the use of community sentences has nearly halved (46%) since 2006 and they now account for just 9% of all sentences. This is despite the fact that they are more effective by 8.3% at reducing one-year reoffending rates than custodial sentences of less than 12 months for similar offences. This would suggest that community sentences can fulfil a rehabilitation aim.

However, the BBC reported, in 2013, that more than 3/4 of people sent to prison the previous year had at least one previous community sentence. Perhaps this suggests that while community orders are not greatly effective they are, at least, more effective than imprisonment at preventing reoffending.

Community orders:

- Offenders carry out unpaid work in the community, thereby achieving an aim of reparation.
- Anyone can nominate a project, within a community, for offenders to work on.
- Ideas acted upon have included ground maintenance, such as clearing litter from communal areas, constructing bin stores, laying paving and rebuilding sections of stone walls.

Key term

Sentencing Council: Provides guidelines on sentencing that the courts must follow unless it is in the interest of justice not to do so.

Activity

Consider your local area and nominate a project for offenders to work on.

Community payback seeks to meet the aim of reparation.

Do financial penalties work?

A fine is a common disposal of a case in a magistrates' court. For relatively minor offences, such as driving offences, a court will take into account the circumstances of the crime and the financial situation of the offender. Often the fine is paid in instalments taken directly from social security benefits.

The main purpose of a fine is to provide deterrence and punishment for the defendants, in an attempt to prevent them from committing repeat offences. It is possible to be sent to prison for failing to pay a fine, but only if the court believes you are deliberately not paying.

According to the *Daily Telegraph* newspaper, a quarter of a billion pounds in court fines have been written off because offenders can no longer be traced. In particular, between 2009 and 2013, a total of £237.1 million of court fines, costs, compensation orders and victim surcharges were 'administratively cancelled' (Whitehead, 2014). The financial penalties were effectively written off because it was concluded there was no realistic chance of collection. In addition, according to the *Daily Mirror* newspaper, 61% of fines are either written off or remain uncollected (Moss, 2015).

Given the above figures, it would appear that fines are not an effective method of achieving deterrence or retribution given the amount that are unpaid. The threat of prison for failing to pay does not seem to impact on the offender.

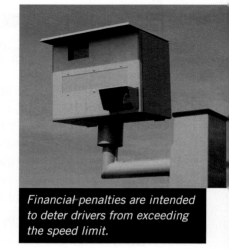

Financial penalties are intended to deter drivers from exceeding the speed limit.

A large proportion of fines remain unpaid.

Do discharges work?

Discharges can be either conditional or absolute. A conditional discharge is frequently used for a minor first-time offence in a magistrates' court. The nature of this punishment is that provided the defendant does not reoffend during the period of the order, no further sanction will be imposed. However, if there is further reoffending during the period of the order, any time up to three years, the courts can give an alternative sentence for the original offence and a second sentence for any reoffending. Almost like a second chance, the aim is one of deterrence.

An absolute discharge is rare but, in effect, no penalty is imposed. It is used in circumstances where the defendant is guilty but morally blameless. It is the lowest level punishment an adult offender can receive. The court believes that the whole experience is sufficient deterrence for the offender. For those offenders who are impacted by the court experience such a sentence is likely to be sufficient. However, for those criminals who are impervious to the system, they are likely to be back before a court. In which case, such a punishment would not achieve its aims.

Example questions

Exam questions in this area:

Unit 4 2017

Assess how two forms of punishment meet their aims.   **[5, 5 marks]**

NOTE that from 2020 the changes in the mark bands would mean that this question would be out of 9 marks.

Explain how a judge might achieve public protection by passing sentences.   **[5 marks]**

NOTE that from 2020 the changes in the mark bands would mean that this question would be out of either 4 or 6 marks.

Unit 4 2019

Identify two aims of a probation order as a court punishment.   **[2 marks]**

Tip

The question requires you to link punishments and aims together. You will need to decide if a punishment works, that is to say, meets its aims or not.

Exam question Unit 4 2017

Assess how two forms of punishment meet their aims.   **[5, 5 marks]**

(i) One form of punishment is prison; this meets the aim of retribution as it is punishing the offender by taking their freedom away. The aim seeks to punish them through 'just desserts' so that the punishment is deserving of the crime. This can be seen through the example of murder, where if you take another's life, then your life will be taken from you. In the UK this is a life sentence. In some states in the USA it is by **capital punishment** or the death penalty. This means prison can be seen as effective as regards retribution. However, prison isn't seen as meeting the aim of rehabilitation because of the high recidivism rates, for example 86% of under 18s committing further crimes within the first year of release from prison. Hence, rehabilitation is not achieved. However, prison can be seen as effective in achieving the aim of deterrence. As the right realist theory of rational choice will mean that offenders and potential offenders are likely to think more rationally about their actions before committing another crime.

(ii) Another form of punishment is a community order, this is where the offender may be given conditions to follow. The punishment meets the aim of rehabilitation because one of the requirements is to attend sessions such as anger management or drug and alcohol workshops. This means that offenders who are given this punishment are more likely to be rehabilitated. Also, this punishment is good at reparation as it involves cleaning the streets, which makes society cleaner.

Key term

Capital punishment: Also known as the death penalty, this is a government-approved practice, where someone is put to death by the state as a punishment for a crime.

Assessment

Under the new mark bands, where the question would be out of 9 marks, this would lie in mark band 7–9 as there is a reasonable focus on the question, with some accurate support and some use of specialist vocabulary. The demands of the question may be only partially addressed.

(i) This answer correctly identifies the punishment concerned and then considers three aims and makes a judgement about whether they are actually achieved. It uses specialist terminology such as retribution and just desserts and includes statistics in support.

(ii) This is again well structured, although it is not as well written as (i). It could be improved by stating that community orders involve unpaid work in the community, for example cleaning overgrown areas. Also, the aim of deterrence could be mentioned, as the idea of unpaid work or being seen by the public on a 'pay back' scheme may deter offending.

Take it further

Research cases involving prosecutions under the Covid 19 legislation where lockdown rules have been breached. Assess which aims of punishment may be achieved by giving out the sentences.

LEARNING OUTCOME 3
UNDERSTAND MEASURES USED IN SOCIAL CONTROL

AC3.1 EXPLAIN THE ROLE OF AGENCIES IN SOCIAL CONTROL

ASSESSMENT CRITERION	CONTENT	AMPLIFICATION

AC3.1 You should be able to …
 	
 Explain the role of agencies in social control
	Role
	 • aims and objectives
	 • funding
	 • philosophy
	 • working practices
	   • types of criminality
	   • types of offenders
	   • reach (local, national)
	
	 Agencies
	 • government-sponsored agencies:
	   • police
	   • CPS
	   • judiciary
	   • prisons
	   • probation
	 • charities
	 • pressure groups
		You should be able to identify agencies involved with social control and explain their role in achieving social control

Synoptic links

You can apply your understanding from Unit 3 to this criterion. Many of the agencies have been explored in that unit through the various stages of a criminal case in the justice system.

The police service – a government-sponsored agency

The first professional police officers, known as 'Peelers' or 'Bobbies', were appointed in London in 1829 by the then Home Secretary, Robert Peel. Today there are:

- 45 territorial police forces in the United Kingdom with regional reach
- 39 in England
- four in Wales
- single forces each covering Scotland and Northern Ireland.

There are also some national law enforcement agencies, including the National Crime Agency and the British Transport Police.

Aims and objectives

The aim of the police is to reduce crime and maintain law and order. This involves the protection of life and property, preservation of the peace, and prevention and detection of criminal offences. They do this by working alongside communities and having the statutory powers of:

- arrest
- detention
- search
- interview.

Their powers are substantially contained in the Police and Criminal Evidence Act (PACE) 1984.

Take it further ≫

Investigate the history of the police service from the time of the Bow Street Runners to the modern day.

Activity

Contact your local police station and ask if you can arrange a class visit to see the workings of the station and in particular the custody suite.

Funding

In England and Wales the main source of income for the police is a central government grant. Some of their income is also raised through council tax.

Philosophy

The main aspects of the philosophy of the police are to act with:

- honesty and integrity – police officers are honest, act with integrity and do not compromise or abuse their position
- authority, respect and courtesy – police officers act with self-control and tolerance, treating members of the public and colleagues with respect and courtesy
- equality and diversity – police officers act with fairness and impartiality. They do not discriminate unlawfully or unfairly.

Working practices

All police forces have teams of officers who are responsible for general beat duties and response to emergency and non-emergency calls from the public. Nearly all police officers begin their careers in this area of policing, with some moving on to more specialist roles. For instance, 'neighbourhood officers' and Criminal Investigation Departments (CIDs) dealing with serious/complex crimes.

There are also 'specialist operations' in the police, with branches covering a wide range of functions, including:

- anti-terrorism
- covert operations and intelligence
- diplomatic protection
- firearms
- drugs
- royal protection
- special branch
- dog handlers
- river police
- mounted police.

Police Community Support Officers (PCSOs)

In addition, supporting the police are Police Community Support Officers (PCSOs) who work on the frontline providing a visible and reassuring presence on the streets and tackling anti-social behaviour. Also, Special Constables who are a trained force of volunteers possessing the full range of policing powers, give up part of their spare time to provide policing support. They are not paid but are entitled to claim reasonable expenses incurred in the performance of their role.

PCSOs give up their spare time to support the police.

Police and Crime Commissioners (PCCs)

Since 2012 there have been regionally elected Police and Crime Commissioners (PCCs). According to the website of the Association of Police and Crime Commissioners (2017) they are 'the voice of the people and hold the police to account with an aim to cut crime and deliver an effective and efficient police service within their force area'.

Take it further »

Find out who the Police and Crime Commissioner is in your area. Invite them to your centre to give a talk about their role.

The Crown Prosecution Service (CPS) – a government-sponsored agency

Aims and objectives

Prior to the Prosecution of Offences Act 1985, the police not only investigated but also prosecuted criminal cases, on behalf of the state. However, in an attempt to promote independence, the CPS became the principal prosecuting authority in England and Wales in 1986. The police maintained their investigatory role.

The CPS:

- Must decide which cases should be prosecuted, keeping them all under continuous review.
- Determine the appropriate charges in more serious or complex cases and advise the police, particularly during the early stages of investigations.
- Prepare cases and present them at court using a range of in-house advocates, self-employed advocates or agents.
- Provide information, assistance and support to victims and prosecution witnesses.

The CPS's values are stated as being:

- independent and fair
- honest and open
- treat everyone with respect
- behave professionally and strive for excellence.

Funding

The CPS is a government-funded body with the majority of its budget being approved by Parliament: the 2016–2017 budget being over £500,000,000. When costs are awarded by courts, the CPS recovers some of the costs of its prosecutions from defendants. In addition, the CPS recovers criminal assets through its confiscation, restraint and enforcement activities.

Director of Public Prosecutions

Max Hill QC is the Director of Public Prosecutions. He was appointed by the Attorney General and took up post on 1 November 2018.

Max was born in Hertfordshire in 1964. He attended state primary schools and, following a family move to Northumberland, the Royal Grammar School in Newcastle upon Tyne. He won a scholarship to study Law at St Peter's College, Oxford 1983-6. He qualified as a barrister in 1987 and was appointed Queen's Counsel in 2008.

While at the bar, Max both defended and prosecuted in complex cases including homicides, violent crime, terrorism, high value fraud and corporate crime. He was instructed in many of the most significant and high-profile murder trials in recent years, including the second set of trials concerning the killing of Damilola Taylor, and the London bombings of 2005.

From March 2017 to October 2018 Max was the Independent Reviewer of Terrorism Legislation. As the Independent Reviewer, he compiled reports including an investigative review of the use of terrorism legislation following the Westminster Bridge attacks.

Max was also the Leader of the South Eastern Circuit from 2014 to 2016, Chairman of the Criminal Bar Association from 2011 to 2012, and Chairman of the Kalisher Trust from 2014 to 2018. Until his appointment as DPP Max was Head of Red Lion Chambers.

Working practices

The CPS consists of 13 geographical areas across England and Wales, and CPS Direct is available 24/7 to provide the police with charging advice. The head of the CPS is the Director of Public Prosecutions, at time of writing this is Max Hill QC.

There is a code of practice used to help decide if a prosecution should take place. It has two parts and both must be satisfied for a prosecution to take place:

(i) evidential test

(ii) public interest test.

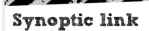

Synoptic link

This refers back to Unit 3 AC2.1.

The evidential test asks, 'Is there enough evidence against the defendant?' When deciding this the Crown Prosecutors must consider whether evidence can be used in court and is reliable and credible. Crown Prosecutors must be satisfied there is enough evidence to provide a 'realistic prospect of conviction' against each defendant.

The public interest test test asks 'Is it in the public interest for the CPS to bring the case to court?' A prosecution will usually take place unless the prosecutor is sure that the public interest factors tending against prosecution outweigh those tending in favour. The questions asked by the Crown Prosecutors are:

a) **How serious is the offence committed?**

b) **What is the level of culpability of the suspect?**

c) **What are the circumstances of and the harm caused to the victim?**

d) **Was the suspect under the age of 18 at the time of the offence?**

e) **What is the impact on the community?**

f) **Is prosecution a proportionate response?**

g) **Do sources of information require protecting?**

None of these questions take precedence over the others and indeed some may not be appropriate. The answers all go towards providing the prosecutor with information to make a decision.

If there is not sufficient evidence for the suspect to be charged, then the threshold test can be applied by the CPS. This allows an immediate charging decision despite not all the evidence being available. This is obviously an infringement of liberty and is made on reasonable suspicion rather than evidence. However, it may only be applied where the suspect presents a substantial bail risk and not all the evidence is available at the time when the suspect is to be released from custody.

Judiciary – a government-sponsored agency

The judiciary is divided into:

- superior judges, those working in the High Court and above
- inferior judges, those working in the lower courts.

Aims and objectives

The role of a judge in a Crown Court criminal case is to make decisions about the law including its interpretation and application, and generally manage the trial. This includes ensuring it is human rights compliant. The judge must also explain the procedure and legal issues to the jury. At the end of a case they will sum up the evidence for the jury and finally pass a sentence if appropriate.

Judges in the appeal courts, such as the Supreme Court and the Court of Appeal, rule on appeal cases. They also interpret the law if it is unclear and set precedent, legal rules, for other courts to follow.

Funding

Judicial salaries are decided following the recommendation of the Senior Salaries Review Body (SSRB). The SSRB provides independent advice to the Prime Minister, the Lord Chancellor and the Secretary of State for Defence on the remuneration of the judiciary. Although judicial salaries are certainly higher than the average wage for England and Wales, it is worth noting that a successful solicitor or barrister from a top firm or Chambers can earn more than even a senior judge.

Judges are independent from the government.

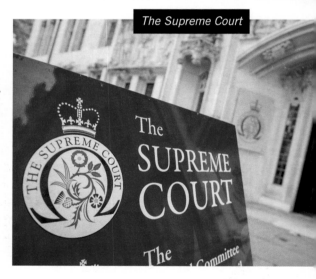

The Supreme Court

Activity

Find out about a day in the life of a judge by reading 'Day in the Life Of ...', at
www.judiciary.uk/about-the-judiciary/who-are-the-judiciary/a-day-in-the-life.

Research carried out in 2008 by Dame Hazel Glenn showed that many highly qualified lawyers were put off applying to join the High Court because they could earn up to three times more in their current post than they could as a judge.

Philosophy

A judge must be loyal to the Queen, as the Monarch is the figurehead of the legal system and in whose name justice is carried out, and law and order is maintained.

In addition, a judge promises to apply the law equally to every person, see the oaths below.

Working practices

When judges are sworn in they take two oaths/affirmations. The first is the oath of allegiance and the second the judicial oath; these are collectively referred to as the judicial oath.

Oath of allegiance

I, _____ , do swear by Almighty God that I will be faithful and bear true allegiance to Her Majesty Queen Elizabeth the Second, her heirs and successors, according to law.

Judicial oath

I, _____ , do swear by Almighty God that I will well and truly serve our Sovereign Lady Queen Elizabeth the Second in the office of _____ , and I will do right to all manner of people after the laws and usages of this realm, without fear or favour, affection or ill will.

One of the most cherished principles of the judiciary is that they are independent. As judges have the ultimate responsibility for decisions regarding freedoms, rights and duties of people, it is vital that they make decisions solely on the basis of the law, evidence and facts, without any improper influence. Therefore, an independent judiciary is an essential requirement for a fair, consistent and neutral administration of justice. They are free from political control and cannot be dismissed by the government. They are not elected but appointed and have security of tenure. Their salary is guaranteed and cannot be altered by the government.

Take it further

Investigate the salaries of the judiciary by searching the Gov.uk website.

Take it further

Investigate the role played by the judges in the theory of separation of powers.

Key term

Security of tenure: Guaranteed permanent employment.

Judges take an oath on appointment.

HM Prison Service – a government-sponsored agency

Aims and objectives

Prison must provide some form of punishment, which involves the deprivation of liberty and all the consequences that has for the prisoner.

In addition rehabilitation should be attempted for the individual, so that when they are released , they return to society as law abiding. This may mean tackling issues and challenges in outside life that have contributed to their criminal behaviour.

Funding

Most prisons are government funded with finances being raised through taxation. In 2015 the budget was £3.4 billion. According to an official study, compiled by the University of Lausanne for the Council of Europe (cited in Barrett, 2015), taxpayers in England and Wales are paying more to run prisons than most other major countries in western Europe. According to the report, expenditure was at £87 a day in 2012, £15 higher than the European average of £72 a day per prisoner. In 2015 it was estimated that the average cost of keeping a prisoner was £36,000 p.a.

Philosophy

The prison service serves the public by keeping in custody those committed by the courts. Their duty is to look after prisoners with humanity and help them lead law-abiding and useful lives while in custody and after release.

Working practices

Most prisons are public sector and run by HM Prison Service (the government), 109 of the 123 prisons in England and Wales are organised on this basis and are run by the National Offender Management Service (NOMS). However, there are 14 private prisons, for example HMP Birmingham, which are contracted to the private security company called G4S.

Prisons are divided into different categories depending on the level of security required to oversee the prisoners:

- **Category A:** high risk/maximum security (e.g. HMP Frankland)
- **Category B:** high risk to others (HMP Nottingham, HMP Pentonville, HMP Durham and HMP Wandsworth)
- **Category C:** lower risk but not trusted to be in open conditions (e.g. HMP Dartmoor)
- **Category D:** very low risk to others and due for release soon, known as open prisons (e.g. HMP Ford, HMP Kirkham)

> **Take it further** »
>
> Find out about life in prison, at www.gov.uk/life-in-prison.

HMP Dartmoor, in Dartmoor National Park, is a lower-risk category prison.

Privileges available to prisoners depend on behaviour, with levels set at basic, standard and enhanced. All prisoners enter prison at standard level. They need to be well behaved and prove themselves to staff to move up to an enhanced level. If rules are broken, or prisoners are badly behaved, they drop back down to basic level. Each level gives you certain rights and activities. For example, if you are on basic level you are not allowed a TV in your room or cell and have to eat meals in your room. If you are on an enhanced level you are allowed more time in the gym, more time out of your room and have access to more visits.

Prisons are divided into categories according to the security risk.

The National Probation Service (NPS) – a government-sponsored agency

Aims and objectives

The National Probation Service (NPS) is a statutory criminal justice service that supervises high-risk offenders released into the community. They work with around 30,000 offenders a year, supporting their rehabilitation while protecting the public. They work in partnership with 21 community rehabilitation companies, the courts, police, and with private and voluntary sector partners in order to manage offenders safely and effectively.

Probation means that someone is serving their sentence out of prison. An offender may be put on probation because of serving a community sentence or have been released from prison on licence or on parole. Anyone released from prison after serving between two days and under two years must be supervised by the probation service for at least 12 months.

While on probation, offenders may have to:

- do unpaid work
- complete an education or training course
- get treatment for addictions, such as drugs or alcohol
- have regular meetings with an 'offender manager'.

Philosophy

The aims of the NPS are to:

- believe in the ability of people who have offended to change for the better and become responsible members of society
- be committed to promoting social justice, social inclusion, equality and diversity
- recognise that full consideration should be given to the rights and needs of victims when planning how a service user's sentence will be managed
- be committed to acting with professional integrity.

Key term

Community rehabilitation companies: The private sector suppliers of probation services for offenders in England and Wales.

Activity

Find out about the life of a probation officer by reading 'A Day in the Life of a Probation Officer', at www.crimeandjustice. org.uk/resources/day-life-probation-officer.

Funding

According to the NPS, its priority is to protect the public by the effective rehabilitation of high-risk offenders, by tackling the causes of offending and enabling offenders to turn their lives around. Served by 35 probation trusts, the NPS is funded by the National Offender Management Service (NOMS), again through income taxation. The community rehabilitation companies are businesses and are self-funding.

Working practices

The NPS also has to prepare pre-sentence reports for courts, to help in the selection of the most appropriate sentence. It also manages approved premises for offenders with a residence requirement on their sentence. Assessing offenders in prison to prepare them for release on licence to the community, when they will be under supervision, is also part of its role. Finally, they must communicate with and prioritise the wellbeing of victims of serious sexual and violent offences, when the offender has received a prison sentence of 12 months or more, or is detained as a mental health patient.

Activity

Research various job roles in prisons and probations by visiting https://prisonandprobation jobs.gov.uk/.

Charities and pressure groups

Both charities and pressure groups play an important role in the criminal justice system. They are not government funded and as such can bring an independent and challenging function to the justice system. Charities and voluntary agencies exist to support and defend the interests of their beneficiaries. They are non-profit making organisations and often enjoy some tax advantages from the government.

The Prison Reform Trust (PRT)

The Prison Reform Trust (PRT) is a charity, established in 1981, which works to create a just, humane and effective penal system. According to its website it aims to:

improve prison regimes and conditions, defend and promote prisoners' human rights, address the needs of prisoners' families, and promote alternatives to custody.

The Prison Reform Trust's main objectives are:

1. Reducing unnecessary imprisonment and promoting community solutions to crime.

2. Improving treatment and conditions for prisoners and their families.

3. Promoting equality and human rights in the justice system.

The charity carries out research on many aspects of prison life and on the composition of prisoners both within prison and their life before being sent into custody. It provides advice and information to not only prisoners and their families but also to other agencies in the criminal justice system such as students, the legal profession and members of the public. It organises lecturers and conferences to help promote its work.

Campaigns to improve the penal system form a main part of their work. For instance, the 'Out of Trouble' campaign, which is seeking to reduce the number of children and young people in prison. Or the 'Out for Good – Lessons for the Future' campaign, a project to secure employment for prisoners on release.

The PRT does not receive any funding from the government and is entirely dependent on voluntary donations to carry out its work.

The Howard League for Penal Reform

This is the oldest penal reform charity in the UK, having been established in 1866. It is named after John Howard, one of the first prison reformers. It aims for less crime, safer communities and fewer people in prison, and seeks to transform prisons for those behind bars. It works with parliament, the media, numerous agencies in the criminal justice system and members of the public to attain these aims.

The Howard League for Penal Reform is entirely independent of the government and is funded by voluntary donations and membership subscriptions.

It has run many successful campaigns, such as the 'Books for Prisoners' campaign, which won a charity award in 2015, and a campaign to reduce the criminalisation of children by working closely with police forces in England and Wales. This resulted in the number of child arrests falling by 58% between 2010 and 2015.

Howard League for Penal Reform

#BooksForPrisoners

Handy hints !

There are many charities and pressure groups that you can research to support your learning in this assessment criterion. Other organisations could include:

- National Association for the Care and Resettlement of Offenders (NACRO)
- the Prince's Trust.

AC3.2 DESCRIBE THE CONTRIBUTION OF AGENCIES TO ACHIEVING SOCIAL CONTROL

ASSESSMENT CRITERION	CONTENT	AMPLIFICATION

AC3.2 You should be able to …
 	
 Describe the contribution of agencies to achieving social control
	Contribution
	 • tactics and measures used by agencies
	  • environmental
	   • design
	   • gated lanes
	  • behavioural
	   • ASBO
	   • token economy
	  • institutional
	  • disciplinary procedures
	   • rule making
	   • staged/phased
	 • gaps in state provision
		You should be able to understand the range of techniques used by the agencies and be able to examine their contribution

Synoptic links

You should be able to apply your understanding of:

- policy and campaigns from Unit 1
- criminological theories from Unit 2 can be seen in some of the concepts of crime prevention
- the processes used to bring an accused to justice in Unit 3

to the role of the different agencies.

CONTRIBUTION

Tactics and measures used by agencies

Environmental design

Environmental design involves what a neighbourhood looks like and how it is designed, both of which have an impact on criminality. This theory, originating from criminologist C. Ray Jeffery, is known as the Crime Prevention Through Environmental Design (CPTED – pronounced *sep-ced*). It is based on the simple idea that crime results partly from the opportunities presented by the physical environment. This being the case, it should be possible to alter the physical environment so that crime is less likely to occur.

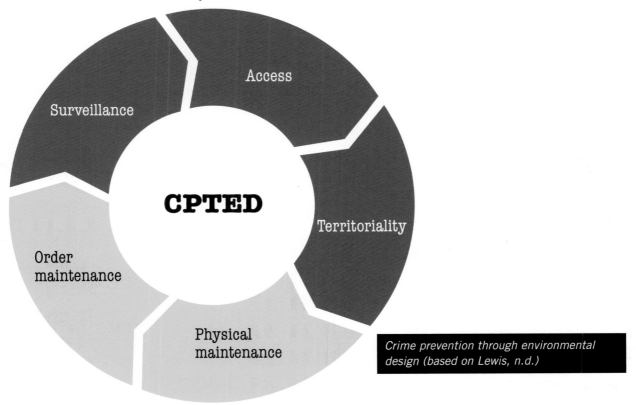

Crime prevention through environmental design (based on Lewis, n.d.)

Crime can be reduced by:

- creating open spaces with strong lighting, especially in doorways, to provide clear visibility
- a lack of hiding places to enable people to see around places such as corners and blind spots
- low-level bushes allowing a clear visible site line.

Closed stairwells result in low-level visibility and easy access and escape. Damilola Taylor died in a concrete stairwell on a condemned housing estate. This senseless murder resulted from a breakdown in society's values and a right realist approach would suggest a tough stance to such crimes.

There are many positives of CPTED, for instance it promotes a sense of ownership, with school exteriors covered in artwork and resident-tended gardens. This could relate to the functionalist view of crime whereby positive boundary maintenance is achieved. Brown and Altman (1981) found that physical modifications suggested resident care and watchfulness help to promote safer residential settings.

Research shows a higher crime rate in cities with high-rise blocks than those with low-level buildings (New York – Brownsville and Van Dyke, 2001, cited in Cozens et al. 2001). In Ohio, a CPTED partnership plan with the housing authority management, residents and police officers has resulted in a 12–13% decline in crime.

However, the CPTED principles suggest criminals operate in hidden places, yet this is not always true, for example graffiti often takes place in very visible locations. In addition, it may be that crime is displaced to another area rather than being prevented.

Activity

Design your own town using CPTED principles.

Prison design

Prison design can also impact on crime. The traditional prison design is the panopticon (all-seeing) shape. The concept of the design is to allow an observer to view all prisoners without the prisoners being able to tell if they are being watched. The building has a tower at the centre, from which it is possible to see each cell in which a prisoner is kept. In other words, visibility is a trap. Prisoners can be seen but cannot communicate with the prison officers or other prisoners. The 'crowd' is abolished. The design ensures a sense of permanent visibility that ensures the functioning of power.

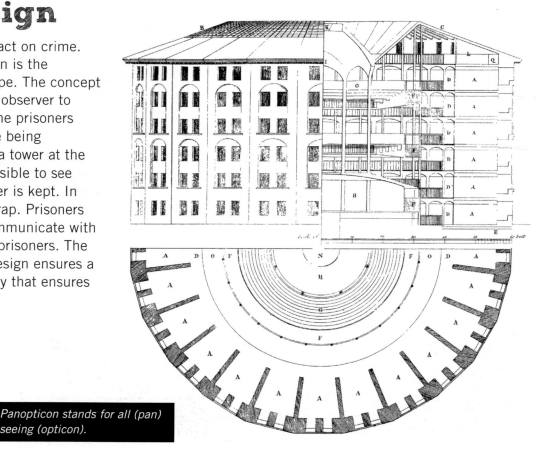

Panopticon stands for all (pan) seeing (opticon).

There are other prison designs such as the American supermax jails. These are the most secure (super maximum) levels of custody. The objective is to provide long-term, segregated housing for prisoners who represent the highest security risks, including those who pose a threat to national and international security. For example, Florence, Colorado, holds some of the most notorious American terrorists and murderers in solitary confinement. The prison is home to about 360 inmates held under ultra-high security. A supermax prison costs two or three times more to build and operate than a traditional maximum security prison.

The UK's most recent prison is HMP Berwyn, in Wrexham, North Wales, and is also the country's biggest – holding 2,106 prisoners. However, the accommodation is divided into smaller units for easier management of the inmates.

The government has promised to increase prison building, with a commitment of £4 billion to build a total of 18,000 prison places. This includes the 10,000 places previously announced as well as the construction of HMPs Five Wells and Glen Parva. The remaining places will be met by: the construction of four new prisons; the expansion of a further four prisons; and refurbishment of the existing prison estate.

HMP Berwyn, the UK's most recent prison

The first new jail will be built next to HMP Full Sutton, in East Yorkshire, and work is underway to identify locations for a further prison in the North-West of England and two in the South-East.

New house blocks will be built at HMPs Guys Marsh, Rye Hill and Stocken, and a new workshop at HMP High Down. These are expected to provide 930 new places and be completed by 2023.

Think theory

A very alternative prison design is that of Bastøy in Norway, which has been classed as a 'human ecological prison'. Critics suggest the design is akin to a holiday camp, where prisoners live in houses that are set in a self-sustaining village, rather than cells. However, this left realist approach to criminality produces a very low reoffending rate of 20% compared to 60% in the UK.

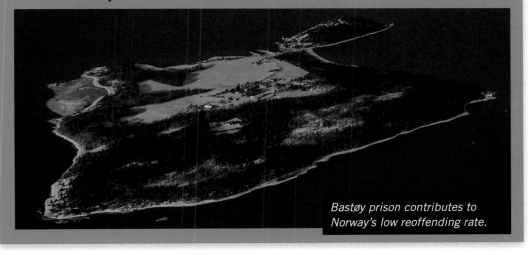

Bastøy prison contributes to Norway's low reoffending rate.

Another environmental design that could influence criminality is gated lanes. These are gates that are installed at the entrance to rear alleyways in order to deter burglars or other criminals from using them to gain unlawful access from the rear of houses. Government regulations came into force on 1 April 2006 giving local authorities powers to erect gates on public highways to combat crime and anti-social behaviour.

A gated lane scheme in Preston, Lancashire, has proved popular with residents, giving them a feeling that they can reclaim their streets. Alley gates have also been erected across Cardiff in an attempt to combat law and disorder. The residents in favour have suggested that it has reduced crime and prevented rubbish from being dumped in the back lanes. However, others have suggested that at approximately £4,000 to provide one gate at either end of an alley, it is too costly to justify.

Gated lanes are used as environmental crime control.

Activity

Copy and complete the summary table below.

TYPE OF ENVIRONMENTAL DESIGN	HOW IT WORKS	POSITIVES OF CONTRIBUTION TO SOCIAL CONTROL	NEGATIVES OF CONTRIBUTION TO SOCIAL COTROL
CPTED			
Prison design			
Gated lanes			

Behavioural tactics

These are tactics used by agencies to change a person's behaviour to make them more socially compliant. Anti Social Behaviour Orders (ASBOs) were introduced in 1998 to limit and correct low-level anti-social behaviour, which would often involve swearing and drinking. However, ASBOs were not without controversy and many critics suggested that persistent offenders viewed them as desirable and as a badge of honour. They were regularly breached and, according to the civil rights group Liberty, 56% of ASBOs were breached in 2009. It is perhaps not surprising, therefore, that such orders were eventually replaced by Criminal Behaviour Orders (CBOs).

An ASBO could be seen as a badge of honour.

The CBO is available under the Anti-social Behaviour, Crime and Policing Act 2014 (ABCPA), for use against anti-social offenders who have committed behaviour that has caused harassment, alarm and distress – the same test that was used for ASBOs. Under the order, a person who has been convicted would be banned from taking part in certain activities or going to certain places, and would be required to try changing their behaviour, for example by attending a drug treatment programme. This positive requirement is the main difference between the old and new orders. A breach could see an adult face up to five years in prison.

Token economies are another method of trying to control behaviour. They are based on the psychological concept of behaviour modification, which means rewarding positive behaviour and punishing negative behaviour. In a typical token economy programme, the institutional management draws up a list of behaviours they wish to promote. This happens in prison in an attempt to control behaviour. For instance, the desired behaviour may be to:

- follow all rules
- keep clean
- keep cell clean
- no fighting
- no intimidation
- no further criminal activity
- be industrious
- seek a job.

In exchange for such positive behaviour, rewards such as extra visiting time or a financial payment will be given.

Key terms

Anti Social Behaviour Order (ASBO): A court order that can be obtained by local authorities in order to restrict the behaviour of a person likely to cause harm or distress to the public.

Criminal Behaviour Order (CBO): An order that tackles the most serious and persistent anti-social individuals where their behaviour has brought them before a criminal court. It can deal with a wide range of anti-social behaviours following the offender's conviction, including threatening violence against others, or frequently being drunk and aggressive in public.

Token economy: A form of behaviour modification that increases desirable behaviour and decreases undesirable behaviour by the use of tokens. Individuals receive tokens after displaying desirable behaviour. These are collected and exchanged for an object or privilege.

Token economy can be seen to be an effective form of social control, as research shows that it is deemed to be effective on a long-term rather than a short-term scale (Hobbs & Holt, 1979). However, a limitation may be that when the offender gets out of prison, they will not have the token economy implemented in their regular day-to-day life. The offender could then not want to behave positively in society because they know they are not going to be rewarded if they do so.

Think theory

The token economies approach can be seen to link to the individualistic theories of criminality. In other words, it is linked to the way an individual learns and reacts to life experiences and how control is exercised.

Institutional tactics

There are institutions that have their own methods or tactics of controlling undesired behaviour. Prison, as mentioned on the previous page, must impose rules to keep control and prevent further crime occurring. The following are examples of rules that must be followed in prison:

- Behaving in a way that could offend, threaten or hurt someone else.
- Stopping prison staff from doing their jobs.
- Causing damage to the prison.
- Not doing what prison staff tell you to do.

The following are examples of punishments if prison rules are broken:

- You could get a caution.
- Your privileges (such as having a TV in your cell) could be taken away from you for up to 42 days.
- Up to 84 days' worth of any money you earn could be stopped.
- You could be locked in a cell by yourself away from other prisoners for up to 35 days. This is called cellular confinement.

Rules must be followed in prison.

As well as prison, other institutions have their own rules for preventing disorder. Schools may impose detention for rule breaking such as wearing the incorrect uniform. Both the Law Society and the General Medical Council (GMC) are institutions that provide rules and punishments for their members. The Law Society can ultimately discipline solicitors by removing them from the Roll of Solicitors and thus prevent them from practising. The GMC can also punish doctors by disqualifying them from the medical profession.

Key term

Cellular confinement: Being restricted to your cell, without socialising with other prisoners, as a punishment.

The police have a staged discipline procedure for dealing with offenders prior to court proceedings taking place. This involves a series of cautions and warnings. They act as a second chance to allow the offender to admit guilt but without having to face court proceedings. Similarly, the National Probation Service allows two minor breaches of the community order to act as a warning before referring the matter back to a court.

Gaps in state provision

Despite agencies in the criminal justice system using tactics or mechanisms to prevent crime taking place, there are still many gaps in the state provision. Unreported crime is often referred to as the dark figure of crime. The police can only detect crime if it is brought to their attention. If they are unaware of the crime it can never be punished. It is estimated that unreported crime can account for a large percentage of crime, even larger than the percentage reported to the police.

Synoptic link

This links to Unit 1 and unreported crime.

- Domestic abuse is often an area that goes unreported. Potentially, the fear of further abuse and violence can prevent offending being reported. Alternatively, the victim does not want the attacker to be in trouble with the police due to a misguided loyalty or affection.

- Likewise, white-collar crime can be unreported due to a lack of proof that a crime has occurred or the time gap between the crime taking place and it being noticed.

Budget cuts can impact upon criminal cases being tackled, especially within the police service. With cries of a lack of police officers on the beat and too many cases being dealt with by cautions, money is inevitably something that produces a gap in state provision.

Domestic abuse often goes unreported.

Often the requirement to adhere to one set of laws can prevent others being implemented and thus create a gap in provision. According to the *Sun* newspaper (Newton Dunn, 2015), a third of those who have won against the UK at the European Court of Human Rights are terrorists, prisoners or criminals. For instance, a number of foreign terrorists have used the Human Rights Act 1998 to remain in the UK and avoid deportation.

Unreported crime is often called the dark figure of crime.

Example questions

Exam questions in this area:

Unit 4 2017

Describe two environmental measures used by agencies to achieve social control. **[4 marks]**

Unit 4 2019

Describe one behavioural tactic used by prisons to achieve social control. **[5 marks]**

NOTE that from 2020 the changes in the mark bands would mean that this question would be out of either 4 or 6 marks.

Tip ✓

Make sure you can show the link between tactics or measures to the criminological theories, as used by agencies.

Exam question Unit 4 2017

Describe two environmental measures used by agencies to achieve social control. **[4 marks]**

One environmental measure is the use of gated lanes. This is where gates are put at the end of an alley, which control access. The gates also prevent crime by restricting the people who can enter. This would help prevent crimes such as fly tipping (leaving rubbish) and burglaries committed by use of rear entrances.

A second measure could be the design of a prison. Traditionally, the panopticon (all-seeing) shape has been used. This involves a tower in the centre from which it is possible to see all the cells. Visibility becomes the trap. Prisoners then conform due to the feeling of being watched.

Assessment

This would lie in the 3–4 mark band. There are two appropriate examples of environmental design appropriately described. For a 4 mark question, the amount of information is at the correct level.

AC3.3 EXAMINE THE LIMITATIONS OF AGENCIES IN ACHIEVING SOCIAL CONTROL

ASSESSMENT CRITERION	CONTENT	AMPLIFICATION
AC3.3 You should be able to ... Examine the limitations of agencies in achieving social control	**Limitations** • repeat offenders/recidivism • civil liberties and legal barriers • access to resources and support • finance • local and national policies • environment • crime committed by those with moral imperatives	You should understand the limitations of social control agencies and be able to examine the implications of these limitations

Synoptic links

You should be able to apply your understanding of criminological theories from Unit 2 in your examination of the limitations. You will also draw on your understanding of policy and campaigns for change in examination of the limitations of agencies.

Limitations

Repeat offenders/recidivism

If offenders fail to rehabilitate and continue to commit crime, then social control will never be achieved. Recidivism is one of the reasons that the prison population has dramatically increased over the last 20 years. According to the Prison Reform Trust, between 1993 and 2015 the prison population in England and Wales has nearly doubled, with an extra 41,000 people behind bars, taking the number of people in custody at the end of June 2016 to 89,332.

Anyone leaving custody who has served two days or more is now required to serve a minimum of 12 months under supervision in the community. As a result, the number of people recalled to custody following their release has increased dramatically. The recall population is now 19% higher than when the changes were introduced in February 2015, with nearly 1,100 more people.

The Bromley Briefings Prison Factfile for Winter 2021 shows that repeat offending limits social control being achieved by prisons. For instance:

- Re-conviction rates within a year of release from prison is very high at 48%.
- However, those serving short sentences of less than 12 months have even higher re-conviction rates at 63% for adults.
- Re-conviction rates for women who were released within the last year after serving a short prison sentence jumps to 73%.
- Re-conviction rates for children released within a year from prison and serving a short sentence is 77%.
- The annual total economic and social cost of re-offending is estimated to be £18.1 billion.

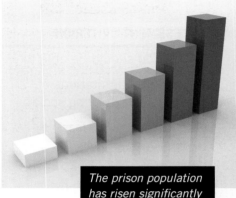

The prison population has risen significantly over the past 20 years.

Think theory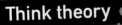

The social learning theory may explain some of these statistics, due to offenders learning and copying from others in the prison system. Prisoners can become 'better' criminals, learning the skills from others to encourage them to continue offending upon release.

Civil liberties and legal barriers

Civil liberties are basic rights and freedoms granted to citizens of a country through the law. They include:

- freedom of speech
- freedom of movement
- freedom from arbitrary arrest
- freedom of assembly
- freedom of association
- freedom of religious worship.

Civil liberties can limit social control, as people have the right to freedom of speech, freedom of movement, etc. Thus, it can be seen as a restriction on agencies such as the police in achieving social control. For instance, there are foreign nationals with criminal convictions who cannot be removed from the UK due to EU regulations. Deportation cannot take place due to prisoners being in danger in their home country.

Civil liberties can limit social control.

CASE STUDY

ABU QATADA

The case of Abu Qatada demonstrates the issue of civil liberties being a limitation to achieving social control, as in 2012 the European Court of Human Rights (ECHR) ruled that the hate preacher could not be deported to Jordan because of the risk he would be tried on evidence obtained by torture. Theresa May, then Home Secretary, said the radical Islamist cleric would have been sent back to Jordan long ago had the ECHR not 'moved the goalposts' by establishing new, unprecedented legal grounds for blocking his deportation. He was eventually deported in 2013.

Abu Qatada

Think theory

The Marxist theory of criminality would suggest that these laws are necessary to protect the working class from the ruling elite making arbitrary judgements against them.

Some argue that civil liberties could be a limitation to social control.

Access to resources and support

Access to resources and support limits prisoners from being able to rehabilitate and therefore bring about social control. Upon release from prison an offender will face problems with finance, accommodation and employment or training opportunities. The following facts are from the Prison Reform Trust's Winter 2021 Bromley Briefings Prison Factfile (Prison Reform Trust, 2021):

- Literacy levels among the prison population remain significantly lower than the general population. Nearly two-thirds (62%) of people entering prison were assessed as having literacy skills expected of an 11 year old – more than four times higher than in the general adult population (15%).
- 78,000 adults in the prison system participated in education in the 2017–2018 academic year – a drop of 12% on the previous year.
- The number of people achieving qualifications fell by 13% in 2017–2018.
- Just over a third of prisons (36%) received a positive rating from inspectors in 2019–2020 for purposeful activity work – continuing the decline from half of prisons in 2016–2017.
- The number of people achieving qualifications fell by 13% in 2017–2018.

The government has announced plans to introduce a Prisoner Apprenticeship Pathway to offer prisoners opportunities that will count towards the completion of a formal apprenticeship on release.

Some people are entitled to receive a discharge grant to help them on release; however, this has remained fixed at £46 since 1997. Thousands more prisoners are ineligible, including those released from remand, fine defaulters and people serving less than 15 days.

Entitlement to housing benefit stops for all sentenced prisoners expected to be in prison for more than 13 weeks. This means that many prisoners have very little chance of keeping their tenancy open until the end of their sentence and lose their housing. One in ten people (11%) released from custody in 2014–2015 had no settled accommodation.

The lack of support or resources available may mean that prisoners are tempted to return to crime. According to the social justice charity NACRO, the National Association of the Care and Resettlement of Offenders, out of the 38,000 people they helped in 2016/2017, 48% of those housed had a primary or secondary support need to manage the risk of offending.

Finance

Public sector funding is inevitably limited and cuts in budget will impact on the effectiveness of agencies providing social control. The police service has faced cuts in its budget over recent years and sees no sign of money being increased over the next few years. Headlines showing this include:

- 'Police Budgets Slashed by £300m Despite Top Officers' Warnings' (Barrett, 2014).
- 'Police Forces all Face Major Budget Cuts' (BBC News, 2015).
- 'Watchdog Says Police Cuts Have Left Forces in "Perilous State"' (Grierson, 2017).

According to the House of Commons Briefing Paper, Police funding Number 7279, 25 February 2016, the central grant to police forces has decreased in 25% in real terms from 2010/11 to 2014/15. Inevitably this will limit the number of police officers available to investigate and detect crimes. Her Majesty's Inspectorate of Constabulary (HMIC) issued a warning that a shortage of detectives and investigators amounts to a 'national crisis'.

The HM Prison Service suffers from budget cuts too. According to the Prisonphone website (2017) from 2011/12 to 2014/15, the National Offender Management Service (NOMS) decreased its budget by a quarter, which equated to £900 million. Clearly this had a significant impact on the prison population, including incidences of suicide, self-harm and attacks on staff. The Prison Officers' Association has warned that inmates with mental health problems are in extra danger without a boost in resources.

In August 2016 police riot squad officers were sent to HMP The Mount twice in 24 hours. According to the *Daily Telegraph* newspaper (Farmer, 2017), prisoners armed with weapons seized control of Nash Wing. Staff shortages and an extended lock-down of prisoners are reported to have left the prison as 'a disaster waiting to happen'. Clearly, a lack of finance impacts on the ability to keep social control inside prisons.

Take it further

Read 'The Prison Service Has Been Cut to the Bone and we Struggle to Keep Control', on the *Guardian*'s website (Anonymous, 2016), which is an account from an anonymous prison officer. This will provide you with an insight into some of the issues caused by budget cuts.

Cuts in public sector spending limit social control by the government agencies.

The agency that prosecutes on behalf of the crown, the CPS, is not immune to financial problems. According to *The Law Society Gazette* (Baksi, 2014), 'staff cuts at the Crown Prosecution Service have led to a marked decline in its performance with inadequate case progression and preparation'. Clearly, this could lead to miscarriages of justice and therefore decreases the effectiveness of social control.

Both charities and pressure groups that focus on social control have their effectiveness limited, as they are substantially funded by voluntary contributions. If they do not receive public donations they are unable to function. In addition, any government grants that the organisations are able to claim also are being reduced. Charities have lost more than £3.8 billion in grants from the government over the last decade.

Local and national policies

Local police forces prioritise certain crimes in preference to others. Inevitably this would mean that some crimes are not investigated. For instance, there have been allegations against the police suggesting that they focus on 'trivial crime' instead of serious offences, in order to meet government targets.

From 2010 to 2015 the government promoted a policy to tackle knife, gun and gang crimes. They introduced new offences, such as gang injunctions to prevent a person from engaging in, encouraging or assisting gang-related violence, to help improve prosecution rates and dedicated £1.2 million to fund support workers in this area. While it was entirely appropriate to set such policies, it can lead to the police focusing on certain crimes and not others.

While national policies may be set by the government, the police have local policies too. The Mayor of London, Sadiq Khan, launched policing plans in March 2017 outlining a series of policies aimed at tackling hate crimes and boosting the Metropolitan Police's armed anti-terror squad.

The CPS also focuses on certain policies over time. In August 2017 the former head of the CPS, Alison Saunders, indicated there would be a crackdown on social media hates crimes. The policy relates to all the different strands of hate crime:

- racist and religious
- disability
- homophobic, biphobic and transphobic.

Official figures show a 20% rise in all forms of hate crime reported to the police in the first quarter of 2017. However, hate crimes are believed to be significantly under-reported.

Take it further »

During periods of lockdown the police focused on policies enforcing breaches of the lockdown rules. Research how the police, in your area, enforced the rules.

Alison Saunders, former Director of Public Prosecutions

Environment

When prisoners are released from custody their home environment has a substantial impact on whether or not they stay out of prison. All too often offenders return to the same social circle involving drug taking or reoffending. There is a lack of employment available or a focus to lead them away from crime. According to the Prison Reform Trust (2016), people are less likely to reoffend if they receive family visits while they are in prison, yet 68% of prisoners had no such visits. Also, offenders are less likely to reoffend if they live with their immediate family on release; however, only 61% do so.

Purposeful activity, including education, work and other activities to aid rehabilitation while in prison, further reduces the risk of reoffending. However, fewer than half (44%) of the prisons received a positive rating from inspectors in 2015–2016 for purposeful activity work (Prison Reform Trust, 2016).

Finally, finding employment after being released from prison has an impact on an effective environment for offenders. However, only one in four (27%) people had a job to go to on release from prison and only 12% of employers surveyed said that they had employed somebody with a criminal record in the past three years (Prison Reform Trust, 2016).

Think theory

From a Marxist perspective it could be argued that the bourgeoisie construct the rules of society to prevent the proletariat from achieving in life, so they have no other option but to commit crimes.

Crime committed by those with moral imperatives

A moral imperative is a strongly felt principle that compels a person to act. In other words, offenders can commit crime as they believe they are doing the right thing from a moral viewpoint.

Assisted suicide could be argued to be a crime committed with a compassionate motive. In the UK, helping someone to die is a criminal offence. However, a family member may resort to such action if they believe it is at the express wish of the victim.

Literacy skills

Can you explain what these words mean?
- Recidivism
- Moral imperatives
- Aiding and abetting suicide
- Civil liberties

CASE STUDY

KAY GILDERDALE

Cases such as Kay Gilderdale, who administered drugs to her daughter to help her die, show that such drastic action can be out of a sense of sympathy and a feeling of being morally right to commit the crime.

Kay Gilderdale admitted a charge of aiding and abetting the suicide of her daughter.

Anti-vivisection protestors also believe their actions are the right thing to do. In attempts to protest at experiments on live animals their actions can result in criminal offences. For example, Luke Steele, head of the Anti-Vivisection Coalition, has twice been imprisoned for attacks on laboratories, along with harassment and intimidation of laboratory workers.

Think theory

From a functionalist viewpoint some crimes can be positive and serve a function in society. The case of Kay Gilderdale may produce boundary maintenance by showing what is acceptable within a society. This is where the majority of right-minded, law-abiding members in society would reaffirm their good values and produce social solidarity.

Activity

Consider what is the greatest limitation to achieving social control and explain why you think so.

AC3.4 EVALUATE THE EFFECTIVENESS OF AGENCIES IN ACHIEVING SOCIAL CONTROL

ASSESSMENT CRITERION	CONTENT	AMPLIFICATION

AC3.4 You should be able to …
 	
 Evaluate the effectiveness of agencies in achieving social control
	Agencies
	 • Government-sponsored agencies
	   • police
	   • CPS
	   • judiciary
	   • prisons
	   • probation
	 • charities
	 • pressure groups
		You should be able to draw together your learning to evaluate the success or failure of agencies in achieving social control

Synoptic links

You should apply the knowledge you developed in Unit 3 to evaluate information in terms of bias, opinion, circumstances, currency and accuracy.

The types of evidence, as set out in Unit 3, include:

- evidence
- trial transcripts
- media reports
- judgements
- Law Reports

Handy hints !

Remember to review the statistics for accuracy and clarity. Do not simply state statistics but consider if they are correct or if is there something behind them that requires consideration and explaining.

Government-sponsored agencies

Police

At times the police can be very effective. The work they do includes:

- Work in the community to prevent crime, keep the public safe and try to combat anti-social behaviour.
- Issuing notices, if necessary, ordering people to cease unacceptable behaviour and referring matters to a court if necessary.
- There are many specialist units trained to deal with issues such as terrorism or incidents involving weapons.

Police working in the community help gain the trust and support of people.

However, inevitably the media tends to report negative aspects of the role of the police in achieving social control. As considered in previous ACs, the police were labelled institutionally racist in the Macpherson Report (1999) following the murder of Stephen Lawrence. In more recent times the police have faced criticism over their effectiveness in achieving social control.

CASE STUDY

THE PUPPY FARM MURDER

In April 2017, in what came to be known as the puppy farm murder, the Surrey police were heavily criticised for returning a killer's shotgun and firearm certificate to him just months before a double murder. Seven months before, John Lowe had his shotguns and certificate seized after his stepdaughter had reported to the police he had threatened to shoot her.

John Lowe

CASE STUDY

DISORDER IN CROMER

In September 2017 the police admitted 'we got it wrong' to the residents of Cromer in a meeting to discuss disorder and anti-social behaviour in the seaside town. During a weekend of disorder by a group of people, police recorded 37 crimes, including rape, theft and assault. However, at the time they failed to provide support to the locals and classed it as 'low-level disturbance' but later said they had 'misjudged' the disorder.

Cromer

Clearly, these examples show ineffective policing and an inability to achieve social control. However, the way the media portray crime and the desire for sensational headlines, which was studied in Unit 1, should be considered when judging the effectiveness of the police.

Statistics can be used to consider the effectiveness of police from both sides of the argument. According to the Office for National Statistics (ONS, 2017), for the year ending March 2017, police forces closed almost half (48%) of offences with no suspect identified. This included around two-thirds (68%) of criminal damage and arson offences. The proportion of offences that resulted in a charge or summons decreased from 14% to 11% over the last year. Such low statistics suggests a lack of effectiveness. The ONS is the UK's largest independent producer of official statistics. The independent aspect suggests reliability as regards the information. However, reliability of such statistics should be considered. In 2016 the chairman of the Treasury Select Committee at that time, Andrew Tyrie, criticised the ONS for falling behind other countries and jeopardising policy decisions with poor quality data.

According to Home Office statistics, the police believe that crime is on the increase, as in July 2017 it had increased by 10%, the largest annual rise for a decade. This includes a 20% increase in gun and knife crime, and a 26% rise in homicide rates. On the face of it, these statistics could suggest that the police are becoming less effective at tackling crime. However, it is important to consider the clarity of such data, which may be affected, in part, by improved crime recording processes by the police. This, according to the ONS, is a factor that has contributed to the increase in police recorded crime. In addition, the homicide figure mentioned above includes the 96 cases of manslaughter that occurred in the Hillsborough disaster in 1989. This reflects the inquest verdicts delivered in April 2016. Interestingly, without them the rise would be reduced to 9%.

The 10% rise in police recorded crime contrasts with a 7% fall in the official crime survey of England and Wales. Again the accuracy of crime statistics can be questioned. It might appear that both sets of research are recording the same information and therefore both cannot be correct. However, it is important to remember that the sources differ in the population and offences they cover. In particular, at least half of the increase in police recorded crime series is in offences not covered by the survey, including shoplifting, public order offences and possession of weapons. Hence, the statistics will inevitably differ from each other.

The lack of accuracy in police statistics was again raised in 2017 when the HM Inspectorate of Constabulary and Fire and Rescue Services (HMICFRS, 2017) said five out of six reported offences were recorded but 38,800 each year were not. In addition, at Leicestershire police one in four crimes currently go unreported. Unrecorded crimes included sexual offences, domestic abuse and rape. It also highlighted the recording of violent crime as a particular cause of concern. Its recording rate is 77.9%; that is, only 77.9% of violent crime reported to the police in the West Midlands is actually recorded by them.

Synoptic link

This refers back to Unit 1 AC1.6 and the recording of crime statistics.

The ONS hit the headlines in September 2017 for IT problems that caused a delay in the publication of retail sales data. This could impact on the reliability of the agency in general.

Office for National Statistics

Synoptic link

This refers back to Unit 1 AC1.6 and the recording of crime statistics.

Activity

Research media headlines relating to the crime rate. What do they say? Are they suggesting that crime is on the increase or decrease?

CPS

The CPS brings an independent element to the charging and prosecution of offences. It is separate to the police but works with them to bring about social control. The Full Code Test provides a uniform and fair approach to its role and allows a due process model of justice to be implemented.

However, there have been occasions when the CPS has failed to bring about social control. It has been beset by funding problems and criticisms that it is centralised, bureaucratic, ineffective and too close to the police. Sir Iain Glidewell produced a report in 1998, stating that the organisation lacked effectiveness and efficiency, and particularly made reference to the number of judge-ordered acquittals of defendants being far too high.

Lord Janner escaped prosecution for serious sexual abuse of boys on three occasions because of failings by the CPS.

As shown in previous ACs, at times there has been a lack of enthusiasm to take formal action against known offenders, such as Abu Hamza. The case of Damilola Taylor is an example of an inappropriate application of the tests resulting in a failed prosecution. There has also been criticism of the failure to produce a successful prosecution concerning female genital mutilation and for the controversy over Lord Janner's prosecution.

Activity

Research the case of Lord Janner. Provide details of not only the case but how it impacts on the effectiveness of the CPS.

Judiciary

One aspect of the criminal justice system that may suggest a lack of effectiveness by the judiciary is the increasing number of appeals alleging an unduly lenient sentence. The Attorney General's Office said that 141 prison terms were increased in England and Wales in 2016 under the Unduly Lenient Sentence scheme. This is a 17% rise from the previous year. It is worthy of note that 41 were sex offences, 16 associated with robbery and 19 were grievous bodily harm cases.

Social control will not be achieved with unduly lenient sentences.

The media has been quick to report cases suggesting that the judiciary are ineffective in achieving social control. Judges are often portrayed as being out of touch with society. The following are questions that have been asked by judges at various times:

- *'Who is Gazza? Isn't there an operetta called La Gazza Ladra?'* (Mr Justice Harman)
- *'What is that?'* referring to a Teletubby. (Judge Francis Appleby)

There have also been many occasions when judges appear to have made inappropriate comments leading to sentences thought to be unsuitable given the circumstances. The following are newspaper headlines:

- Judge Who Spared Aspiring Oxford Student From Jail After She Stabbed her Partner is Cleared Following Investigation into Three Complaints (Harley, 2017)
- Judge Lets Former Drug Dealer off Unpaid Work Because of Transport Issues (Discombe, 2017)
- Judge Lets off Sex Abuser then Blames Victim (Rantzen, 2013)
- 'Manchester United Can Afford It', Says Judge as he Lets off Thieving Burger Kiosk Workers (Scheerhout, 2017)
- Judge Lets off Thief and Commends his 'Enterprise' (Court News UK, 2017)
- Model Caught Stealing from Harrods Spared Jail After Judge Praised her 'TALENTS' (Pilditch, 2017)

Prisons

Overall, it could be argued that prison is not effective at achieving social control. There are many statistics from the Prison Reform Trust (2016, 2017b, 2020) that would support this suggestion as regards preventing further offending.

For instance:

- Anyone leaving custody who has served two days or more is required to serve a minimum of 12 months under supervision in the community. As a result, the number of people recalled back to custody has increased, particularly among women. 8,931 people serving a sentence of less than 12 months were recalled to prison in the year to June 2020.
- Scotland and England and Wales have the highest imprisonment rates in Western Europe.
- The prison population has risen by 70% in the last 30 years, but it has steadied in the last 6 years.
- Fewer than one in 10 people surveyed said that having more people in prison was the most effective way to deal with crime. Early intervention, such as better parenting, discipline in schools and better rehabilitation, were all rated as more effective.

Handy hints !

Make sure that you can include both the positives and negatives of each agency when you evaluate them. The exam question may ask for both or one of them.

As well as the above statistics there is evidence to suggest that social control is not maintained inside prisons. There has been a significant rise in prison disturbances and the call out of the National Response Group, the prison's riots squad. In December 2016 a riot occurred in HMP Birmingham that lasted 15 hours during which time staff were sprayed with fire hoses and pictures of prisoners in riot gear were posted on social media. Keys to key doors and gates were stolen from a prison officer and the cells of 500 prisoners were opened by other prisoners.

The use of drugs and their wide availability inside prisons again suggests a lack of achieving social control. The Centre for Social Justice (CSJ), in the report 'Drugs in Prison' (2015), states:

Prisons in England and Wales have a serious drug problem – they have done for decades.

According to the report, the use of drugs impacts on social control as it undermines prison security through leading to the build-up of debt and violence. It makes prisoners less likely to engage constructively in their rehabilitation and it significantly contributes towards high reoffending rates. For instance, more than two in five prisoners in England and Wales reported committing offences in order to get money to buy drugs. In December 2017 Holme House prison in Teesside was found to have a very serious drug problem. HM Inspectorate of Prisons said a quarter of the 1,200 male inmates of Holme House needed help.

Violence within prison impacts on the effectiveness of social control. This refers to assaults on both prison officers and prisoners. Such attacks are on the increase and according to Mark Fairhurst, from the Prison Officer's Association (Johnson, 2017), the attacks are taking place at the rate of 19 per day. As a consequence of this, he suggests that prison officers should be routinely armed with Tasers and stab-proof vests in order to tackle rising violence in jails.

The increase in attacks has been highlighted recently following a number of high-profile incidents.

Take it further »

Read the report entitled *Drugs in Prison* (2015) on the Centre for Social Justice's (CSJ's) website. This will provide you with details of the problms of drug use in prison.

CASE STUDY

INCIDENTS IN PRISON

An inmate at HMP Pentonville in north London was stabbed to death in October 2016. Weeks later, the same prison saw two inmates escape. Shortly after that, officers lost control at HMP Bedford when hundreds of prisoners rioted. As previously mentioned, a riot also occurred in HMP Birmingham in December 2016.

Statistics, from the Ministry of Justice (Wright & Palumbo, 2016), show an enormous rise in prison attacks over the last five years. In the year ending June 2016, there were 23,775 assaults in prisons, which amounted to a 62% rise from 2010, with officers and offenders now seeing an average of 65 assaults behind bars every day. Included in the statistics are an unprecedented number of attacks on prison staff, doubling from about 3,000 to 6,000 between 2010 and 2016.

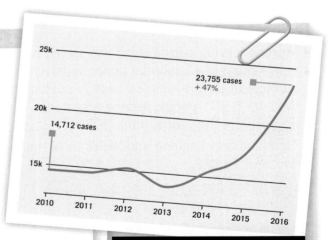

Figures from the Ministry of Justice show the rise in the number of attacks in prison on both prison officers and prisoners.

Source: Wright and Palumbo (2016)

Probation

The National Probation Service has been part privatised, this means that it now works in partnership with other organisations or companies, known as Community Rehabilitation Companies (CRCs). The then director of the service, Sarah Payne, said privatisation would enable the National Probation Service to nurture collaboration, working to get to the root cause of reoffending. She said:

I think people who have the right expertise should get involved in this. Reoffending is a complex societal issue; offenders will muck up, they will get things wrong, but we must not give up. It is a complex thing and needs a lot of people to give it the attention it deserves. **(Rutter, 2013)**

Such a view clearly contains bias given her position within the organisation. However, there have been many suggestions that this makes the service less effective. The National Audit Office has warned that the government has no way of knowing how well companies responsible for running the country's probation services are performing (see Fenton, 2016). There are fears that companies are not subject to adequate oversight or scrutiny.

A joint report, in June 2017 (HM Inspectorate of Probation and HM Inspectorate of Prisons, 2017), by the former chief inspectors of probation and prisons says that staff are focused on paperwork and targets at the expense of prisoners. Dame Glenys Stacey, the then chief inspector of probation, and Peter Clarke, the then chief inspector of prisons, say that the work done by the 21 community rehabilitation companies are having a negligible impact on reducing prisoner offending rates. The report contains many criticisms that impact on the effectiveness of the probation service, including that:

- Too many prisoners have been released not knowing where they would sleep that night.
- In too many cases, prisoners' risk to the public has been inadequately assessed before release.
- Despite much talk about the use of mentors, they could find only one prisoner out of a sample of 98 who had been mentored.

An inspection report by HM Inspectorate of Probation August 2016 in the Durham area found that, overall, the quality of work undertaken by the National Probation Service was 'good, and leadership was strong'. However, one of the issues it found was that pre-sentence reports, used by the courts to help decide sentencing, were not good enough, and led in many cases to 'poorly focused proposals and inappropriate sentences'. In addition, quality of:

some core probation work had deteriorated since our previous inspection. Assessments and plans, while not helped by a lack of required information from court, were often not good enough. Rehabilitation work that should have been started six months into the sentence was often not being done. Consequently, reducing reoffending and public protection outcomes were less likely to be achieved.

HM Inspectorate of **Probation** Arolygiaeth Prawf EM

HM Inspectorate of Probation reports to the government on the effectiveness of people who have offended, with an aim to reduce reoffending and protect the public.

Take it further

Research the latest inspection report by HM Inspectorate of Probation in your area by searching 'Quality and impact inspection. The effectiveness of probation in …' then add area. You can make brief notes to help you consider the effectiveness of the NPS.

Charities and pressure groups

The Prison Reform Trust

The Prison Reform Trust has championed many campaigns to work towards a just, humane and effective penal system. Mental health is an area that has fought for change.

Working with the Women's Institute (WI) they launched the 'Care not Custody' campaign to ensure people with mental illness were given treatment and not placed into the prison system. Some success was achieved in 2011 when the Secretaries of State for Health and for Justice jointly announced their commitment to develop services within police stations and courts for vulnerable suspects and defendants. This was developed by 2014 with parliamentary reports showing an investment of £50 million towards the development of such schemes. There is also a variety of groups and organisations that have come together to join the campaign and support the government in keeping the 'care not custody' promise. Such organisations include the:

Care not Custody was inspired by the death of the son of a Norfolk WI member.

- NHS Confederation Mental Health Network
- Bar Council
- Police Federation
- Royal College of Nursing.

The campaign clearly has had some success and the backing of a large number of high-profile groups. However, they can only put pressure on the government to agree to their requests, they cannot force them to take action.

The Prince's Trust

The Prince's Trust, which helps young people including those who have been in trouble with the law, could be said to be an effective charity as regards social control. It was founded in 1976 and, at time of writing, has helped 825,000 young people across the UK. It helps 13- to 30-year-olds who are unemployed or struggling at school to transform their lives. More than three in four people will achieve a positive outcome, moving into jobs, education and training. There are several initiatives, including one that aims to help ex-offenders make a positive transition back into the community.

The Howard League for Penal Reform

The Howard League for Penal Reform is the oldest penal reform charity in the UK, having been established in 1866. It aims for less crime, safer communities and fewer people in prison. It has run many successful campaigns such as the 'Books for Prisoners' campaign, which won a charity award in 2015, and a campaign to reduce the criminalisation of children by working closely with police forces in England and Wales. This resulted in the number of child arrests falling by 58% between 2010 and 2015. Individual success stories should also be credited.

Activity

Produce a 'newspaper report' on a successful charity or pressure group that has had an impact on social control, for example the Women's Aid with domestic violence law reform campaign or the 'Not with my Name' campaign to reduce identity fraud.

UNIT SUMMARY

By working through this unit:

- You have learned about the criminal justice system in England and Wales and how it operates to achieve social control.
- You will have gained an understanding of the organisations that are part of our system of social control and their effectiveness in achieving their objectives.
- You will be able to evaluate the effectiveness of the process of social control in delivering policy in different contexts.

USEFUL LINKS

Bromley Briefings Prison Factfile:
www.prisonreformtrust.org.uk/Publications/Factfile.

CPS: www.cps.gov.uk/.

Crime Statistics for England and Wales:
www.gov.uk/government/collections/crime-statistics.

CrimeStoppers: https://crimestoppers-uk.org/.

Crime Survey for England and Wales: www.crimesurvey.co.uk/.

Crown Prosecution Service: www.cps.gov.uk/.

Guardian 'Beyond the Blade':
www.theguardian.com/membership/series/beyond-the-blade.

Home Office: www.gov.uk/government/organisations/home-office.

Howard League for Penal Reform: http://howardleague.org/.

Jeremy Bamber Campaign: www.jeremy-bamber.co.uk/.

ManKind Initiative: http://new.mankind.org.uk/.

Police.UK: www.police.uk/.

Restorative Justice Council: https://restorativejustice.org.uk/.

Stop Hate UK: www.stophateuk.org/.

The Witness Charter (Ministry of Justice):
www.gov.uk/government/uploads/system/uploads/attachment_data/file/264627/
witness-charter-nov13.pdf.

Tips from Former Smokers (Centers for Disease Control and Prevention):
www.cdc.gov/tobacco/campaign/tips/.

Women's Aid:
www.womensaid.org.uk/?gclid=CMrGw_P6sMsCFXMzOwodr-ULJg.

You be the Judge: www.ybtj.justice.gov.uk/.

FREQUENTLY ASKED QUESTIONS

1. Is Criminology an A level?

This qualification is not an A level, nor is it a BTEC, but is a Level 3 course. It is classed as the same level of qualification as an A level. It is also known as an applied general qualification.

2. Which topics will I study?

You will learn about different types of crime and reasons why people do not report them, including theories of why people commit crime and how crimes change over time, place and even in different cultures. You will also learn about many aspects of the criminal justice system including the process of a case through court and the role of agencies such as the police and prison service.

3. Can I select which units to study?

No, there are no optional units. For the Certificate Units 1 and 2 must be studied, while the additional Units 3 and 4 must also be studied for the Diploma.

4. What are the units called?

Unit 1 – Changing Awareness of Crime

Unit 2 – Criminological Theories

Unit 3 – Crime Scene to Court Room

Unit 4 – Crime and Punishment

5. Can the assessments be sat electronically?

The controlled assessments can be sat with the use of a computer or on paper. In addition, the external exams can be sat both electronically and in the traditional paper-based way.

6. What skills will I develop if I study the qualification?

As well as gaining knowledge and understanding you will also learn how to describe and explain. In addition, higher order skills will also be developed. These are the ability to evaluate, analyse, discuss, assess and examine.

7. Does the qualification qualify for UCAS points?

Yes, the qualification carries the same UCAS points as grades awarded for an A Level. The Certificate, awarded for 2 units, carries 50% of the points awarded for the Diploma. This is shown in the following table.

Grade	Certificate	Diploma
A*		56
A	24	48
B	20	40
C	16	32
D	12	24
E	8	16

8. Can I see the briefs for Units 1 and 3?

Not prior to the start of the controlled assessment.

9. How long do the controlled assessments last?

Both Units 1 and 3 last for a total of 8 hours. This time is divided up at the discretion of your teacher. However, for Unit 1 there is a 3-hour and 5-hour spilt due to internet access restrictions.

10. How long do the external exams last?

Both Units 2 and 4 last for 1 hour 30 minutes.

11. Are Units 3 and 4 more difficult than Units 1 and 3?

No, they are all worth the same percentage towards your final grade. All are weighted at 25% towards the Diploma qualification. Units 1 and 2 are worth 50% towards the Certificate.

12. What resources can I take into the controlled assessments?

Class notes, including those supplied by your teacher and those you have prepared, can be taken into the assessments. This could include research that you have carried out. You should note that you are always encouraged to put any research or information from a textbook into your own words. This will mean that the work you produce in the controlled assessments is original.

13. What resources cannot be taken into the controlled assessments?

Textbooks or work copied directly from them. This is to avoid plagiarism, which could result in marks being downgraded. Pre-prepared answers or designed materials are also not allowed. It is important that everything is produced in the controlled assessments time.

14. Are there any optional questions in the external exam?

No, all questions are compulsory.

15. Do I have to study everything on the specification?

Anything listed in the content section of the specification must be studied, as this can form the basis of an exam question. However, the wording in the amplification section is a guide as to the type of information that can be used to answer a question. If your teacher uses other examples, theories or ideas, that is perfectly acceptable.

16. Is there preparation work I can do in advance of studying the course?

Attend any open events or taster sessions offered by local schools or colleges, as this will give you a feel for the course. Also, try to watch or listen to the news and keep up to date with current affairs that impact on the criminal justice system. In addition, if you enjoy watching crime or criminal investigation programmes on television, that too may be helpful. But please remember Criminology is about much more than serial killers.

17. Which other subjects go well with Criminology?

Many other subjects go with Criminology such as Sociology, Law and Psychology. Level 3 Criminology can be studied alongside A levels, BTECs and other Level 3 courses.

18. Do all universities accept this qualification?

Many universities accept this qualification, and it carries the same UCAS points as grades at A Level. However, you are advised to contact the university of your choice to gain its individual advice.

19. What can I do after the qualification?

Many students use it to help gain entry into university. Alternatively, you may consider a career in the Police Service, Prison Service, or work as a probation officer, social worker or youth worker. You could also consider an apprenticeship such as a police constable apprenticeship or a prison officer apprenticeship.

20. What are the benefits of studying this qualification?

There are many benefits of studying this course. These include:

- If you are unable to complete the 2-year qualification you can still gain the Certificate in a year.
- The Certificate carries 50% of the full UCAS points.
- Criminology is an interesting subject, you study the how, why, when, what and who of crime.
- It is a multi-disciplinary course that allows you to gain aspects of sociology, psychology and law.
- There is a variety of assessments, with both a controlled assessment and an external exam in each year of the course.
- You gain an understanding of how society operates within the criminal justice system.

REFERENCES

Adler, P.B., Hille Ris Lambers, J. & Levine, J.M. (2007) 'A Niche for Neutrality', *Ecology Letters*, 10, pages 95–104.

Ainsworth, P. (2001) *Offender Profiling and Crime Analysis*, Willan.

Allyon, T. & Milan, M. (1979) *Correctional Rehabilitation and Management: A Psychological Approach*, John Wiley & Sons.

Amnesty International (2021) Death Penalty, www.amnesty.org/en/what-we-do/death-penalty/.

Andrews, D.A., Zinger, I., Hoge, R.D., Bonta, J., Gendrea, P. & Cullen, F.T. (1990) 'Does Correctional Treatment Work? A Clinically Relevant and Informed Meta-Analysis', *Criminology*, 28, 369–404.

Anonymous (2016, 6 August) 'The Prison Service Has Been Cut to the Bone and we Struggle to Keep Control', *The Guardian*, www.theguardian.com/public-leaders-network/2016/aug/06/crisis-managing-violence-prison-service-cut-to-the-bone.

Association of Police and Crime Commissioners (2017) Role of the PCC, www.apccs.police.uk/role-of-the-pcc/.

Baksi, C. (2014, 10 July) 'Health Check Shows Impact of Cuts at CPS', *The Law Society Gazette*, www.lawgazette.co.uk/practice/health-check-shows-impact-of-cuts-at-cps/5042113.article.

Barrett, D. (2014, 17 December) 'Police Budgets Slashed by £300m Despite Top Officers' Warnings', *The Telegraph*, www.telegraph.co.uk/news/uknews/law-and-order/11299163/Police-budgets-slashed-by-300m-despite-top-officers-warnings.html.

Barrett, D. (2015, 11 February) 'England and Wales Near Top of Prison Spending League', *The Telegraph*, www.telegraph.co.uk/news/uknews/crime/11405588/England-and-Wales-near-top-of-prison-spending-league-table.html

BBC News (2013, 23 December) '"Sarah's Law" Sees 700 Paedophiles Identified', www.bbc.co.uk/news/uk-25489541.

BBC News (2015, 7 March) 'Police Forces all Face Major Budget Cuts', www.bbc.co.uk/news/uk-31771456.

Blackburn, R. (1993) *The Psychology of Criminal Conduct: Theory, Research and Practice*, John Wiley & Sons.

Bowlby, J. (1944) 'Forty-four Juvenile Thieves: Their Characters and Home Lives', *International Journal of Psycho-Analysis*, XXV, pages 19–25.

Brown, B.B. & Altman, I. (1981) 'Territoriality and Residential Crime: A Conceptual Framework', in P.L. Brantingham & P.J. Brantingham (eds), *Environmental Criminology*, Sage.

Burrell, I. (2014, 14 February) 'BBC Accused of Political Bias – on the Right, not the Left', *The Independent*, www.independent.co.uk/news/uk/politics/bbc-accused-ofpolitical-bias--on-the-right-not-the-left-9129639.html.

Butcher, M. & Taylor, S. (2007, 3 April) 'Jurors Biased in Sentencing Decisions by the Attractiveness of Defendant', *Psychology & Crime News*, https://crimepsychblog.com/?p=1437.

Campbell Collaboration (2013) Restorative Justice Conferencing (RJC) Using Face-to-Face Meetings of Offenders and Victims: Effects on Offender Recidivism and Victim Satisfaction, www.campbellcollaboration.org/library/restorative-justice-conferencing-recidivism-victim-satisfaction.html.

Centre for Social Justice (2015) Drugs in Prison, www.centreforsocialjustice.org.uk/library/drugs-in-prison.

Children's Society (2020) The Good Childhood Report, www.childrenssociety.org.uk/good-childhood?gclid=CjOKCQiA-OeBBhDiARIsADyBcE5HxPhgIyZf4UTIBGsJH9TkGMWS0J3JcbwRVW8O4QbqR8emVr4-TP4aAnm1EALw_wcB

Cohen, S. (1973) *Folk Devils and Moral Panics: The Creation of the Mods and Rockers*, HarperCollins.

College of Policing (2013) The Effects of CCTV on Crime, http://library.college.police.uk/docs/what-works/What-works-briefing-effects-of-CCTV-2013.pdf.

Court News UK (2017, 8 June) 'Judge Lets off Thief and Commends his "Enterprise"', http://courtnewsuk.co.uk/judge-lets-off-thief-commends-enterprise/.

Cozens, P., Hillier, D. & Prescott (2001) 'Defensible Space: Burglars and Police Evaluate Urban Residential Design', *Security Journal*, 14(4), pages 43–63.

Christiansen, K.O. (1977) 'A Review of Studies of Criminality amongst Twins', in S. Mednick & K. Christiansen (eds), *Biosocial Bases of Criminal Behaviour*, Gardener Press.

Cumberbatch, G. (1997) 'Is Television Harmful?', in R. Cochrane & D. Carroll (eds) *Psychology and Social Issues*, Falmer.

Death Penalty Information Center (2017) Federal Court Finds Intentional Misconduct by Alabama Prosecutor, but Lets Death Penalty Stand, https://deathpenaltyinfo.org/.

DeLisi, M. (2012) 'Revisiting Lombroso', in F.T. Cullen & P. Wilcox (eds), *Oxford Book of Criminological Theory*, Oxford University Press.

Devlin Committee Report (1976) *Report of the Committee on Evidence of Identification in Criminal Cases* (Cmnd 338), 134/135, 42.

DeYoung, C.J. (2010) 'Personality Neuroscience and the Biology of Traits', *Social and Personality Psychology Compass*, 4(12), pages 1165–1180.

Discombe, D. (2017, 4 May) '"Thank You Very Much" – Judge Lets Former Drug Dealer off Unpaid Work because of Transport Issues', *Gloucestershire Live*, www.gloucestershirelive.co.uk/news/gloucester-news/thank-you-very-much-judge-45395.

Edwards, J.S.A., Hartwell, H.J. & Schafheitle, J. (2001) *Prison Foodservice in England*, Foodservice and Applied Nutrition Research Group, Bournemouth University.

Farmer, B. (2017, 1 August) 'Prison Riot Squad Officers Sent into HMP The Mount for Second Time in 24 Hours as "Inmates Seize Wing Again"', *The Telegraph*, www.telegraph.co.uk/news/2017/08/01/prison-riot-squad-officers-sent-hmp-mount-second-time-24-hours/.

Farrington, D.P., Loeber, R., Stouthamer-Loeber, M., Van Kammen, W.B. & Schmidt, L. (1996) 'Self-reported Delinquency and Combined Delinquency Seriousness Scale Based on Boys, Mothers, and Teachers: Concurrent and Predictive Validity for African-Americans and Caucasians', *Criminology*, 34, pages 493–517.

Fenton, S. (2016, 2 May) 'Watchdog Criticises Government's Privatisation of Probation Services', *The Independent*, www.independent.co.uk/news/uk/politics/national-audit-office-watchdog-savages-governments-disastrous-privatisation-of-probation-services-a7010496.html.

Flood-Page, C., Campbell, S., Harrington, V. et al. (2000) Youth Crime: Findings from the 1998/99 Youth Lifestyles Survey, Home Office Research Study 209, Home Office Research, Development and Statistics Directorate.

Fo, W.S. & O'Donnell, C.R. (1975) 'The Buddy System: Effects of Community Intervention on Delinquent Offenses', *Behavior Therapy*, 6, pages 522–524.

Gesch, C.B., Hammond, S.M., Hampson, S.E., Eves, A. & Crowder, M.J. (2002) 'Influence of Supplementary Vitamins, Minerals and Essential Fatty Acids on the Antisocial Behaviour of Young Adult Prisoners. Randomised, Placebo-Controlled Trial', *British Journal of Psychiatry*, 181, 22–28.

Glenn, H., Dame (2008) 'The Attractiveness of Senior Judicial Appointment to Highly Qualified Practitioners', Report to the Judicial Executive Board, www.ucl.ac.uk/laws/judicial-institute/files/The_Attractiveness_of_Senior_Judicial_Appointment_Research_Report.pdf.

Glidewell, Sir Iain (1998) The Review of the Crown Prosecution Service Summary of The Main Report with the Conclusions and Recommendations Chairman: Rt Hon. Sir Iain Glidewell Presented to Parliament by the The Attorney General by Command of Her Majesty (Cmd 3972), Stationery Office.

Glueck, S. & Glueck, E. (1956) *Physique and Delinquency*, Harper.

Goring, C. (1913) *The English Convict: A Statistical Study*, HMSO.

Grierson, J. (2017, 2 March) 'Watchdog Says Police Cuts Have Left Forces in "Perilous State"', *The Guardian*, www.theguardian.com/uk-news/2017/mar/02/inspectorate-police-engaging-dangerous-practices-austerity-cuts-diane-abbott.

Hale, C., Hawyard, K., Wahidin, A. & Wincup, E. (2013) *Criminology*, Oxford University Press.

Harley, N. (2017, 29 September) 'Judge Who Spared Aspiring Oxford Student From Jail After She Stabbed her Partner is Cleared Following Investigation into Three Complaints', *The Telegraph*, www.telegraph.co.uk/news/2017/09/29/judge-spared-oxford-student-jail-bright-stabbed-partner-investigation.

Hinsliff, G. (2003, 22 September) 'Diet of Fish "Can Prevent" Teen Violence', *The Guardian*, www.theguardian.com/politics/2003/sep/14/science.health.

HM Inspectorate of Constabulary and Fire and Rescue Services (2017) West Midlands Police: Crime Data Integrity Inspection 2017, www.justiceinspectorates.gov.uk/hmicfrs/publications/west-midlands-police-crime-data-integrity-2017/.

HM Inspectorate of Probation (2016) Probation Work in Durham – Much Good Work but Some Improvements Needed, www.justiceinspectorates.gov.uk/hmiprobation/media/press-releases/2016/08/durhamqi/.

HM Inspectorate of Probation and HM Inspectorate of Prisons (2017, June) An Inspection of Through the Gate Resettlement Services for Prisoners Serving 12 Months or More, www.justiceinspectorates.gov.uk/cjji/wp-content/uploads/sites/2/2017/06/Through-the-Gate-phase-2-report.pdf.

HM Prison Service (n.d.) About Us, www.gov.uk/government/organisations/hm-prison-service/about.

Hobbs, T.R. & Holt, M.M. (1976) 'The Effects of Token Reinforcement on the Behavior of Delinquents in Cottage Settings', *Journal of Applied Behavior Analysis*, 9, pages 189–198.

Hobbs, M.M. & Holt, T.R. (1979) 'Problems of Behavioural Interventions with Delinquents in an Institutional Setting', in A.J. Finch & P.C. Kendall (eds), *Clinical Treatment and Research in Child Psychopathology*, SP Medical and Scientific Books.

Howitt, D. (2008) *Introduction to Forensic and Criminal Psychology*, Pearson Education.

Hutchings, B. & Mednick, S.A. (1975) 'Registered Criminality in the Adoptive and Biological Parents of Registered Male Criminal Adoptee', in R. Fieve, D. Rosenthal & H. Brill (eds), *Genetic Research in Psychiatry*, The Johns Hopkins Press.

Jacob, P.A., Brunton, M., Melville, M., Brittain, R.P. & McClemont, W.F. (1965) 'Aggressive Behaviour, Mental Sub-normality and the *XYY* Male', *Nature*, 208, pages 1351–1352.

Johnson, B. (2006, 22 June) 'Colin Stagg Shows Why Trial by Judge, Not by Media, is Right', *The Telegraph*, www.telegraph.co.uk/comment/columnists/borisjohnson/3625868/Colin-Stagg-shows-why-trial-by-judge-not-by-media-is-right.html.

Johnson, B. (2017, 10 July) 'Prison Officers "Need Tasers and Stab Vests" to Cope with Rising Violence in Jails', *Sky News*, http://news.sky.com/story/prison-officers-need-tasers-and-stab-vests-to-cope-with-rising-violence-10943089.

Kelling, G.L. & Wilson, J.Q. (1982) 'The Police and Neighborhood Safety: Broken Windows', *Atlantic Monthly*, 249(3): 29–38.

Lange, J. (1929) *Crime as Destiny: A Study of Criminal Twins*, Unwin.

LawTeacher (2019) Labelling Theory its Strengths and Weaknesses, www.lawteacher.net/free-law-essays/criminal-law/labelling-theory-its-strengths-and-weaknesses.php.

Leeson, N. (1997) *Rogue Trader*, Warner Books.

Lewis, A. (n.d.) Understanding CPTED Principles + School Safety, www.dpsdesign.org/blog/understanding-cpted-principles-school-safety.

Lombroso, C. (2006) *Criminal Man*, M. Gibson & N. Hahn Rafter (eds), Duke University Press.

Macpherson, W., Sir (1999) The Stephen Lawrence Inquiry, www.gov.uk/government/publications/the-stephen-lawrence-inquiry.

Martin, J. (2016) *English Legal System*, 8th edn, Hodder Education.

McLeod, S.A. (2014) Bobo Doll Experiment, www.simplypsychology.org/bobo-doll.html.

McIsaac, K.E., Moser, A., Moineddin, R., Keown, L.A., Wilton, G., Stewart, L.A., Colantonio, A., Nathens, A.B. & Matheson, F.I. (2016) 'Association between Traumatic Brain Injury and Incarceration: A Population-based Cohort Study', *CMAJ Open*, 4(4), pages E746–E753.

Meadow, R., Sir (1997) *ABC of Child Abuse*, BMJ Books.

Mednick, S.A., Huttunen, M.O. & Machón, R.A. (1994) 'Prenatal Influenza Infections and Adult Schizophrenia', *Schizophrenia Bulletin*, 20(2), pages 263–267.

Moss, V. (2015, 24 January) 'Criminals Dodge £549 Million in Unpaid Court Fines as Taxpayers are Hit in the Pocket', *Mirror*, www.mirror.co.uk/news/uk-news/criminals-dodge-549million-unpaid-court-5037017.

Newburn, T. (2007) *Criminology*, Routledge.

Newton Dunn, T. (2015, 17 August) 'European Court of Killers' Rights', *The Sun*, www.thesun.co.uk/archives/politics/204465/european-court-of-killers-rights/.

Novaco, R.W. (1975) *Anger Control: The Development and Evaluation of an Experimental Treatment*, Heath.

Office for National Statistics (ONS) (2017) Crime in England and Wales: Year Ending March 2017, www.ons.gov.uk/peoplepopulationandcommunity/crimeandjustice/bulletins/crimeinenglandandwales/yearendingmar2017.

Office for National Statistics (ONS) (2020) 'Crime in England and Wales: Year Ending September 2019', www.ons.gov.uk/peoplepopulationandcommunity/crimeandjustice/bulletins/crimeinenglandandwales/yearendingseptember2019#:~:text=The%20Crime%20Survey%20for%20England%20and%20Wales%20(CSEW)%20provides%20the,compared%20with%20the%20previous%20year.

Osborn, S.G. & J West, D.J. (1979) 'Conviction Records of Fathers and Sons Compared', *British Journal of Criminology*, 19(4), pages 120–133.

Packer, H.L. (1968) *The Limits of Criminal Sanction*, Stanford University Press.

Pilditch, D. (2017, 4 August) 'Model Caught Stealing from Harrods Spared Jail After Judge Praised her "TALENTS"', *Daily Express*, www.express.co.uk/news/uk/836761/Model-stealing-Harrods-Natalia-Sikorska-Westminster-court.

Prison Fellowship (2017) Does Restorative Justice Work?, www.prisonfellowship.org.uk/what-we-do/sycamore-tree/does-restorative-justice-work/.

Prison Reform Trust (2014) Incentives and Earned Privileges, www.prisonreformtrust.org.uk/Portals/0/Documents/IEP%20Briefing%20Prison%20Reform%20Trust.pdf.

Prison Reform Trust (2016) Bromley Briefings Prison Factfile, Autumn 2016, www.prisonreformtrust.org.uk/Portals/0/Documents/Bromley%20Briefings/Autumn%202016%20Factfile.pdf.

Prison Reform Trust (2017a) Prison: The Facts, www.prisonreformtrust.org.uk/Portals/0/Documents/Bromley%20Briefings/Summer%202017%20factfile.pdf.

Prison Reform Trust (2017b) Bromley Briefings Prison Factfile, Autumn 17, https://pdf4pro.com/view/bromley-briefings-prison-factfile-prison-reform-c208a.html

Prison Reform Trust (2021) Bromley Briefings Prison Factfile, Winter 2021, www.prisonreformtrust.org.uk/Portals/0/Documents/Bromley%20Briefings/Winter%202021%20Factfile%20final.pdf.

Prisonphone (2017) Prison Budget Cuts – The Actual Statistics, www.prisonphone.co.uk/prison-budget-cuts-the-actual-statistics/.

Putwain, D. & Sammons, A. (2002) *Psychology and Crime*, Routledge.

Raine, A., Buchsbaum, M.S., Stanley, J., Lottenberg, S., Abel, L. & Stoddard, J. (1994) 'Selective Reductions in Prefrontal Glucose Metabolism in Murderers', *Biological Psychiatry*, 36(6), pages 365–373.

Rantzen, E. (2013, 9 February) 'Judge Lets off Sex Abuser then Blames Victim', *Mirror*, www.mirror.co.uk/news/world-news/judge-lets-off-sex-abuser-then-blames-1599608.

Restorative Justice Council (2016) Evidence Supporting the Use of Restorative Justice, https://restorativejustice.org.uk/resources/evidence-supporting-use-restorative-justice.

Rutter, T. (2013, 29 November) 'Meet the Woman on a Mission to Cut Reoffending in Wales', *The Guardian*, www.theguardian.com/public-leaders-network/2013/nov/29/probation-services-devolved-nation.

Sample, I. (2010, 14 September) 'Psychological Profiling "Worse than Useless"', *The Guardian*, www.theguardian.com/science/2010/sep/14/psychological-profile-behavioural-psychology.

Scerbo, A. & Raine, A. (1993) 'Neurotransmitters and Antisocial Behavior: A Meta-Analysis', in A. Raine (ed.), *The Psychopathology of Crime: Criminal Behavior as a Clinical Disorder*, Academic Press.

Scheerhout, J. (2017, 12 April) '"Manchester United Can Afford It", Says Judge as he Lets off Thieving Burger Kiosk Workers', *Manchester Evening News*, www.manchestereveningnews.co.uk/news/greater-manchester-news/manchester-united-can-afford-it-12886475.

Schoenthaler, S.J. (1982) 'The Effect of Sugar on the Treatment and Control of Anti-social Behavior: A Double-blind Study of an Incarcerated Juvenile Population', *International Journal of Biosocial Research*, 3, pages 1–9.

Sheldon, W.H. (with Hartl, E.M. & McDermott, E.) (1949) *Varieties of Delinquent Youth: An Introduction to Constitutional Psychology*, Harper and Brothers.

Sheldon, W.H. (1954) *Atlas of Men: A Guide for Somatotyping the Adult Male of All Ages*, Harper.

Sutherland, E.H., Cressey, D.R. & Luckenbill, D.F. (1992) *Principles of Criminology*, General Hall.

Theilgaard, A. (1984) 'A Psychological Study of the Personalities of XYY- and XXY-Men', *Acta Psychiatrica Scand*, 69 (suppl. 315), pages 1–133.

Travis, A. & Rogers, S. (2011, 18 August) 'Revealed: The Full Picture of Sentences Handed Down to Rioters', *The Guardian*, www.theguardian.com/uk/2011/aug/18/full-picture-of-riot-sentences.

Victim Support (2006) Victims Code, www.victimsupport.org.uk/help-and-support/your-rights/victims%E2%80%99-code.

Virkkunen, M., Nuutila, A., Goodwin, F.K. & Linnoila, M. (1987) 'Cerebrospinal Fluid Monoamine Metabolite Levels in Male Arsonists', *Archives of General Psychiatry*, 44, pages 241–247.

Whitehead, T. (2014, 26 April) 'Quarter of Billion in Court Fines Written Off', *The Telegraph*, www.telegraph.co.uk/news/uknews/law-and-order/10788130/Quarter-of-billion-in-court-fines-written-off.html.

Wilson, D. (2014) *Pain and Retribution: A Short History of British Prisons, 1066 to the Present*, Reaktion Books.

WJEC (2015) WJEC Level 3 Applied Certificate & Diploma in Criminology, www.eduqas.co.uk/media/yzqlsmq4/wjec-applied-diploma-in-criminology-spec-e-03-06-2020-1.pdf.

Wolfenden, Lord (1957) The Report of the Departmental Committee on Homosexual Offences and Prostitution (Cmnd 247), The National Archives.

Wright, P. & Palumbo, D. (2016, 15 November) 'UK Prisons Crisis: Five Graphs Showing Why Officers are Striking as Chaos Erupts Behind Bars', *International Business Times*, www.ibtimes.co.uk/uk-prisons-crisis-five-graphs-showing-why-officers-are-striking-chaos-erupts-behind-bars-1591687.

GLOSSARY OF KEY TERMS

Accidental death: A verdict at an inquest given where a death is considered to be as a result of an accident.

Acquittal: Verdict of a court when someone is found not guilty of a crime they been charged with doing.

Actus reus: Latin for guilty act.

Amnesty: To officially pardon or give official confirmation that no criminal action will be taken.

Anomie: Loss of shared principles or norms.

Anti Social Behaviour Order (ASBO): A court order that can be obtained by local authorities in order to restrict the behaviour of a person likely to cause harm or distress to the public.

Antecedents: The defendant's family and social background.

Atavistic: Relating to something ancient or ancestral.

Atrocity: A horrific and, usually, violent act.

Automatism: A defence in law where the defendant is not in control of their actions.

Barnum effect: When individuals give high accuracy ratings to descriptions of themselves. However, the descriptions are in fact vague and very general, capable of being applied to a wide range of people.

Biased: Unfairly prejudiced for or against someone or something.

Bill: A proposed piece of legislation that attempts to proceed through the stages of parliamentary law making.

Biological determinism: A person's personality or behaviour is caused by the genes they've inherited, rather than by social or cultural factors, i.e. by nature rather than nurture.

Broadsheet: A more serious newspaper that used to be printed on large sheets of paper but is now often printed on smaller sheets.

Brothel: A place where men go to pay to have sex with a prostitute.

Burden of proof: The duty of proving the charge.

Campaigns for change: Relate to a set of planned activities that people carry out over a period of time in order to achieve something such as social or legal change.

Capital punishment: Also known as the death penalty, this is a government-approved practice, where someone is put to death by the state as punishment for a crime.

Capitalism: The social system in which the means for producing and distributing goods (the country's trade and industry) are controlled by a small minority of people for profit (the capitalist class). The majority of people must sell their ability to work in return for a wage or salary (the working class/proletariat).

Cellular confinement: Being restricted to your cell, without socialising with other prisoners, as a punishment.

Civil liberties: Basic rights and freedoms granted to citizens of a country by the law.

Civil partnership: Legally recognised agreement for both same-sex couples and heterosexual couples.

Coercion: The use of force to achieve a desired end.

Combination order: A sentence of the court that combines a probation order and a community service order.

Community rehabilitation companies: The private sector suppliers of probation services for offenders in England and Wales.

Community sentence: A punishment from a court that involves activities carried out in the community.

Concordance: In agreement or harmony.

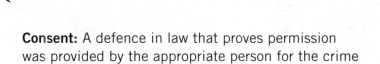

Consent: A defence in law that proves permission was provided by the appropriate person for the crime to occur.

Constitutional law: The fundamental principles according to which a state is governed.

Control: Regulate, govern, manage, organise.

Control group: A group in an experiment or study that does not receive treatment by the researchers and is then used as a benchmark to measure how the others subjects tested did.

Covert surveillance: Undercover or not obvious monitoring.

Criminal: Actions that will constitute an offence under English and Welsh law and are punishable by the state.

Criminal Behaviour Order (CBO): An orders that tackles the most serious and persistent anti-social individuals where their behaviour has brought them before a criminal court. It can deal with a wide range of anti-social behaviours following the offender's conviction, including threatening violence against others, or frequently being drunk and aggressive in public.

Crown Prosecution Service: The principal prosecuting authority for England and Wales, which acts independently in criminal cases investigated by the police.

Custodial sentence: A punishment of being sent to prison.

Custody officer: The police officer, of at least the rank of sergeant, who is responsible for the care and welfare of an arrested person.

Cyber-bullying: A form of bullying using electronic devices, for example mobile phones, tablets or computers. It is becoming increasingly common, especially among teenagers.

Dark figure of crime: The amount of unreported or unknown crime.

Decriminalisation: Stop something from being illegal.

Denunciation: Aims to show offenders that society disapproves of their behaviour and that it is unacceptable conduct.

Deterrence: Aims to dissuade the offender, or anyone in society, from committing crime by a fear of punishment.

Deviance: Any behaviour that violates social or cultural norms or accepted standards. Much of society will generally disapprove of deviant behaviour.

Deviancy amplification: A process often performed by the media, in which the extent and seriousness of deviant behaviour is exaggerated, creating a greater awareness and interest in deviance.

Differential associations: Interactions with others.

Diminished responsibility: A partial defence for murder resulting in a conviction for manslaughter instead of murder.

Dignity in Dying: A campaign group who believe that assisted dying for terminally ill, mentally competent adults should be legal in the UK.

Dizygotic: Non-identical (fraternal) twins.

DNA or deoxyribonucleic acid: The chemical that carries genetic information and is contained in chromosomes found in the nucleus of most cells. Sometimes called our genetic code as it determines all our characteristics.

Entomology: The scientific study of insects.

European Convention on Human Rights (ECHR): A treaty or agreement to protect human rights and fundamental freedoms in Europe.

Event: An occasion that takes place, especially one of importance, to promote a campaign's cause.

Examination-in-chief: The questioning of a witness by the party who has called that witness to give evidence, in support of the case being made.

Execute: To kill someone as a legal punishment.

Extraversion: Being mainly concerned with and gaining pleasure from things outside of the self.

Facilitator: Someone who assists in making a task easier or helps someone to find a solution.

Folk devils: A person of bad influence on society.

Forensic odontologist: Someone who can present dental knowledge in legal cases.

Forms: Types, ideas, theories, ways of, methods.

Funding: Money provided for a particular purpose.

Genocide: Any action with the intention to destroy, in whole or in part, a national, ethnic or religious group.

Geographical profiling: Considers patterns revealed in the location and timing of offences to make judgements about where the offender lives (circle theory).

Historic offences: Crimes that were committed many years ago but are being prosecuted now, often due to a delay in reporting them to the police.

Imprisonment: A sentence given by a court compelling the offender to be sent to prison.

Incapacitation: A sentence of the court to prevent further offending. This could include a term of imprisonment.

Incarcerated criminals: People who have been found guilty of a criminal offence and received a term of imprisonment as a punishment.

Indictable offence: A serious offence that must be dealt with at a Crown Court.

Inference of guilt: It is possible to decide, on the evidence given, that the person is guilty.

Internet troll: A person who upsets people on the internet by starting arguments or by posting inflammatory messages.

Introversion: Directing your interests inwards or to things within the self.

Investigative psychology: A profiling technique based on psychological theory and research to provide support for suspect identification and crime linking to evidence.

Islamophobia: A dislike of or prejudice against Islam or Muslims.

Jury equity: A jury can bring in a verdict that is morally right rather than one that complies with the law and previous cases.

Juvenile delinquent: Someone under the age of 18 years who has broken the law.

Kerb crawling: Driving slowly along a road, close to a pavement or walkway, in order to ask a prostitute for sex.

Latent: Not visible to the naked eye.

Law Lords: Also known as the 12 Lords of Appeal in Ordinary, and are judges who hear cases in the Supreme Court.

Legalise: Make an act legal within the law.

Lenient: Not as harsh in punishment as would be expected.

Locard's exchange principle: Dr Edmond Locard was a French forensic scientist, often informally referred to as the 'Sherlock Holmes of France'. He was a pioneer in forensic science techniques including the exchange principle that something is added to and removed from an environment every time someone enters it.

Mandatory: Required by law.

Manslaughter: An unlawful killing, without malice, aforethought and in circumstances when it is not murder.

Marxism: The political and economic theories of Karl Marx, which state that capitalism is unequal and undemocratic, being based on the exploitation of the working class by the capitalist class/bourgeoisie.

Mens rea: Latin for guilty mind.

Miscarriage of justice: The conviction and punishment of a person for crime that they had not committed.

Monozygotic: Identical twins.

Moral panic: Used to describe the consequence of the media presentation of something that has happened where the general public react in a panicky manner. The reporting is usually exaggerated and consequently the public reaction is inflated.

Neuroticism: To have feelings of anxiety, worry, anger or fear.

Nobbled: Bribed or intimidated.

Observational learning: When an observer's behaviour changes after viewing the behaviour of a model.

Paedophile: A person with a sexual attraction to children.

Paranoid schizophrenic: Someone with an illness of psychosis of varying intensity, which makes them lose touch with reality.

Parliament: Made up of three parts. Firstly, the House of Commons, the elected representatives, or Members of Parliament, voted by the people in an election. Secondly, the House of Lords, which still contains some hereditary peers (Lords) and now many lifetime appointed peers who do not pass on their title after death. For example, Sir Alan Sugar, Baroness Doreen Lawrence (Stephen Lawrence's mother) and Sir John Prescott. Lastly, the Monarch, who provides approval to the finalised Bill.

Parole Board: An independent body that carries out risk assessments on prisoners to determine if they can be safely released into the community.

Patent: Clearly visible to the naked eye.

Perpetrators: People who commit criminal acts (offenders).

PET scan: Positron emission tomography (PET) scans are used to produce detailed three-dimensional images of the inside of the body.

Petition: A formal written request, typically one signed by many people, appealing to authority in respect of a particular cause.

Phishing: A scam or an attempt to persuade someone to give out personal information, such as bank account numbers, passwords and credit card details.

Pilot scheme: Used to test an idea before deciding whether to introduce it on a large scale.

Privatisation: The transfer of a business or service from public to private ownership and control.

Probation order: A punishment from a court where you serve your sentence in the community. While on probation, you may have to do unpaid work, complete an education or training course, get treatment for additions, such as drugs or alcohol, and have regular meetings with an 'offender manager'.

Probative value: How useful evidence is to prove something important in a trial.

Psychoticism: A personality pattern that is typified by aggression and hostility towards other people.

Punitive laws: Laws that intend to punish.

Recidivism: The tendency of a convicted criminal to reoffend.

Referendum: A general vote by the electorate on a single political question that has been referred to them for a direct decision.

Reformation: To reform or rehabilitate.

Rehabilitation: Aiming to alter the offender's mindset so that future reoffending can be prevented.

Reparation: Aiming to ensure the defendant pays back to the victim or society for the wrongdoing.

Retreatist: Rejection of society's prescribed goals and the conventional means of attaining them.

Retribution: Aiming to punish an offender to the level that is deserved.

Ritualistic: Performing in the same way.

Rules of evidence: Legal rules that explain when evidence, as in a court case, is admissible and when it will be disallowed or ruled inadmissible.

Safeguarding: Protecting from harm or damage with an appropriate measure.

Scaremonger: To spread stories that cause the public fear.

Security of tenure: Guaranteed permanent employment.

Self-defence: A defence in law allowing the use of reasonable force to avoid a conviction.

Sentencing Council: Provides guidelines on sentencing that the courts must follow unless it is in the interest of justice not to do so.

Sex Offenders Register: Contains the details of anyone convicted, cautioned or released from prison for sexual offences against children or adults since September 1997. It is kept by the police and has around 9,000 people on it.

Simitator: A website that allows you to produce a fake Facebook or Twitter account.

Social: Society, public, community, collective, common, shared, group.

Soliciting: To offer sex for money, usually in a public place.

Somatotype: Body shape.

Stability: Unlikely to move or change.

Statute: An Act of Parliament or legislation.

Stereotyping: A widely held but fixed, over-enlaraged image or idea of a type of person.

Stigma: A mark of disgrace associated with something bad.

Surveillance: Keeping a close watch over something or someone.

Tabloid: A type of popular newspaper with small pages, many pictures and short stories.

Token economy: A form of behaviour modification that increases desirable behaviour and decrease undesirable behaviour by the use of tokens. Individuals receive tokens after displaying desirable behaviour. These are collected and exchanged for an object or privilege.

Typological profiling: Considers characteristics of the offender by analysing the crime scene and crimes.

Victim surveys: Occur where the intention is to interview a representative sample of a particular population and to ask a series of questions about their experience of victimisation. These surveys started in the USA; the first such survey in the UK was in 1972. It later became the British Crime Survey and from 2012 has been called the Crime Survey for England and Wales.

Vigilante: A person who tries an unofficial way to prevent crime occurring or to catch and punish a criminal, usually as they believe the police are unable to do so.

Vulnerable witness: Anyone under the age of 17, or a victim of a sexual offence, or a person whose evidence or ability to give evidence is likely to be diminished by reason of mental disorder, significant intelligence or physical impairment.

Whole-life tariff: An order that having been convicted of murder the defendant must serve all of it in prison and not be allowed parole.

Young Offenders Institution: A type of prison for 18- to 20-year-olds.

INDEX

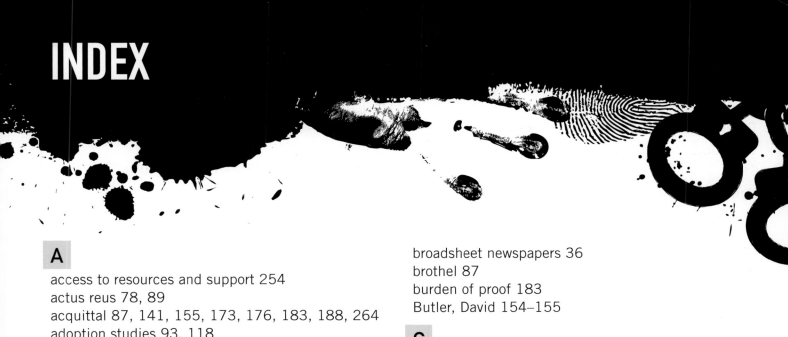